BOBCAT BOOKS PRESENTS THE STORY OF

NINE INCH NAILS

D1341636

THE UNAUTHORIZED BIOGRAPHY

Front cover photograph: Ashley Maile/Retna Ltd.
Back cover photograph: Sean Michaels/Retna Ltd

Photographs courtesy of Steve Jennings/Corbis, Sin/Corbis, David Samuel
Robblns/Corbis, Mitchell Gerber/Corbis, Martin Philbey/Redferns, Jon Super/Redferns,
Rune Hellestad/Corbis, John Shearer/WireImage, Barry Brecheisen/WireImage, Lester
Cohen/WireImage, Leslie McGhie/WireImage, Jason Squires/WireImage, Kevin
Mazur/WireImage, John Shearer/WireImage, Kelly A. Swift/Retna, Jeff Kroll/Retna,
Lili Wilde/All Action/Retna Ltd., Myriam Santos- Kayda/Retna Ltd.,
and Jay Blakesberg

Order No: BOB11583US
ISBN-10: 0-8256-7348-8
ISBN-13: 978-0-8256-7348-1

Exclusive Distributors
Music Sales Limited,
14 - 15 Berners Street,
London W1T 3LJ, UK.

Music Sales Corporation,
257 Park Avenue South,
New York, NY 10010, USA.

Macmillan Distribution Services,
53 Park West Drive,
Derrimut, Vic 3030,
Australia.

To the Music Trade only:
Music Sales Limited,
8/9 Frith Street,
London W1D 3JB, UK.

Every effort has been made to trace the copyright holders of the photographs in this
book but one or two were unreachable. We would be grateful if the photographers
concerned would contact us.

Printed and bound in the United States of America by Quebecor World
A catalogue record for this book is available from the British Library.

Visit Omnibus Press on the web at www.omnibuspress.com

NINE INCH NAILS

TOMMY UDO

**BOBCAT
BOOKS**

THE UNAUTHORIZED BIOGRAPHY

Contents

Preface And Acknowledgements

Most of what I write is business. This is personal.

Nothing is of less interest to me than a critic getting personal and telling you what someone's art means to them, but Reznor's music has been a constant companion through addiction, detox and the long drug and booze-free aftermath. The music didn't 'help' me through anything, but it was there as a soundtrack. Nor did I feel that Trent Reznor was communicating with me personally, though I recognised a lot of the territory that he was delving into.

I am not an obsessive fan of Nine Inch Nails, though anyone who is into the music of Trent Reznor tends to overanalyze, tends to know too much, tends to be too familiar with them. It goes with the territory of making 'serious' music. By serious I don't necessarily mean po-faced or miserable, but I am heartily sick of the dumb-it-down attitude that sneers at music that isn't happy clappy. It's a kind of inverse inverse inverse snobbery about pop criticism that dictates that you aren't allowed to be 'too' serious. While I don't for one minute buy the Morrissey/Radiohead party line that 'miserable' music is somehow more profound and worthy than 'happy' music – personally, I've always found more deep truths in the music of Martha Reeves And The Vandellas than Mahler, The Smiths and Diamanda Galás combined – there is still more great music born from unhappiness, heartbreak and sorrow than from contentedness, satisfaction and happiness. It's one of those clichés that holds true – the best comes from the most tragic, whether that is Van Gogh, Nick Drake or Edgar

Allan Poe. And it's especially true in pop music: the real motivations for great music are desperation and pain. The great songs are churned out by desperate and lonely people, maybe reaching out to others, maybe trying to make a few bucks but mostly just doing it because it's the last thing left to do. The songs may not necessarily be sad - desperate people can be desperately upbeat and optimistic, driven by a faith that tomorrow might not be like today - but they touch something deep inside us.

Pop music has always been about turning a buck, with art squeezing in sometimes unnoticed, but in recent years, as the scene has become dominated by a few mega-corporations, art has been downsized. And there are elements in the press who have gone along with this.

Anyone not making out and out comedy music - Leonard Cohen, Nick Cave, Belle And Sebastian, Tindersticks - will be mercilessly ribbed. Sometimes the ribbing is well deserved, but often it makes it difficult to discuss it on the level it really merits.

Nine Inch Nails/Trent Reznor are one of the walls that our back is against. If we care about the commitment that drives people to make great music - whether that is Sun Ra, Muddy Waters, Black Sabbath, Marvin Gaye, Primal Scream, Miles Davis, Bessie Smith, PJ Harvey, Led Zeppelin, Ministry, John Coltrane, Dr Dre, The Clash or (fill your own names in here) - then the fight of Nine Inch Nails against corporate mediocrity is our fight.

I first saw Nine Inch Nails live at Wembley Stadium in the August of 1991. Almost as soon as Trent Reznor walked onstage, a group of meatheads sitting next to me - they were beefy Home Counties lads in their late 20s or early 30s, sporting poodle perms and 'mullets', wearing fringed leather jackets over tiger-print cap-sleeved t-shirts and ridiculously tight jeans tucked into cowboy boots - started booing loudly and screaming out 'FUCK OFF POOFTER!' at the top of their voices. They weren't alone; several thousand of their spiritual brothers were joining in, while plastic glasses full of urine flew across the heads of the crowd towards the stage (though few landed anywhere near). It actually became impossible to hear the band over the catcalls. I half expected – even wanted – Reznor to jump into the crowd and start beating people up. But they just soldiered on bravely. The set lasted around 40 minutes and while the old-school metal types calmed down or drifted off to drink more lager, the smattering of industrial fans in the crowd – as well as few converts from the bouffant-'n'-bullet-belt set – got their first taste of Nine Inch Nails.

Looking around the crowd there were a few dissidents. They were mostly male or in couples, and could best be described as post-goth. Shaven headed, dressed in full length leather coats, one even wore a gas mask and an army surplus NATO Atomic Biological Chemical suit spray painted with the distinctive NIN logo, with the reversed 'N'.

Pretty Hate Machine had only been released in the UK that year, two years on from its US debut, though like many hardcore industrial fans, I suspect that we had all managed to get hold of import copies. It was hard to know what to make of the show: I had been eager to see the band since I first heard 'Head Like A Hole' at the start of the year. I had been set to fly out to one of the Lollapalooza shows in the US to see Nine Inch Nails play on the bill along with Jane's Addiction – another favourite band – Ice-T, The Butthole Surfers and Siouxsie And The Banshees as a feature for the rock weekly *Sounds*. Unfortunately the paper folded – murdered by men in suits – shortly before I was due to go. So there I was, desperately trying not to be disappointed, watching 50,000 gimps giving them the finger.

It was a neat illustration of the seemingly unbreachable barrier at that time between heavy metal and other, more 'progressive', forms of music. Metal was dominated by American bands – though a few major league British acts like Iron Maiden and Def Leppard commanded international respect – but seemed to have reached such a dead end that it had become embarrassing. Thrash had revitalised the genre in the early '80s and bands like Metallica and Slayer were at, or approaching, their artistic peak. But the bands who really dominated the scene were the likes of Bon Jovi, Poison, Warrant, Extreme and Skid Row. As a long-time fan of hard rock, it was a mystery to me why a lot of these fans would listen to Bon Jovi – whose groin-straining 'power' ballads seemed at best to be middle of the road soft rock – but not, for example, The Rollins Band, Pixies, Dinosaur Jr, Mudhoney or Nirvana. That was, of course, a situation that would change almost overnight in the wake of *Nevermind*.

Reznor seemed to be making a new kind of hard rock that was forward thinking, technologically savvy and righteously angry. How could you possibly prefer Skid Row's stale, retro licks and absurd cock rock posturings to that?

These days, of course, I'm a lot more forgiving of absurd cock rock posturings and Skid Row generally, but in 1991 it felt like a revolution brewing. Trent walked offstage and Skid Row came on. The crowd went wild but I remember thinking: *adieu l'ancien régime!* A few months after this gig traditional rock was in disarray, increasingly under siege from younger, harder and faster artists like Reznor, Kurt Cobain and a whole generation who would follow. Suddenly men in bandanas pulling tortured faces when they played guitar solos seemed – once again – sad, old and in the way.

Speaking to *Kerrang!* in 2002, Reznor looked back on the early-'90s scene with something approaching nostalgia. While this was hardly a 'golden age', it did at least allow a wide variety of bands to thrive: 'At that time it was probably hard to say. But now – and I don't mean to sound old – things are so bad that it makes me think that things must have been really good then. Looking back into the early '90s and bands like Jane's Addiction and Tool and Rage Against The Machine, it seemed like it was a time of more freedom. The hair metal bands were getting stabbed in the heart and it seemed like a time of great upheaval. But what happened was that the major labels realised there was a marketing label they could stick on all these bands and that term was "alternative". And this would apply to everything from Nirvana to The Dead Kennedys to The Barenaked Ladies. And then everything became homogenised.'

Britain and Europe have traditionally been more tolerant of electronic music than America but, brilliant as they were, European artists have always been 'experimentalists' rather than merely performers who happen to use electronics. From the early days of so-called krautrockers like Can, Kraftwerk, Tangerine Dream, Neu! And Cluster through post-prog bands like Roxy Music (during the Brian Eno era) and early Hawkwind, and up to the first wave of 'industrial' bands – Throbbing Gristle, Cabaret Voltaire, The Human League – there has always been an element of 'look ma, no guitars!' showing off. In America, on the other hand, there is less of a tendency to make quirky experimental music as there is simply to use the available technology to make comparatively mainstream music. While European composers were pushing back the frontiers of sound in the '50s, their American counterparts, like Louis and Bebe Barron, were composing film music for sci-fi hits like *Forbidden Planet*. The really big US 'synthesiser' albums of the '70s were things like Stevie Wonder's soul-meets-synth *Innervisions* or even Todd Rundgren's latter-day Brian Wilson rock and soul. Disco, early hip hop and later house all incorporated electronics without necessarily trumpeting the fact. They weren't interested in necessarily creating something innovative – though many of these records actually are – as they were in making hit records, something that you could never accuse Tangerine Dream of.

But even in the early stages of electronic music there was a cold war between the traditional 'rock' fans – and musicians – and the new school. Electronic music, they said, 'lacked a soul', or wasn't 'proper music'.

Industrial music, as it was defined in the US, seemed to me to be very different from the Throbbing Gristle school of British/industrial music. It was like an attempt to marry rock and electronics together, to put a ghost in the machine as it were, as well as enhancing what was then a tired form. Nine Inch Nails seemed to do this better than anyone else. Theirs was a new kind of rock 'n' roll. Trent got into the charts, onto MTV whereas – with the exception of Ministry and Skinny Puppy – none of the other industrial bands like Frontline Assembly, Laetherstrip, KMFDM, My Life With The Thrill Kill Kult or X

Marks The Pedwalk were ever going to matter outside of a small, but loyal, cult following.

I met Reznor a few days later at an aftershow party for an MTV gig where they had been, bizarrely, added to a bill that included The Wonder Stuff and EMF. The Wonder Stuff – essentially a glorified pub-rock band – were, inexplicably, the darlings of the British music press at the time while EMF were just a one-hit-wonder pop act who were never quite able to make it as an 'albums' band.

Reznor had not fared as badly as he had at Wembley – many in the audience were merely indifferent though a larger concentration of fans had turned up – but there was a lot of carping from the scenemakers hanging around the other band. Predictably, the reviews in the UK weeklies were scathing.

'Reheats leftovers from electric body music as purveyed by Skinny Puppy, Ministry and Front 242,' said the *NME*'s Dele Fadele, who at least actually understood Reznor's aesthetic.

Reznor tried to seem unphased but it was clear that he was seriously pissed off. My interview went badly – he was sullen and monosyllabic – and he only really came to life when we discussed science fiction, especially the films of David Cronenberg (we were both massive fans of *Videodrome* and the under-rated body horror flick *Dead Ringers*).

Reznor was scathing about the new school of Euro techno such as The Orb, The Shamen, LFO and Future Sound Of London and just seemed a bit whiney that nobody understood him. In retrospect, I'm annoyed that I didn't spot then that he was destined to be one of the most important artists of the decade, still making vital music today, while Skid Row, EMF and The Wonder Stuff have returned to the dustbin of history.

Ten years on, Reznor has made two classic albums – *The Downward Spiral* and *The Fragile*, respectively the *Pet Sounds* and *What's Going On?* of the nose-piercings and PVC set – and has turned in some of the most stunning live performances I have ever seen (Woodstock 94 for example, where it was hard to imagine that Trent's angst could actually improve an already hellish event). His constant reworking of tracks, started early in his career with Flood and the Sherwood/LeBlanc remixes, is always interesting and, while occasionally throwing up the odd diamond, you would not necessarily want to listen to every single Jim Thirlwell mix of *The Downward Spiral*. It's hard to think of another American artist who has managed to remain true to this spirit of invention and innovation, still capable of selling a shedload of records and not showing any signs of pegging out artistically (or literally) like so many of his contemporaries. He has outlasted Kurt Cobain, Billy Corgan and Al Jourgensen as the voice of a generation and, while I acknowledge the greatness of Marilyn Manson as an idea, as a media figure who pokes a stick into the cage where they keep the Christian fundamentalist nutters and Republican psychos, as a performer, songwriter and musician, compared to Trent he's thin beer.

Words like 'genius' are bandied around too often and without thought: Trent is no genius – he is, rather, a savant, a man of learning; a person eminent for acquirements. He has, like Phil Spector before him, made the studio his instrument. He has found new ways to write songs and tell stories in a connected age.

Trent in the '90s was the living embodiment of cyberpunk, the new school of science fiction created in the 1980s by William Gibson, Bruce Sterling, Rudy Rucker, Greg Bear and John Shirley. If everyone from Kraftwerk to Gary Numan had made electronic music that would fit as the soundtrack to some antiseptic utopia like Fritz Lang's *Metropolis* or the perspex art-deco future in *Things To Come*, then Reznor's dirty and dangerous music was part of something harsher. He is part of the noir future depicted in films like *Blade Runner*. *Pretty Hate Machine* almost seemed like the soundtrack to Gibson's bleak, urban future where computer hackers were part of a criminal underworld like drug dealers, where the gee-whizz technological McGuffins of traditional science fiction – ray-guns, spaceships, artificial intelligence machines – had found their way into the hands of the mafia, the Yakuza, the Hell's Angels, Rastafarians and Voodoo

Guerrillas. If they ever get around to making Gibson's *Neuromancer* into a film, they could do worse than to cast Reznor as the burned-out anti-hero Case, tapping his mind into the data galaxy in cyberspace, hacking reality itself.

I am indebted, as always, to all at *Metal Hammer*, to Martina for support when it counted, and especially to Richie the unpaid information monkey who actually managed to track down just about every word ever written on the subject of Trent Reznor, Nine Inch Nails, every former member of Nine Inch Nails and everyone who ever met Reznor between 1988 and the present day and reviews – including two by me that I had forgotten that I wrote – from publications from the UK to Uzbekistan (no exaggeration!). And the fact that it would have taken over ten years to sift through it all was no deterrent: there is no such thing as information overload!

1 Pre-Load

'I actually thought I was the Antichrist after I saw *The Omen* when I was 13.'

- Trent Reznor, 1994

He is the electric Lord Byron, the dark Orpheus and the technological Luciferian. For over a decade, Trent Reznor has been at the forefront of high technology rock 'n' roll, a beacon to the misfits, the individualists and the outsiders. An unapologetic technophile, Reznor is one of rock's great 'early adopters', dabbling in every new technology including MIDI, digital recording and holographic sound, years in advance of his contemporaries. He has also made some of the bleakest, the most uncompromising and the most hurt-filled rock 'n' roll ever recorded. Few have ever gone so far into the heart of despair as Reznor on 1999's *The Fragile* and few would want to. Yet, in a world where unhappy music has become the norm, even the most dour black-clad teen malcontent can find something in Reznor's music to shake them up and upset their world.

This book will attempt to trace the history of Trent Reznor and Nine Inch Nails from inception in the dog days of the '80s to the present day, looking at the albums, live shows, side projects, film soundtracks, remixes, production, collaboration and videos, as well as the lyrics of the songs, and attempt to decode the overt and covert meanings and see why they have found such a place in the hearts of the 'lost' generation of discontented youth. It will also try and put Nine Inch Nails into context as part of a culmination of several different strands of rock 'n' roll, from industrial, to goth, to punk. It will look at Trent Reznor the performer in the context of antecedents like

David Bowie, Peter Murphy of Bauhaus, Depeche Mode's Dave Gahan and Ministry's Al Jourgensen. It will look at him as a theatrical performer in a tradition that goes back to the *grand guignol* 'theatre of blood' as well as more recent practitioners like extreme mime artist Lindsay Kemp and rock 'n' roll's greatest pantomime dame Alice Cooper. And, in a wider sense, it will put Reznor into a deeper historical context as a resolution of the romantic Byronic 'vampyre' persona and the early 20th-century avant-garde art movements such as Dada, its successor Surrealism and the techno-fetishistic anarcho-fascists the Futurists. It will look at the influence that Reznor has had on others and forward to the next decade of Nine Inch Nails.

Dismissed by critics as pretentious, life-hating and cacophonous, these are actually all strengths for Reznor. He is unrepentantly pretentious, though perhaps he is really pretentious using the definition given by composer and artist Brian Eno in his 1996 book *A Year With Swollen Appendices*: 'Pretension is the dismissive name given to people's attempts to be some-"thing other than what they really are". It is vilified in England in particular because we are so suspicious of people trying to "rise above their station".

'In the arts, the word "pretentious" has a special meaning: the attempt at something that the critic thinks you have no right even to try. I'm very happy to have added my little offering to the glowing mountain of things described as "pretentious" – I'm happy to have made claims on things that I didn't have any "right" to, and I'm happy to have tried being someone else to see what it felt like.

'I decided to turn the word "pretentious" into a compliment. The common assumption is that there are "real" people and there are others who are pretending to be something they're not. There is also an assumption that there's something morally wrong with pretending. My assumptions about culture as a place where you can take psychological risks without incurring physical penalties make me think that pretending is the most important thing we do. It's the way we make our thought experiments, find out what it would be like to be otherwise.

'Robert Wyatt once said that we were always in the condition of children – faced with things we couldn't understand and thus with the need to guess and improvise. Pretending is what kids do all the time. It's how they learn. What makes anyone think you should sometime give it up?'

While many rock 'n' roll stars from Iggy Pop (particularly in his early Detroit incarnation) onwards have wallowed in negativity, few have made life-sickness such an art as Reznor. Of course it is a pose he affects, part of the act, but it is effective nonetheless.

Onstage, Reznor's violence can be shocking; various members of his band have been attacked midway through the set. During the Lollapalooza tour, he destroyed ten guitars a night and, unlike The Who's Pete Townshend who pioneered 'auto destruction' onstage, he wasn't faking it by smashing up sub-standard cheap ones. Speaking to *NME* journalist Terry Staunton after one show, Reznor recounted an incident that resulted in keyboard player James Woolley being injured: 'It was just one of those shows,' explains an almost apologetic Trent, a couple of weeks after the 'Frisco Incident', as it has become known among the Lollapalooza entourage. 'Every single thing was fucking up; monitors weren't on, guitars were out of tune, the mic stand was nowhere to be seen. Every fuck-up that could happen happened. Also the crowd were a little weird, and I just snapped... I just went totally violent, really scared a lot of people. I picked up my out-of-tune guitar, and smashed the fuckin' thing on the keyboard. Then I turned around and went about my business of the next song. A couple of songs later our road manager ran by and said "It's OK, the medics are finally here." I just looked at him and said "Medics? What fuckin' medics? What for?" Then I turned around and saw James scowling at me, with all this blood trickling down his face. Seems a piece of guitar busted off and hit him in the head. Oh well, that's showbiz.'

Offstage, however, Reznor is neither moody nor aggressive. Thoughtful, intelligent, capable of great charm and wit, he is one of the few great rock 'n' roll stars capable of giving a revealing interview where every answer seems to be an intense revelation about him personally or else he hands you the key that unlocks all the secrets of his music. Yet he still remains veiled in enigma, clinging onto the mystique that raises him above the company of mere rock 'n' roll workhorses, and lends him a glamour that endures because he seems ultimately unknowable.

In 1997 Trent Reznor was named one of *Time* magazine's 25 most influential people, sharing the honour with the cartoon character Dilbert, political shock jock Don Imus and the then US Secretary of State, Madeline Albright. Reznor is called 'the anti-Bon Jovi' by *Time*. His 'vulnerable vocals and accessible lyrics led an industrial revolution: He gave the gloomy genre a human heart... Reznor's music is filthy, brutish stuff, oozing with aberrant sex, suicidal melancholy and violent misanthropy. But to the depressed, his music...proffers pop's perpetual message of hope: There is worse pain in the world than yours. It is a lesson as old as Robert Johnson's blues. Reznor wields the muscular power of industrial rock not with frat-boy swagger but with a brooding, self-deprecating intelligence.'

The recognition of Reznor as the poet laureate of teen despair by *Time*, house journal of the American establishment, marked his transition from cult underground megastar to mainstream household figure. But, more importantly, it also marked the high watermark of Reznor as a major force in American music. In the brief period between the suicide of Kurt Cobain and the rise of nu metal, Trent became the poster boy for black-clad American teen angst; he was the country's most popular nihilist.

'People come up to me like I'm this grim, have-a-noose-around-my-neck-at-all-times kind of person. That's not the case at all,' he told *Spin* magazine in 1990. 'I'm not the happiest guy in the world. I'm not sure why. But I can't say, "It's because someone stole my bike."'

Industrial music – a term coined to describe bleak synthesiser heavy post-punk rock – had been around in one form or another since 1977 (Throbbing Gristle's *Second Annual Report* – actually not released until 1978 – was the album for which the term was coined in the now defunct rock weekly *Sounds*) and even before that (Suicide were recording in the early '70s, and German experimentalists like Kraftwerk, Can and Faust in the '60s). But it was Trent's *Pretty Hate Machine* that made it commercial enough for mass consumption.

Trent Reznor could have ploughed the same 'fork in the eyeball' (as he describes it) groove forever, but it was his desire always to push his art forward that took his career upward and – ultimately – backward. One of the few really authentic rock 'n' roll auteurs, Reznor guards his control jealously. He will collaborate with others but only on his terms: when he ventured beyond the studio to take Nine Inch Nails on the road – most famously on the first Lollapalooza tour – there was never any suggestion that the musicians in the band were anything other than hired hands. They were just the gilt on the frame and Reznor was the icon in the centre.

The Downward Spiral cemented his reputation as a rock 'n' roll Dostoievsky, trawling through the underworld to create his art. Critics in Europe and America were dismissive of the album: *Select* magazine's Andrew Perry called it '...the kind of sad, 2-D take on life you'd expect from an early-adolescent goth. Unlike, say, Polly Harvey's vision of pain, it's not humane. It's not mad. It's just stupid. It's also pretty misguided to think that a rock lyric that goes "your God is dead and no one cares" ("Heresy") will really shock the world in this day and age.' But fans were less sniffy and purchased the album by the truckload: it entered the *Billboard* charts at number one, something unheard of at the time for an album as 'difficult' as this. It was in fact the birth of NIN as a phenomenon. Reznor has been compared with other artists such as Al Jourgensen (a comparison he is happy with), Nick Cave, Marc Almond and Alan Vega, but they were all 'cult' artists, critics favourites who never sold more than a few thousand albums at any one time. Reznor, on the other hand, was a pop star, entering – however gingerly – the vacuous world of international celebrity.

For somebody with impeccable underground credentials, this success could be a two-edged sword. As he told *Huh* magazine in

1995: 'The price you pay is that the media that was aware of you and the fan base that was there from the start, they turn their backs on you because you "sold out". Even though it's the same record they bought six months ago. And then it's not cool to like these guys if you're really cool because other people that aren't cool like 'em now. Bullshit. I felt really bad about it at first. I wish people would quit liking us and we could go back to play the cool club and, you know, stay in the cool magazines and worry about the cool people. Then I thought fuck the cool people. Do what you do. The cool people that are worth a shit are still gonna like you if they liked you for the right reasons in the first place. The ones that are trend hoppers, fuck them. It's not about the music for them anyway, it's more about the statement of "look how aware I am. I found a band that nobody's gonna wanna hear, and that makes me cool".'

Quite why it was that Reznor should hit the right chord at this time has much to do with the mood of young people (teenagers up to people in their mid 20s) in the US in the late '80s and early '90s. There was a lot of anger and frustration that was bewildering to older people, particularly the generation of their parents who had lived through the cultural upheavals of the 1960s and '70s. Spoiled, brattish and indulged, these middle-class children weren't so much biting the hand that fed them as whining about it at great length. Angry, cynical and even nihilistic music, then as now, was in vogue not just in rock 'n' roll but in every other field of popular music. Pop music had given up any pretence that it was anything other than a marketing exercise to sell merchandizing to pre-teens and corporate rock was going the same way. Mainstream bands were closer in spirit to fast food franchises like McDonald's and Starbucks than to any spirit of rebellion that rock 'n' roll had once represented. Those who were outside had to adopt ever more extreme and militant positions. The initially upbeat and optimistic hip hop of the early '80s – music that had grown out of a party spirit – had given way to the more brutal gangsta rap at the end of the decade. The big albums of the time were Niggaz With Attitude's *Straight Outta Compton*, Public

Enemy's brilliant *It Takes A Nation Of Millions To Hold Us Back* and Ice-T's rap/rock band Body Count's debut with the controversial track 'Cop Killer', which revived the interest of Congress in censorship for rock and rap records.

Rock had split into a bewildering array of sub genres – grunge, death metal, hardcore – but what united them all was the same spirit of anger and resentment against targets as nebulous as 'society' to a more focussed 'mom and pop' anger. Nirvana, Pearl Jam, Stone Temple Pilots, Alice In Chains, Smashing Pumpkins, Hole – early-'90s rock was awash with despair, angst and loathing. Classics of negativity – Nirvana's *In Utero*, Hole's *Live Through This*, Smashing Pumpkins *Melon Collie And The Infinite Sadness* – all vied with each other to plumb the depths of sadness and inner rage.

And as well as this anger, teenage depression was being recognised as something more serious than the run of the mill angst and insecurity of growing up. According to statistics compiled by the (American) National Institute of Mental Health in 1996, more teenagers and young adults died of suicide than from cancer, heart disease, AIDS, birth defects, stroke, pneumonia and influenza, and chronic lung disease combined. In 1996 suicide was the second-leading cause of death among college students, the third-leading cause of death among those aged 15 to 24 years and the fourth-leading cause of death among those aged 10 to 14 years.

It's perhaps significant that Reznor, like Kurt Cobain, Courtney Love and any number of prominent young rock and rap artists, came from a broken home. With divorce rates continually rising throughout the '80s and '90s, it was also statistically likely that a large section of the audience, perhaps even a majority, also came from one parent families. The social impact of this radical shift in the pattern of the average Western family from the extended network of the pre-industrial age through the compact 'nuclear family' ideal of the post-war era to the normalization of absent parents or unstable two parent families (where partners change) has not yet been definitively studied.

Although there is nothing glaringly obvious in Reznor's songs – nor indeed those of any of his contemporaries – the generalised rage and frustration that he articulated certainly found kindred souls who felt that he was communicating directly with them.

As one fan wrote in an online essay 'From Machine to Man: An Interpretation of *The Fragile* by Nine Inch Nails': 'I suggest the one thing that really sets Nine Inch Nails apart from other industrial bands, the main reason so many don't merely enjoy but actually love Trent's music, is the fact that this is music we can really connect to; the honesty and passion with which Trent examines his life and the world, in some dark way, touches us. He explores topics we never wanted to touch by ourselves, he makes it acceptable to feel the way we feel – he lets us know that someone actually understands what we're going through, because he's gone through it too.

'This is not to say that only depressed, angry people can enjoy Trent's music; even if we don't feel the way he does, the sincerity with which he shares his life with us, in some way, allows us to truly see inside another human being – something we get precious little of, especially from celebrity figures and rock bands. Trent, in an odd roundabout way, actually encourages compassion – because he opens up to us completely, because he shares his soul with us and lets us see, truly see, inside his mind.'

Reznor attracted a smart, hip, if cynical and disaffected, fan base. Some of this audience was stolen away by the more populist and accessibly 'nu metal' bands in the second half of the decade: Limp Bizkit, Korn and The Deftones. And the gothic sensuality of NIN's *The Downward Spiral* era was delivered in a purer and again more accessible form by Marilyn Manson.

For whatever reasons, Trent Reznor has never recaptured the notoriety he enjoyed in the wake of his phenomenal second album, *The Downward Spiral*, nor the critical or popular acclaim. The cruelest twist of fate was that he saw his protégé Marilyn Manson – an artist he had discovered, produced, nurtured and signed to his own record imprint Nothing – eclipse him as America's favourite prince of darkness. Manson drew the ire of concerned parents, Christian fundamentalist fanatics, Congressional committees and outraged newspaper pundits. He also sold more records than Reznor, and in fact all but scooped up and took as his own the neo-gothic black-clad malcontents who had listened to NIN's *Pretty Hate Machine* and *The Downward Spiral* as though they were words of fire inscribed on tablets brought down from Mount Sinai by their dark Moses. The resulting feud with Manson – and later battles of words with the likes of Limp Bizkit frontman Fred Durst – smacked slightly of sour grapes. It was perhaps a bit of a 'pissing contest' to see who was king of all the goths.

Goth was a romantic tradition that flourished in the '80s in the wake of bands like Siouxsie And The Banshees, New Order/Joy Division and Bauhaus, who had all emerged from the British punk rock scene but soon eschewed its minimalism and anti-intellectualism for a dreamier, almost psychedelic music heavily influenced by David Bowie and imagery informed by German expressionist cinema, Weimar Republic-era cabaret, Expressionist horror movies and a hint of Luciferianism. Manson, painfully thin and pale with long raven black hair, was in the mould of Byronic goth pin-up boys like Peter Murphy of Bauhaus and Andrew Eldritch of The Sisters Of Mercy. And Reznor, though he was far more extreme.

The band had a minor hit in 1995 with their Eurythmics cover 'Sweet Dreams (Are Made Of This', taken from their Reznor-produced debut album *Portrait Of An American Family*. In the early stages of his career Manson was often seen as merely Trent Reznor's puppet, a sort of 'Mini Me' clone that followed his master around. It was advantageous for Manson; the tours with NIN and David Bowie brought Manson to a huge new audience. Reznor, who composed the soundtrack for David Lynch's *Lost Highway*, was instrumental in having Manson appear in the film. During the recording of Manson's third album, the breakthrough *Antichrist Superstar*, however, Reznor and Manson's relationship broke down, resulting in an ugly public feud.

Reznor took exception to tell-all revelations in Manson's autobiography *The Long Hard Road Out Of Hell*, which describes in lurid detail on-the-road escapades involving groupies that would make Led Zeppelin blush, including one '95 escapade that involved burning a woman's pubic hair and a party with the Jim Rose Circus Sideshow where they held a contest to see which groupie could hold an enema the longest before ejecting into a bowl of Froot Loops.

Ironically, when Reznor and Manson supposedly buried the hatchet in 2000, with Trent directing the video for Manson's 'Starfuckers, Inc', a song attacking the cult of celebrity at any cost, it drew him into the ongoing cold war with Fred Durst, who took exception to seeing his image smashed in the clip.

Durst told *Revolver* magazine: 'Trent Reznor is pissing me off. I'm a huge NIN fan; *Pretty Hate Machine* was a huge part of my life. Big. Trent really took industrial music to another level. So to have him smashing a plate that's got my image on in his 'Starfuckers, Inc' video for no other reason than jealousy is really small. I understand his record isn't doing what he'd hoped it would, but that doesn't mean he has to bring everyone else down with him. Despite everything, I'd like to collaborate with him. That would be fantastic and our fans would love it. But instead, he's out there talking shit, and he's hurting himself.'

Durst responded with the refrain 'You want to fuck me like an animal/You want to burn me on the inside/You like to think I'm your perfect drug/But just know that nothin' you do will bring you closer to me' – all references to Reznor songs – on 'Hot Dog' from *Chocolate Starfish And The Hotdog Flavored Water* over a sample from NIN's 'Closer'.

With Limp Bizkit riding high in the charts it could be seen as the age old story of 'A Star Is Born' – the conflict between the one on the way up and the one on the way down. Yet Trent was far from past his peak: five years on from *The Downward Spiral* he released *The Fragile* at the close of the millennium, an awe-inspiring work that took industrial rock to its absolute outer limits.

It was an undisputed masterpiece but, coming five years after *The Downward Spiral*, it may have been one whose time had already passed. The generation of industrial bands that had preceded NIN was in disarray: Ministry, Reznor's major influence, had been dropped by the Warner Brothers label amidst reports of mainman Alain Jourgensen's increasingly bizarre drug-induced behaviour; Skinny Puppy were no more, with one member dead from a heroin overdose; others, like Front 242, The Young Gods and Laibach, continued to play but with little attention from press or public. A new generation of artists influenced by industrial music as well as post-Prodigy techno were springing up around the world: Berlin's Atari Teenage Riot and EC8OR made the likes of Ministry sound very old. And a new school of young bands influenced by Reznor – Static X and Orgy at the forefront – were springing up and stealing away the remaining fans of the old school. Trent's parent label Interscope didn't understand where he was going with *The Fragile* and, he claims, failed to market the album correctly, never cashing in on the praise – albeit reserved – that the album received from critics and fans alike.

Writing in *Metal Hammer* magazine at the time, Dan Silver said: 'Two and a half years in the making, its 23 tracks consuming two CDs and over an hour and a half of your time, *The Fragile* is an intense labour of hate and decidedly uneasy listening, the result of a sustained bout of fear and self-loathing in New Orleans. Or rather half of it is. That this writhing behemoth of a record is a colossal artistic achievement is beyond doubt, but as a listener you can't help but wish alternative music's genuinely deranged *enfant terrible* had brought in some outside ears to temper his seemingly unstemmable flow of ideas and invention.'

Rolling Stone, never one of Reznor's champions, said: 'It's been five years since the Nine Inch Nails auteur dropped *The Downward Spiral*, crunching punk and goth and Depeche Mode and God knows what else into the diary of a teenage death-disco vampire... But the world was a much more innocent place in 1994. You remember the carefree days of grunge – it was a time before Heaven's Gate, before

Oklahoma City, before Justine Bateman's announcement that she was accepting Jesus Christ as her personal savior. Michael and Lisa Marie were just a couple of crazy kids in love. Korn was just what white people called maize. Trent has to show and prove for a more jaded world – he's a vampire version of an aging action hero, and he's getting too undead for this shit. But *The Fragile* isn't the music of a man going quietly. Trent comes on like an avenging disco godfather returned for the big payback. *The Fragile* is his version of Pink Floyd's *The Wall*, a double album that vents his alienation and misery into paranoid studio hallucinations, each track crammed with overdubs until there's no breathing room. The stun-volume guitar riffs, intricate synth squeals and interlocking drum-machine patterns flow together as a two-hour bubble bath in the sewer of Trent's soul. Even beautiful moments like the piano ballad "La Mer" are full of tension; acoustic bass and an African mbira decorate the piano until a live drum kit shows up to splatter itself all over the studio walls.'

Reznor has always been unsatisfied as an artist, always pushing his work a little bit further. Even when he has finished a song, he keeps going back to it, reworking and remixing. It's as though there is no actual definitive version of a Nine Inch Nails song, as though the version he releases on record is only the latest one, and that others – equally good – preceded it and will follow it.

Having released a live album – *And All That Might Have Been*, a companion piece to a DVD filmed on the Fragile tour – he also made a short album to accompany it, available as a limited edition. On this mini-album called *Still* Trent 'deconstructs' songs from *The Fragile*, performing them at a piano in a live setting. Reznor is adamant that *Still* is a little curiosity rather than a signpost to the future direction that NIN will take and that while an acoustic club tour is on the cards, it's not necessarily the only path that Reznor will take in future. Nevertheless, it is closer in spirit to recent albums by Radiohead, Björk and PJ Harvey – all artists that he admires – than anything he has done previously and he makes no secret of his dissatisfaction with the way NIN are perceived.

He was annoyed at the perceived 'failure' of *The Fragile*: 'I knew it was a pretty difficult record in a disposable climate but I guess I'm more disappointed in the fact that the media seem to equate commercial success with things being good. I have to admit that I get defensive when that starts coming up because it's an album that I loved and I still love. If you'd asked me when I put out *The Downward Spiral*, I'd never have thought then that it would even sell a tenth of what it did and I think in the long run the success of that album was damaging to career in a way in that now the stakes have gone up. As a musician you're put into this competitive race to see who sells more records in the first week than the other guy. And that's not a good thing if you're in music for the reasons that I'm in it. My anger at the distributor stems from their inability to understand what they're trying to sell. When you push my record through the same hole that Eminem goes through, it doesn't fit, and when it started to not fit, it was left to die on the floor.'

'I love Radiohead and this isn't anything against them. Those albums *Kid A* and *Amnesiac* were two of my favourite records of last year,' he says. 'With the distributors I have, if they had tried to understand or put a little more thought into presenting it to the right people. On that label alone, the Radiohead machinery, the people behind them, succeeded. Our machinery failed. Radiohead's team of people that sold you that record also sold you the perception that it worked, it was a success. The actual numbers would challenge that (*The Fragile* actually sold more than *Kid A*, shifting 800,000 double albums in the US to Radiohead's 300,000) but it didn't matter. They won, you didn't question it. Interscope dropped the ball.'

That he is now looking at a drastic overhaul of the very concept of Nine Inch Nails itself – which has been everything from Trent playing all the instruments in the studio to the fully fledged 'proper' band who went on the road with *The Fragile* – is hardly a surprise. The release of *And All That Might Have Been* at the start of 2002 was a way for Trent to lay one incarnation of NIN to rest before unleashing another.

Everything from the line-up of the band to the music that he plays and the sort of venues that he performs in will change. As an experiment he expressed his intention of going out on the road playing 'unplugged' shows at smaller venues.

'My favourite venues are clubs, where you can see the audience and the audience can see you without 30 feet [10m] of security barriers in between.'

But whether this acoustic sound – Trent onstage with a piano – actually heralds a new direction for Reznor remains to be seen.

Reznor, whose movie credits involve compiling and overseeing soundtracks for both Oliver Stone's *Natural Born Killers* and David Lynch's *Lost Highway*, told me of his major ambition: to actually compose the score for a major motion picture.

'Actually my big dream is that David Cronenberg calls me up and tells me that he's got a project that he wants me to work on from start to finish. I'd love him to say "I've got an uneasy film and I need some uneasy music to go with it". I'm not saying that this would replace what I want to do with Nine Inch Nails, but I'd like to go in and find out what I don't like about it!'

At the time of writing, NIN were in the studio with producer and long-time collaborator Alan Moulder, a British-born engineer who worked on *Pretty Hate Machine, The Downward Spiral* and *The Fragile*, whose other credits include The Jesus And Mary Chain, My Bloody Valentine and Smashing Pumpkins.

In a posting on a NIN fan site, Jerome Dillon said of the next album: 'As far as NIN...there are new songs and ideas that were worked on with Alan Moulder and Dave Ogilvie...and I really like the direction it's heading...very brutal and stripped down.'

Trent, more obliquely, referred to music that he was listening to at the time: Radiohead, Julian Cope's *Autogeddon* and *20 Mothers*, Spiritualized, Mercury Rev and Beethoven's piano sonatas.

As Reznor told me in early 2002: 'I need to risk failure to move into whatever is next. The whole format of the band needs to evolve.'

2 Neurotic Boy Outsider

'Mercer is a nice little picturesque one-horse, one-McDonald's kind of town. I go back there now and it's like "what a nice pleasant place", but not a place to grow up in.'

– Trent Reznor, 1990

Born Michael Trent Reznor in Mercer, Pennsylvania to Mike Reznor and Nancy Clark on 17 May 1965, he would be joined six years later by a sister called Tera. Shortly after she was born his parents decided to separate. Trent was raised by his maternal grandparents. His sister, Tera, lived with their mother.

Mercer is a town with a population of just under 2000, north of the industrial mill town of Pittsburgh, a pleasant, normal American heartland town. Like most small towns, however, there is little to interest smart, ambitious kids like Reznor. Despite the separation of his parents, Reznor had a reasonably happy childhood and remained close to both parents. His father Mike was a commercial artist who came from a family who owned the rights to the Reznor Furnace (a sort of industrial heater) and, although not rich, was comfortably off. He remained in touch with his son, Mike Jr, throughout his childhood and later he would attend Nine Inch Nails shows. To avoid confusion, Mike Jr became known by his middle name, Trent. When he was six his father sat him down for a man to man talk. 'I'm leaving,' he said. 'When are you coming back?' was Trent's reply.
'I'm not coming back.' Trent didn't understand what that meant.

'I was raised by my grandparents, the greatest people in the world,' Trent told *Spin* magazine in 1990. 'I try to tell them "You're not going to hear my music on the radio. I'm not going to be on soap operas singing this." I can imagine what my grandfather tells people: "It's called Nine Inch Nails – here's the video. And here he is lying dead at the end of it." I warned my grandfather that the church might be after him.'

There seems to be little bitterness or resentment. Reznor told *Alternative Press*: 'It was just easier on my mother having my sister and me stay with my grandparents because they lived near each other. My grandparents are good people and good parents, but I feel like anybody does whose parents split up – kind of ripped off. I'm not going to make it out to be some big fucking kind of deal. Subconsciously, it may have some kind of effect, but it didn't seem to be that bad. You just realise you're not on *Happy Days*. It's the real world – you need to ignore what you are programmed by sitcoms to think your life should be. I don't really think about it and I don't put any blame on anybody. My parents were young. I would have done the same thing, I'm sure.'

Trent's mother, Nancy, was an amateur bluegrass musician and the child soon developed a strong interest in what would become his path in life. His parents would prove to be supportive of his ambitions: 'My dad and I are best friends. He's pretty much responsible for the way I turned out,' Reznor told *Alternative Press*. 'He would provide a little artistic inspiration here and there in the form of a guitar, stuff like that. My family has always been supportive of what I do.'

'He was always a good kid,' his grandfather Bill Clark told *People* magazine. A semi-retired furniture salesman, Bill recalled idyllic days spent cane-pole fishing with his grandson – a boy scout who loved to skateboard, build model planes and play the piano. 'Music was his life, from the time he was a wee boy. He was so gifted.'

In the same feature, *People* magazine dug up Trent's piano and high school teachers.

Reznor's playing 'always reminded me of Harry Connick Jr,' says his former piano teacher, Rita Beglin. Remembered in Mercer as a clean-cut, handsome and popular kid, Trent Reznor, who played tenor sax and keyboards, starred in his Mercer Area Junior and Senior High

School jazz and marching bands, was voted best in drama by his classmates and performed with various local rock groups before and after graduating in 1983. 'I considered him to be very upbeat and friendly,' says Mercer's band director Hendley Hoge, 40. 'I think all that "dark avenging angel" stuff is marketing – Trent making a career for himself.'

He appeared in two high school musicals *The Music Man* and *Jesus Christ Superstar*. The role he played in *Jesus Christ Superstar*, the hit '70s musical written by Tim Rice and Andrew Lloyd Webber, was Judas Iscariot. It's worth noting that the Judas in the musical is a complex, Hamlet-like figure, wracked with self doubt rather than a straight villain from less imaginative interpretations of the New Testament.

Jesus Christ Superstar chronicles the last seven days in the life of Jesus of Nazareth as seen through the eyes of his disciple, Judas Iscariot. Judas has become disillusioned with the 'movement', which draws some ham-fisted parallels with the 'movement' in the '60s. At the opening of the play, Judas agonises over his perception that Jesus' followers have become fanatical and unrealistic, hailing him as a god and twisting his words into monstrous prophecies. After all, in Judas' mind, Jesus is only a man – a man with certain inconsistencies, as evidenced by his relationship with Mary Magdalene. As the crowds in the street grow more and more out of control, the rift between Jesus and Judas grows. After watching Jesus lose control in the temple, lashing out at the moneylenders and merchants, then begging to be left alone when a crowd of cripples surround him asking to be healed, Judas is more convinced than ever that the man from Nazareth is just that – a man, and nothing more. He decides that Jesus, having lost control of the mob, has become dangerous and must be stopped. He goes to the priests and gives them all the information they need to catch Jesus alone so that they can take him prisoner without risking violence by the mob. After leading the soldiers to Gethsemane, however, and watching the events that unfold, Judas soon realises that he has been tricked by God into being the instrument of Jesus' martyrdom. Furious that the man from Nazareth will be remembered as a 'superstar', Judas hangs himself.

When it was first performed on Broadway in the early '70s, *Jesus Christ Superstar* was attacked by doctrinaire Christians both Protestant and Catholic as 'blasphemous'. Judas, in the original production, was portrayed by the flamboyant black musical star Ben Vereen, something else that upset traditional Christians. Although it seems anodyne and its authors examples of everything that is awful about stage musicals, *Jesus Christ Superstar* is perhaps the most popular work of heresy (as opposed to blasphemy) of recent times. The portrayal of Judas as a complex, ambiguous figure rather than a thoroughly evil villain – his usual role in the Christian pantomime – was unusual. It was to be Trent's first step on the road to 'the dark side'.

Trent was not raised a fanatical fundamentalist but, like most small-town Americans, he attended church. Contemporaries like Marilyn Manson (né Brian Warner) and Tori Amos tell such horror stories about religious upbringings that some of their art is explained.

According to Manson in *The Long Hard Road Out Of Hell*, his grade school teacher Miss Price told the class that President Ronald Reagan was the Antichrist. (His name 'Ronald Wilson Reagan' had six letters contained within each word): 'The Antichrist was here on Earth and we must prepare for the coming of Christ and the rapture. My teachers explained all of this not as if it was an opinion open to interpretation, but as if it were an undeniable fact ordained by the Bible.

'It was then that I began having nightmares – nightmares that continue to this day. I was thoroughly terrified by the idea of the end of the world and the Antichrist. So I became obsessed with it, watching movies like *The Exorcist* and *The Omen* and reading prophetic books like *Centuries* by Nostradamus, *1984* by George Orwell and the novelised version of the (strange campy 1972 Christian apocalyptic sci-fi) film *A Thief In The Night*, which described very graphically people getting their heads cut off because they hadn't received 666 tattoos on their forehead. Combined with the weekly harangues at Christian school, it all made the apocalypse seem so real, so tangible, so close that I was constantly haunted by dreams and worries about what would happen if I found out who the Antichrist was. Would I risk my life to save everyone else? What if I already had the mark of the beast somewhere on me where I couldn't see it? What if the Antichrist was me? I was filled with fear and confusion.'

Tori Amos recalled her grandparents, both Pentecostal ministers, always praying. She even once witnessed them speaking in tongues. Her father, also a preacher, used to take her to sing in bars when she was eight.

Reznor, by contrast, seems to have enjoyed a comparatively normal childhood and adolescence.

'Trent was a quiet guy, real good looking. There were kids who were religious and some quite freaky about it, but he wasn't one of them,' recalled a former high school classmate. 'He didn't seem like an unhappy sort of guy or a screwed up guy. He wasn't like a ray of sunshine or anything but he wasn't, you know, Darth Vader.'

'I believe in God,' he told *Spin*. 'I was brought up going to Sunday school and church, but it didn't really mean anything. Things upset me a lot. It was just a theme I kept coming back to – religion, guilt and doubting. I believe there's a God but I'm not too sure of His relevance.'

The rash of quasi-theological horror movies seem to have made more of an impression than any mainstream religious upbringing.

'*The Exorcist* ruined my childhood,' he told *Details* magazine in 1990. 'It was the ultimate scary thing because it couldn't easily be disproved.' Then there was *The Omen*. After that he was convinced he was the Antichrist. He went looking around his scalp for the three sixes that would confirm the truth. He was terrified of the Devil. He would make imaginary deals to sell his soul. In bed at night he would lie a certain way because if he lay on the other side he knew he would be in for bad things.

Yet the song 'Heresy' on *The Downward Spiral* seems to hint at some deeper disillusion with Christianity: 'He sewed his eyes shut because he was afraid to see/He tries to tell me what I put inside of me/He's got the answers to ease my curiosity/He dreamed a god up and called it Christianity/He flexed his muscles to keep his flock of sheep in line/He made a virus that would kill off all the swine/ His perfect kingdom of killing, suffering and pain/Demands devotion – atrocities done in his name.'

His childhood world, his early role models, were characters on TV, like Steve Austin (played by Lee Majors) in the hit sci-fi series *The Six Million Dollar Man*. Reznor, by his own admission, was a massive fan. Based on the novel *Cyborg* by Martin Caidin, *The Six Million Dollar Man*, about an astronaut transformed into a part-robotic superman after an accident left him shattered, was one of the first popular dramas involving the idea of a man-machine interface, that the boundaries between what is human and what is machine would start to melt away.

Trent always loved science fiction. *The Six Million Dollar Man* struck a chord, he told *Details* magazine, 'probably because I wasn't the biggest kid in the class and I wasn't cool. The day the Bionic Woman died on *The Six Million Dollar Man*, that was a tearful day in our household. When I think back, I had a degree of feeling mildly depressed, of melancholiness.

This proto-cyberpunk theme would become important years later when Reznor became one of the first rock 'n' roll stars to try to integrate himself with his own machinery. And there would be more than six million dollars involved.

At this time the young Reznor also discovered rock 'n' roll.

For anyone who grew up male, white and provincial in '70s America, getting into KISS was simply part of the process of growing up. It has been suggested that the government actually issued every teenage boy with a copy of KISS' *Destroyer* when he reached his 14th birthday! When *Rip* magazine asked what he listened to while growing up he said: 'KISS. Just KISS, nothing else. The Partridge Family a little bit. Before KISS. Then KISS. You know, Supertramp, REO Speedwagon thrown in. Just kidding about the Speedwagon.'

Reznor had been studying classical piano but now began to see other possibilities.

KISS were the first band to truly realise the potential of a rock 'n' roll band that aspired to be a recognised corporate brand. Most bands wanted to be as big as The Beatles but KISS wanted to be as big as Coca-Cola. Led by the hyper-intelligent and ambitious Israeli American frontman Gene Simmons, KISS only ever appeared in public wearing their full kabuki-influenced makeup – their individual styles protected by copyright in the manner of clowns or real kabuki actors – and their image was licensed to appear on everything from posters and t-shirts to lunchboxes. There were KISS comic books, KISS movies, KISS action figures and – more recently – Simmons launched the KISS coffin (for the die hard fan). KISS had total market penetration in '70s America, they had a profile that was the envy of other bands. Musically they were a competent if rather unoriginal rock 'n' roll band; despite the imagery of Simmons as a demon blowing fire onstage, they sounded very poppy and enjoyed major hits with lush ballads like 'Beth' and even had forays into disco (the band were in fact signed to Neil Bogart's Casablanca Records, the quintessential American commercial disco label – KISS were part of the same stable as P-funk superstars Parliament, disco diva Donna Summer and camp macho collective The Village People). But they suggested that they were part of the 'dark side'. Though there was nothing overtly Satanic or occult about KISS – they were closer to Scooby Doo than to real occultists – they were often lumped alongside horror rockers like Alice Cooper and the quasi-occultic art-metal band The Blue Oyster Cult. KISS were also one of the first bands to be targeted by loopy Christian fundamentalists: their name, so the rumour went, stood for Knights In Satan's Service!

Although punk was breaking in the UK at this time, outside of cities like New York, Detroit and LA, it meant little to the youth of middle America. The first show that Reznor attended was, by his own admission, The Eagles with Fleetwood Mac and Boz Scaggs. In small towns like Mercer, people only liked what they heard on Top 40 radio and could buy from their local Wal-Mart. As he grew, so the culturally backward and narrow-minded life in the backwater town started to chaff against Reznor's skin. He started thinking about escaping but without a clear plan as to how he would go about it. He left school early and practiced the piano, originally planning a career as a concert pianist. But as raging hormones – and the influence of KISS – kicked in, he realised that he wasn't going to get laid regularly wearing a tuxedo and playing Chopin. Opportunities in Mercer were limited for careers: Reznor saw himself pumping gas at the local service station and was appalled.

Adept on piano, tenor sax, tuba and guitar, Reznor, in his teens, began to pester his parents for a synthesiser as his interest in electronic music grew.

'When I was in high school, I begged my parents to get a cheap Moog. Now I could play "Just What I Need". Whoo-oo-whoo-oo. (whistles synth line from the Cars song). When that kind of explosion of synth music came around in the early 80's, it really was exciting; sequencers were just coming out. I thought, I love music, I love keyboard instruments – maybe I can get into synthesiser design. The excitement of hearing a Human League track and thinking, that's all machines, there's no drummer. That was my calling. It wasn't The Sex Pistols.'

His father had already bought him an electric piano and he played with a few local garage bands, mostly Top 40 covers. And after leaving high school in 1983, he enrolled to study computer programming at Allegheny College, in Meadville, PA, one of the top 80 national liberal arts colleges in the US. Also at this time Reznor became aware of the post-punk British new wave acts making their impact on the US charts thanks to the fledgling MTV, which broadcast videos by The Human League, Culture Club, ABC, The Associates, Billy Idol, Blancmange, Depeche Mode, Duran Duran and Tears For Fears in heavy rotation. The 18-year-old Reznor adopted a new-wave look, dying his hair first peroxide blonde then red. He was a member of a local band called Option 30, a covers band playing new wave songs by the likes of U2 and The Cars. Talking to *Spin* in 1996 he said: 'Option 30. That was actually about one-third originals, two-thirds covers, from Elvis Costello to Wang Chung. For what it's worth, Wang Chung put a record out before the "Dance Hall Days" record, when they spelled their name differently, H-U-A-N-G Chung. All guitar-bass-drums. Still a real good record.'

Reznor was living with his father at this time and began to spend less and less time attending classes and more time holed up writing songs. He also started playing three or four gigs a week with the band, often making little more than expenses playing bars and lounges in the Midwest. Option 30 played around Pennsylvania and Ohio, as far south as Cleveland which – to a boy from Mercer – actually seemed like a fantastically cosmopolitan urban sprawl.

'It was the most whorish part of my career,' he later recalled. 'Three hundred bucks [£200] a week. I played keyboards and sang. My destiny was lounge bands.'

Trent eventually dropped out of college altogether after the first year, leaving the band for a short succession of equally forgettable semi-professional covers bands including another local covers outfit called The Urge. Although Reznor is dismissive of his work at that time, friends and acquaintances from that period were impressed by his charisma and energy as a performer. He was also writing his own songs and performed them with both Option 30 and The Urge, though they bore little resemblance to anything he would later do with Nine Inch Nails as they were essentially his own attempts to compose lightweight, catchy early-'80s synth-pop like the artists he was covering.

In 1984, aged 19, Trent made the move to Cleveland. He got a job working at a music shop that sold keyboards and synthesisers that, although it sometimes bored him hearing a stream of wannabes trail through to play the intro to 'Stairway To Heaven', it gave him an opportunity to familiarise himself with state-of-the-art musical kit as it became available. By the early to mid '80s there was an explosion in the sort of synthesisers that were available on the retail market. Early synthesisers were cumbersome, unstable and looked like telephone exchanges. They were also hugely and prohibitively expensive, often being custom built, and it was only the rich-as-Croesus progressive acts like Emerson, Lake And Palmer, Pink Floyd and Yes who were able to afford to buy them in the early '70s. Musicians needed a working knowledge of electronics and engineering to be able to coax even comparatively simple sounds out of them. But as soon as mass production began, cheaper and simpler instruments started to come onto the market, pioneered by the WASP synthesiser (a simple monophonic instrument with a printed keyboard) in the late '70s and even 'toy' products. Sequencers – simple computers that automate keyboard patterns, essential in most forms of electronic music – were also starting to appear on the market in a more affordable form.

Reznor also joined a succession of small-time Cleveland bands. The most embarrassing seems to have been a mainstream 'hard rock' band called The Innocent: 'Foreigner crap...dinosaur AOR bullshit rock.' Although he didn't play on their album *Livin' On The Streets,* his photograph did appear on the record sleeve. As ghosts from the past go, there are worse, more embarrassing pictures to be found. With a keyboard slung over his shoulder and bearing in mind that nobody in the '80s ever looked good, he is recognizable albeit just. He is still extremely touchy about the picture. Talking to *Details,* whose writer had dredged up a copy to confront him with, he called himself: 'Stupid. Dumb. A ridiculous 1983 [sic – it was taken in 1984] sissy. You got me. I'm an idiot. I've tried to hide it. It was the one thing I was waiting for someone to throw at me.'

He left after three months. He also had his first brush with the movies at this time. He appeared in a flop film that starred Michael J Fox and Joan Jett called *Light Of Day* as a member of a po-faced synth trio who were known as The Problems (though the line-up may have been the same as The Exotic Birds, which was the germ of the first touring incarnation of Nine Inch Nails) – they appeared as objects of derision. The film is a confused and downbeat family drama; Fox and Joan Jett play a brother and sister who sneak off to play in a local rock 'n' roll band. It says much about the movie that Michael J Fox's singing is not the worst, nor is Joan Jett's acting the poorest performance. Reznor does not have a speaking role but appears for several minutes: 'They used to be called The Sins, now they're called The Problems,' one of the characters says of them. The film is awful despite being written and directed by Paul Schrader (screenwriter of *Taxi Driver* and *Raging Bull*, director of *Blue Collar, Hardcore* and *American Gigolo*) but has become a cult item among Nine Inch Nails devotees with copies of the now-unavailable VHS trading on eBay for around $50 (£35).

Reznor's contribution to the film – not included on the soundtrack album – was a cover of Buddy Holly's 'True Love Ways', which he arranged and sang. The song was chosen by the film's producers, no doubt to highlight how ridiculous it is for a 'soul-less' electronic trio to be playing 'real' rock 'n' roll, represented throughout the movie by Jett/Fox's dire AOR 'rawk'.

Actually, there are many similarities between Buddy Holly and Trent Reznor. Both were 'geeky' kids regarded as dweebs by their schoolfriends, both came from small towns and both were happiest in the studio using the best available technology and techniques at the time – Reznor with MIDI, sampling and drum machines, Holly with tape delay, 'click' tracks and orchestration. Both were accomplished pianists who incorporated elements learned from classical music as well as marrying classic pop songs to the hard rock of their time. Holly's drummer and closest collaborator Jerry Allison, like Chris Vrenna, was a schoolfriend. Both are known for their production talents as well as their unique-yet-readily-imitable singing and songwriting styles. Norman Petty and Flood were both mad-as-hatter producers who coaxed the best from Holly and Reznor. And both were almost ruined by larger-than-life figures responsible for their early success; Norman Petty also filling the role of TVT's Steve Gottlieb in Holly's career.

Cleveland is a city with an undeserved bad reputation. While it is hardly a major art centre like New York or San Francisco, there has always been a healthy music scene in Ohio. Alan Freed, who coined the term rock 'n' roll, was one of the first radio DJs to play black R&B records to a white teenage audience on a Cleveland radio station. The first ever major rock 'n' roll show – the March 1952 Moondog Coronation Ball – was held in Cleveland. Top black acts were booked for the show. Six thousand fans crashed gates in addition to the thousands already in the 10,000-seater hall. Two-thirds of the audience was white. This partly explains why the Rock 'n' Roll Hall of Fame is based there.

Anglophile pop band The Raspberries and early punks The Dead Boys hailed from Cleveland. In the late '70s, Cleveland – and the nearby city of Akron, America's 'rubber capital' – had a cult scene including bands Pere Ubu, Devo, Jane Aire And The Belvederes, Chi Pig and Rachel Sweet who enjoyed international fame way beyond Ohio thanks in part to the patronage of British punk labels Stiff and Radar. Influenced by Frank Zappa, Captain Beefheart and by a knowing retro-futurist art scene, these bands were largely prophets without honour in their home town. Local tastes tended to be conservative. Pere Ubu's brand of disturbing industrial blues may have been just the thing for the hip post-punk crowd in London and New York, but back in Cleveland they preferred beer-swilling plaid-shirted plain boogie bands like local hero Michael Stanley and a host of anonymous bar bands who sounded (a bit) like Bruce Springsteen.

And because it had a vast population of Russian and Eastern European immigrants who settled there in the early part of the century – you will see the onion domes of Russian and Serbian Orthodox churches all over the Ohio/Pennsylvania region and sometimes the landscape looks more like the Russian steppes or the wheatfields of the Ukraine than America – there is an overabundance of polka music blaring out from radios, TV and from car stereos. Turn on your TV in Cleveland at any hour of the day and you will probably find one of the grainy locally produced shows featuring pensioners dancing around to an accordion band, like a transmission from another era. And, as manufacturing plants withered throughout the recession in the '80s, the landscape was notable for having huge tracts of abandoned rusting factories and empty warehouses. This post-industrial wasteland was a major influence on the music and concepts of Devo and Pere Ubu and the post-apocalyptic flavour of the city at night was inspirational to Trent.

Sadly, despite the fact that Ohio has produced and nurtured a wealth of maverick talent – perhaps springing up there in isolation from the scenes in the rest of America and becoming militantly individualistic in the conservative milieu – they all ultimately leave to find success. Trent quickly became aware that he had traded in one kind of small town with its blinkered worldview for another: Cleveland was just a small American town like Mercer on a much bigger scale.

Desperate to learn about recording, Reznor landed a job as a dogsbody at Right Track, a local recording studio. The work mostly entailed tidying the place, cleaning the toilets and mopping the floor. But it was a chance to be around the process of recording music.

'I heard stuff other people were recording and I always thought, "This stuff sucks." I thought I could do better, but for a long time I wasn't doing anything about it. I was arranging other people's music. I was playing keyboards on other people's bullshit demos. I was playing live, taking drugs and being a fucking idiot – fooling myself that I was doing something when really I wasn't. Then when I got in that studio I realised that there's an opportunity here. I could make it happen.'

Continuing to play in bands he started to evolve as a musician and to find his feet, to discover the kind of music he wanted to play. Trent did keyboards, programming and backing vocals with a group called Slam Bam Boo – a terrible '80s name if ever there was one – and played keyboards in Lucky Pierre (name from a cult soft porn film directed by schlockmeister Hershell Gordon Lewis) around 1984-5.

He also played saxophone on their 1988 'Communique' EP, though this was more of a favour to Kevin McMahon, the main man behind this band who became a friend of Trent's. Later, when McMahon formed a new band called Prick, Reznor produced and engineered them as well as getting his producer/collaborator Alan Moulder involved. He also released their eponymous debut album on his Nothing Records imprint in 1994.

Lucky Pierre and Kevin McMahon became a serious influence on Reznor. McMahon was later to affect a vampiric style that saw him unfairly compared with Reznor, though even in Lucky Pierre he was experimenting with theatricality – based on glam rockers such as David Bowie, Iggy Pop and Lou Reed – as well as making a poppier version of the nascent industrial music coming from groups like Test Dept, SPK and Ministry.

He also played in an outfit called The Exotic Birds with drummer Chris Vrenna, whose later credits would include stints with Nine Inch Nails as well as Stabbing Westward, KMFDM, Die Warzau and industrial 'supergroup' Pigface. He is now a prominent remixer whose credits include David Bowie, Smashing Pumpkins, Marilyn Manson, Green Day, The Wallflowers, Hole, Rob Zombie and Xzibit featuring Dr Dre and Snoop Dogg.

Vrenna told *Face* magazine that he and Trent met: '...In 1985 or 1986. I was still a senior in high school. I'm from Erie, Pennsylvania and he's from Mercer, which is 45 minutes south from Erie, and there's a town in the middle of our two towns. And I was playing in a band there, and the keyboard player from that band and Trent were friends already and I got introduced to him. He would always come see our band and we would drive to Cleveland to see him play. We were roommates and I helped him do demos in the studio. He had all his gear in his bedroom in our little apartment.'

They lived the sort of squalid poverty level existence common to all penniless struggling artists around the world. They lived on instant noodles, and when work was scarce lived by selling albums to second hand shops or to friends and acquaintances. Although the music came first, a sizeable portion of the income also went on getting wasted. There is no suggestion that Trent was ever a junkie during this time, but low-level hedonism is a fact of life even on the breadline.

The Exotic Birds were a rock band, though at this time Reznor had discovered a whole new world of electronic music and was edging closer to formulating the idea for the band he wanted to lead.

'If anyone ever asks me about influences I always say Ministry. I'm not embarrassed of that,' Reznor told *Alternative Press* after he worked with Ministry founder Al Jourgensen, singing vocals with one of his many side projects, The Revolting Cocks. 'Al's been a hero of mine and it was just cool to walk in a room and have him go, "Trent, I gotta talk to you about a lotta shit, man." I was like, wow. I couldn't believe it. I have to admit before I met him I thought, "Is he going to fucking throw a bottle at me?" But he's a nice, intelligent guy. He's got that aggressive side to him, but it wasn't like he was an animal loose, peeing on people. He's got his shit together.'

By the mid '80s, there was a wave of American alternative bands who had grown up in the wake of punk, been influenced by electronic pop from Europe, who were forging their own futuristic sound. There were pioneers in New York, in hip hop, such as Afrika Bambaataa and The Jonzun Crew. There were the early stirrings in the clubs of Chicago and Detroit of the music that would take the world by storm as house and techno. And alongside Ministry there were bands like Big Black, The Butthole Surfers and My Life With The Thrill Kill Kult incorporating harsh electronic drums, synth bass and heavy distorted guitars, taking punk rock beyond the ghetto of four piece thrash, which had been around in one form or another since the '60s.

Although he later claimed that he had never written songs before – there's evidence that he had, though never anything that he was particularly proud of – Reznor knew that the time was right. His first song that he will admit to writing is 'Down In It', a despair-laden hymn to depression: 'I used to be so big and strong/I used to know my right from wrong/I used to never be afraid/I used to be somebody/I used to have something inside/Now just this hole it's open wide/I used to want it all/I used to be somebody/I'll cross my heart, I'll hope to die/But the needle's already in my eye/And all the world's weight is on my back/And I don't even know why/What I used to think was me is just a fading memory/I looked him right in the eye and said goodbye/I was up above it/I was up above it/Now I'm down in it.'

With the masses of electronic kit that he and Vrenna had accumulated and crammed into their apartment, he started work on the songs that would become *Pretty Hate Machine*.

3 The Family Of Noise

'After hearing Gary Numan's "Cars" on the radio, I knew I wanted to make music with synthesisers.'

- Trent Reznor

To say that Trent Reznor is hardly an original or an innovator is not to insult him. The history of music is divided between those who are the innovators and those who build on the work of innovators and hone it to perfection. JS Bach, for example, was hardly an original composer in the sense that he was not the inventor of a particular revolutionary leap forward in music. Bach took music as it existed at the time, drew together a lot of threads and simply did it better than his contemporaries. Similarly, while The Beatles were to make innovative music late in their career, their early - and most popular - music was completely unoriginal, drawing heavily on contemporary R&B, particularly Motown, as well as the hard rock and roll of Chuck Berry and Little Richard. They did, however, popularise the music, bringing it to a much wider public than the tiny cult of hardcore enthusiasts who eagerly consumed the scarce American import records.

Just as it took The Byrds to put Bob Dylan in the Top 40, Reznor's sound did not come fully formed from his head. In fact, what he did was to make an already existing genre of music - 'industrial' - palatable to a mass audience. That, in many ways, is as much of an achievement as being the inventor of a sound.

By the time that *Pretty Hate Machine* was released in 1989, the concept of a rock band being just one or two members was no longer a novelty. The traditional pattern - guitar, bass, drums, vocals - was not so much obsolete as it was now just one of many competing templates for what a rock 'n' roll band could be like.

The lineage of Nine Inch Nails extends back through near contemporaries like Ministry and Skinny Puppy, through the post-punk 'futurist' bands like Throbbing Gristle, Depeche Mode and (especially) Gary Numan, to David Bowie (particularly the albums *Station To Station, Low, Heroes* and *Lodger*), Lou Reed and Tangerine Dream.

And the roots of this electronic music go all the way back to the domestication of electricity itself. Alexander Graham Bell, Nikolai Tesla and Thomas A Edison are as much godfathers of industrial music as Kraftwerk.

Just as rock 'n' roll could not exist without electronic technology – the first electric amplifier was developed in the 1920s, the first electric guitar (the so-called 'Frying Pan') was launched in 1931 – so industrial music is a culmination of developments in the field of electronic instruments as well as in music theory and practice. The roots of industrial music are inextricably entangled with the European and American avant-garde.

Electronic music has been around in one form or another since the late 19th century. Elisha Gray would have gone down in history as the inventor of the telephone if Alexander Graham Bell hadn't got to the patent office an hour before him. He did, however, invent the first electronic musical instrument, the Musical Telegraph, in 1876, a spin off from his research into the electronic transmission of sound. Basically his discoveries led to the invention of a basic single note oscillator using steel reeds whose vibrations were created and transmitted, over a telephone line, by electromagnets. Gray also built a simple loudspeaker device in later models consisting of a vibrating diaphragm in a magnetic field to make the oscillator audible. Similar electronic keyboards employing variable voltage to control sound emitted by electric arcs are the 'Telharmonium' or 'Dynamophone', which broadcast performances (usually involving two musicians to control its vast keyboard) over telephone lines.

In 1913 the Futurist composer Luigi Russolo demonstrated his 'Intonorumori' – noise making machines – to the incredulous public. The machines generated sounds rather like engines, and were intended to be used in performances of works simulating the noise of a modern city. Futurist founder, leader and poet FT Marinetti described the public's stunned and hostile reaction as like 'showing the first steam engine to a herd of cows'. Another Futurist composer wrote works intended to be performed by orchestras and aeroplane engines.

But the first really significant electronic instrument was invented in the USSR in 1918 by Leon Termen, who utilised body capacitance as a control mechanism for an electronic tone generator. By moving nearer to and further away from the instrument's field generator, the player could change the pitch, creating the truly eerie sound that has graced everything from Bernard Herrmann's music from *The Day The Earth Stood Still* to The Beach Boys' 'Good Vibrations'. Termen called it the 'Theremin' or the 'Aetherophone'. The instrument made its public debut at the Moscow Industrial Fair in 1920 where Lenin was suitably impressed and requested lessons on the instrument. Termen left the Soviet Union in 1927 for the United States where he was granted a patent for the theremin in 1928. The theremin was marketed and distributed in the USA by RCA during the 1930s and continues, in a solid state form, to be manufactured by Robert Moog's 'Big Briar' company. Termen himself was kidnapped in New York in 1938 by NKVD agents of Lenin's successor Josef Stalin and put on trial in Moscow for alleged anti-Soviet activities. He was sentenced to death and reports of his execution circulated in the US. Yet he was actually transported to the brutal Siberian guklaga at Magadan where he was put to work on secret Soviet projects. He invented the first practical electronic listening device (or bug), a staple tool of both Soviet and Western espionage. Rehabilitated and given a position at the Moscow Conservatory of Music, he once again took up studying electronic music. This contravened the official Soviet view – Termen was reportedly told that electricity should be reserved for the execution of traitors. Termen returned to the USA in 1993 after living quietly as a provincial music teacher; he had been completely unaware of the impact that his instrument had had on both serious Western music and on popular music.

Indeed it was an article by Robert Moog in *Electronics World* on how to built a theremin in kit form that started him on the path to develop the first electronic synthesiser. The first Moog synthesiser was built in 1963 and manufacturing began soon afterwards. Musician Walter (now Wendy after a high profile sex-change operation) Carlos popularised the instrument with the hit album *Switched On Bach* in 1967. Although they were prohibitively expensive and difficult to play, bands like The Beatles and The Rolling Stones bought them (though Jagger, frustrated at his inability to coax even a simple sound from his, later sold his on to the German progressive electronic pioneers Tangerine Dream).

Although the Moog was not the first synthesiser (RCA had designed and built a prototype instrument in the 1950s that utilised a punched-paper input system), nor even the most significant development in electronic music (the creation in Paris in 1948 of the the first electronic music studio by Pierre Schaeffer, French radio broadcaster, working for the Radiodiffusion-Television Française [RTF], and the birth of *musique concrète* holds that distinction), it was the first almost affordable instrument. The Moog helped to make electronic music accessible.

The Walter Carlos album established the Moog as a novelty instrument that could (badly) approximate the sounds of conventional acoustic instruments such as the piano, harpsichord and organ. The electronic albums that followed from Carlos and others would take familiar pieces and play them using ham-fisted Moog settings rendering them at best merely distressing and at worst downright irritating. The Velvet Gentlemen released an album of music by Erik Satie performed on synthesisers while Japanese pioneer Isao Tomita made albums of synthesised interpretations of Debussy (*Snowflakes Are Dancing*), Stravinsky (*The Firebird Suite*) and Mussorgsky (*Pictures At An Exhibition*) that have acquired a certain kitsch value over the years. The Moog became the staple sound of 'test' discs – albums made for in-store testing of stereo equipment. The sound of a synthesiser in the late '60s seemed incredibly futuristic and conjured up images of the latest NASA space shot, with the album sleeves usually making use of the blocky computer font Westminster. Quickie, easy-listening synthesiser albums by Jean-Jacques Perrey, Enoch Light, Dick Hyman, Mort Garson and Gershon Kingsley – particularly their seminal *The In Sound From Way Out*, which utilised the spacey synthesiser the Ondioline – created the genre known in retrospect as Space Age Bachelor-Pad Music.

Although it would be stretching a point to suggest any firm connection between these early popularisers of electronic music and Trent Reznor, these were in fact the first stirrings – in the arena of popular music – of the sound that was to have such an impact in the aftermath of punk. It was the 'wild west' period in electronic music when there were no rules, when it was possible to make it up as you went along.

While serious composers like Edgar Varèse had been working since the 1950s using tape recorders to create electronic music such as *Déserts* for wind, percussion and tape (1954) and *La Poème Électronique* (1957-8), written for the Philips pavilion at the Brussels Exposition of 1958, this was the first time that popular music had really started to punch above its weight intellectually.

Electronics and rock 'n' roll had always been confined to novelty records but with the increasing adoption of special effects such as wah-wah and fuzz pedals by guitarists like Link Wray in the late '50s and early '60s, trying to create a more distinctive style, using the electric guitar as an instrument in its own right, not merely a much louder version of an acoustic, saw an increasing awareness of the possibilities of instruments and studios to create new sounds.

The first relatively successful rock band to utilise electronics as part of their *raison d'être* was a folk rock combo from Denver

Colorado called Lothan And The Hand People. Formed in 1965, they relocated to New York, and became friends with the unknown guitarist Jimi Hendrix. Lothar And The Hand People predated Brian Wilson's use of the theremin in The Beach Boys' 1967 classic 'Good Vibrations'.

'We were at the Exodus one night, and whenever I'd play a theremin solo, this one guy would start thrashing around,' Lothar And The Hand People's singer/theremin player John Emelin recalled in an article in *Westword* magazine in 2000. 'He seemed to be going into ecstatic paroxysms. But as it turned out, he had a metal plate in his head, and the theremin was causing some kind of horrible short in his nervous system. When we found out, we felt terrible.'

Signed to Capitol Records, the band went into the studio with a budget of $8000 (£5,500), choosing as their producer Robert Margouleff, who had access to the country's then-largest Moog synthesiser. Margouleff had been doing engineering work for commercials and TV shows such as *Star Trek*. He would later work on *Talking Book* and *Innervisions*, Stevie Wonder's brilliant early-'70s electronic funk albums, and working as a producer, engineer or performer with acts as diverse as Quincy Jones, David Sanborn, Devo and 2 Live Crew.

The resulting album *Presenting...Lothar and the Hand People*, finally released in 1968, is an unusual if not entirely successful blend of country rock and electronics. Particularly interesting is the song 'It Comes On Anyhow', a sound collage that preceded the very similar 'Revolution Number 9' on The Beatles' eponymous 'white' album that same year and the disturbing 'Machines', with its almost Beefheartian structure, which pre-figures much later electronic rock such as Cabaret Voltaire and Throbbing Gristle. The follow-up *Space Hymns* sold poorly and the group are now remembered mostly by rock historians and archeologists of the psychedelic sound.

Other acid rock bands like The Grateful Dead began experimenting with electronics, particularly on the insane cut-up 'What's Become Of The Baby' on their acclaimed *Aoxomoxoa* album. New York's Silver Apples, a two piece featuring Simeon Coxe (electronic) and Dan Taylor (percussions) utilised an instrument that they constructed themselves involving rows of oscillators to create a unique sound years ahead of its time. They also pioneered the idea that a group could consist of only one or two people with their hand-knitted synthesiser filling in the gaps of bass, guitar and conventional keyboards. The United States Of America, another New York art ensemble, used synthesisers and tape cut-ups to add effects to an otherwise fairly conventional late-'60s rock sound.

In 1969, Robert Margouleff and partner Malcolm Cecil worked with Robert Moog to develop additional modules for the centrepiece unit of Moog's keyboard empire. They built a supersynthesiser called TONTO – The Original New Timbral Orchestra – the world's largest Moog synthesiser. The instrument was used on a number of studio projects for other artists (including Stevie Wonder) before, in 1971, they recorded their own compositions under the name TONTO's Expanding Head Band. *Zero Time*, still considered to be a turning point in the use of synths, created vivid musical soundscapes, utilizing the vast array of sounds that it was possible for TONTO to create rather than simply imitating existing sounds or adding novelty effects to conventional records. *Zero Time* used sequences, electronic drum patterns and a dizzying variety of noise. Although in retrospect it sounds like any other ambient album, it was a revelation at the time.

Jazz, too, undergoing its most febrile period, saw musicians hungry to experiment. Just as Miles Davis and John Coltrane had pushed the limits of jazz as far as they would stretch, so electronics and synthesisers began to appear on jazz albums. Roland Kirk had used a Moog in the mid '60s, but it was Herbie Hancock who became the most important electronics pioneer in jazz. Having left the Miles Davis Band in 1968, he worked on a number of projects including the soundtrack for Michelangelo Antonioni's 'swinging London' movie *Blow-Up*. Hancock then recorded an funk album *Fat Albert Rotunda* in collaboration with comedian Bill Cosby and in 1969 formed a sextet that evolved into one of the most vital, progressive jazz bands of the time. Hancock added the synthesiser to the band's line-up alongside his Echoplexed, fuzz-wah-wah pedalled electric piano and clarinet. The records he made became more cosmic and more complex rhythmically and structurally. *Mwandishi*, his critically successful though poorly selling 1970 album and its impressive follow-up *Crossings* were less frantic than Miles, almost harking back to his more contemplative albums like *In A Silent Way*. The music – and the concept – was Afrocentric (all of the band adopted Swahili names) and intellectual. It was 'head' music. Hancock split the band in 1973 after they went broke and, as a convert to Buddhism, he decided that rather than push the boundaries of composition and performance, he just wanted to make people happy. Hancock's next group, The Head Hunters, were a Sly Stone-influenced good times funk band, who enjoyed popular success with their 1974 single 'Chameleon', and though Hancock remained adventurous throughout his career – his 1983 hit employed electro, hip hop and proto-industrial rock prior to embarking on an exploration of African music with Gambian kora virtuoso Foday Musa Suso – he never returned to the powerful, emotional fusion of those two early-'70s albums.

But the first true direct link between the electronic experimentation of the '50s, '60s and '70s and the music of Nine Inch Nails was to appear in the modern, recently rebuilt cities of post-war West Germany.

The influence of everything from avant-garde jazz, psychedelic rock, the avant-garde in European music – Stockhausen, Milhaud, Boulez – as well as American minimalists like Steve Reich, LaMonte Young and Tony Conrad, all found fertile ground in which to spawn a new hybrid in Germany. Kraftwerk emerged from the same German experimental music community of the late 1960s, which also included Can, Faust, Neu!, Cluster and Tangerine Dream. Florian Schneider and Ralf Hütter first met at the Dusseldorf Conservatory. After a foray into rock, they formed Kraftwerk and set about building their own studio where they recorded their eponymous 1971 debut. Like Silver Apples they utilised home-made instruments, attempting to create mechanical rhythms using oscillators and modified instruments.

Their fourth album, 1974's *Autobahn*, was a perfect integration of the Moog synthesiser with their radical pro-technology early-adopter stance. The roots of everything – industrial music, disco, house, synth pop – are contained on this one record, a sprawling electronic song about driving on a motorway. The follow-ups, *Radioactivity* and *Trans Europe Express*, marked an increased use of this musical mechanization as well as an image that was calculatedly retro-futurist, hinting at the Futurists and Expressionists of the early years of the 20th century.

In 1975 they outlined their concept of Kraftwerk as the sum of everything they did. Speaking to *Triad* magazine, Ralph Hütter said: 'We've had this idea for a long time but it has only been in the past year that we've been able to create what we feel is a loudspeaker orchestra. This is what we consider Kraftwerk to be, a non-acoustic electronic loudspeaker orchestra. The whole thing is one instrument. We play mixers, we play tapes, we play phasers, we play the whole apparatus of Kraftwerk. That's the instrument. Including the lights and the atmosphere. '

Kraftwerk seemed to be out on a limb in the mid '70s. British progressive bands like ELP, Yes and Pink Floyd had all integrated synthesisers into their live and studio set-ups, but seemed content to use them to simulate the sounds of an orchestra, creating increasingly turgid rock pastiches of 19th-century Romantic music. Contemporaries like Can and Faust were not primarily electronic units, though they utilised tapes, electronic effects and even primitive drum machines to extend the possibilities of conventional instruments. Tangerine Dream, however, were, like Kraftwerk, a synth band, though their cosmic space rock appealed more to the sort of '70s hippie hangers-on who continued to smoke pot and expand their minds with LSD a decade after it had been fashionable. But on their 1974 album *Rubicon*, they hit on a sound utilizing early sequencers to create rhythm tracks that would later be employed by disco producer Giorgio Moroeder, particularly on American diva Donna Summer's massive hits 'Love To Love You Baby' and 'I Feel Love'. Significantly, this would be the first time that electronic music would be used to create a truly erotic, sensual kind of pop music rather than the more cerebral music of these art bands.

David Bowie, collaborating with former Roxy Music keyboards player Brian Eno on his seminal 1977 album *Low*, was heavily influenced by Kraftwerk both musically and image-wise. As well as comparatively conventional Bowie songs, the album included some bleak electronic soundscapes like 'Warszawa', 'Art Decade', 'Weeping Wall' and 'Subterraneans'. Bowie had adopted a consciously Eurocentric persona on the earlier *Station To Station* and, dubbed 'The Thin White Duke', he had even briefly flirted with fascism. But the overall feel of *Low*, its follow-up *Heroes* and the albums he produced for Iggy Pop, *The Idiot* and *Lust For Life*, was a sort of futuristic Weimar Republic, laden with portents of apocalypse, the electronic music adding an intentional element of dehumanization and alienation to the lyrics.

Adrian Belew, who played guitar with Bowie at this time, would later be drafted in by Trent to play on *The Downward Spiral*: 'He was an inspiration,' Trent said at the time. 'To be honest, I've been listening to a lot of music I avoided when I grew up – like Led Zeppelin – because people who I didn't like liked them. Flood (legendary producer and long time Nine Inch Nails collaborator) and I have been on a big Bowie kick, *Low/Heroes* era, *Hunky Dory* – stuff that I never heard growing up in rural western PA. But we were infatuated with that whole *Low*/Belew style of playing, and we wondered if he'd be into doing it.'

Reznor was also to play on the 1995 Outside tour with Bowie and produced the track 'I'm Afraid Of Americans' on Bowie's album *Seven*, as well as six remixes released on an EP.

But Bowie's influence was to come to Trent initially filtered through an intermediary generation of neurotic boy outsiders.

In Britain, punk sharply divided rock audiences. Compared to the new, short, sharp, sock of bands like The Clash and The Sex Pistols, the previous generation of rock bands such as Yes, Pink Floyd and

Genesis seemed hopelessly reactionary and obsolete. Yet punk itself was capable of being equally as staid and reactionary and stifling to innovation. Concurrent with the rise of punk a new underground scene germinated in London and Sheffield. This Heat, Cabaret Voltaire and Throbbing Gristle had been around in one form or another for a couple of years but, as the excitement about young spiky youths died down in 1978, their debut releases elicited a wave of interest in a new kind of electronic music. Other bands followed, such as The Human League, Thomas Leer and Robert Rental And The Normal, which was actually just one man, Daniel Miller, who released the record on his own label called Mute; this 1978 one-off single 'Warm Leatherette'/'TVOD' was to have repercussions way beyond its sales (in the low thousands). Dubbed 'the cold wave' in a genre-defining article in the rock weekly *Sounds*, these bands differed from progressive bands like Pink Floyd and Tangerine Dream in that they weren't attempting to make 'head' music to comfort tripping hippies. They were using electronic music to reflect the alienation and despair of life in the crumbling backward-looking Britain of the late '70s in the same way as the likes of Generation X and The Buzzcocks.

The first band to be dubbed 'industrial' were Throbbing Gristle, who used a phrase coined by San Francisco performance artist Monte Cazazza. They began life as COUM Transmissions, a performance art group that featured two of the founding members of Throbbing Gristle: Genesis P Orridge and Cosey Fanni Tutti. Recalling his pre-Throbbing Gristle stage act, Genesis told one journalist: 'I used to do things like stick severed chicken's heads over my penis, and then try to masturbate them, whilst pouring maggots all over it. In Los Angeles, in 1976, at the Institute of Contemporary Arts (LAICA), Cosey and I did a performance where I was naked, I drank a bottle of whiskey and stood on a lot of tacks. And then I gave myself enemas with blood, milk and urine, and then broke wind so a jet of blood, milk and urine combined shot across the floor in front of Chris Burden and assorted visual artists. I then licked it off the floor, which was a not-clean concrete floor. Then I got a 10-inch [25cm] nail and tried to swallow it, which made me vomit. Then I licked the vomit off the floor and Cosey helped me lick the vomit off the floor. And she was naked and trying to sever her vagina to her navel with a razor blade – well, she cut it from her vagina to her navel with a razor blade, and she injected blood into her vagina which then trickled out, and we sucked the blood from her vagina into a syringe and injected it into eggs painted black, which we then tried to eat. And we vomited again, which we then used for enemas. Then I needed to urinate, so I urinated into a large glass bottle and drank it all while it was still warm. (This was all improvised.) And then we gradually crawled to each other, licking the floor clean ('cause we don't like to leave a mess, y'know; after all, it's not fair to insult an art gallery). Chris Burden, who's known for being outrageous, walked out with his girlfriend, saying, "This is not art, this is the most disgusting thing I've ever seen, and these people are sick".'

Although none of the later industrial bands went to quite these extremes, Skinny Puppy at various times showered their audiences with animal guts. Throbbing Gristle first performed in 1976, involving Genesis, Cosey, Sleazy and Chris Carter. They used synthesisers, a primitive sampler constructed by Carter, tape loops, effects pedals, conventional instruments that they could not play plus other home-built machines. They released their music through their own label, called Industrial Records, as well as material by other artists including Cabaret Voltaire, Monte Cazazza, The Leather Nun, Clock DVA and William Burroughs. Musically they sounded like an ambient rumble, occasionally interspersed by 'songs', snatches of attempted disco-motorik in the style of Giorgio Moroeder and calming sub-muzak. They parodied real industrial concerns, calling their first two releases *The First Annual Report* and *The Second Annual Report*. Although by their very nature their appeal was limited to an art cult, their influence – and the influence of the bands that grew out of their split, most notably Psychic TV and Coil – was to have a profound effect on later electronic music. But, in 1977, Throbbing Gristle were treated with great hostility by the press and the increasingly reactionary punks who were content to listen to badly played conventional rock 'n' roll and were suspicious of any sort of innovation.

This was further demonstrated when the New York electronic duo Suicide visited the UK to support The Clash. Suicide – who had been around since 1972, contemporaries of glam-punks The New York Dolls, KISS and Patti Smith – were a duo consisting of Martin Rev on instrument and Alan Vega on voice. The instrument was a modified organ built by Rev and an early drum machine. Vega, looking like a New York greaser, would scream at the front, his voice filtered through an array of effects pedals to create an almost post-human howl. They were genuine innovators, they sounded like nobody else. But when they appeared in front of The Clash audience, they found themselves showered with bottles and abuse, rarely managing to complete their set without some injury to one or other of them. This was ironically a pattern repeated whenever an electronic band appeared on the same bill as a more conventional band. The Human League actually constructed cages to play inside to protect their equipment as much as the musicians from hurled glasses. Yet despite the perception of Suicide as a failure, for a tiny minority of the people at those Clash shows, they were an inspiration. Later bands like Soft Cell and even The Pet Shop Boys acknowledge their debt to them.

Soon, electronic music became massively popular with original punk bands like Ultravox retooling their sound to incorporate synthesisers, drum machines and a low-rent copy of Bowie's imagery.

When Tubeway Army released their one and only album *Replicas* on Beggars Banquet in 1978, they seemed like a real division three band, imitating Ultravox imitating Bowie (imitating Kraftwerk). The album spawned one minor classic single 'Down In The Park', an eerie synth-washed slice of contemporary fashionable alienation. But when the singer of that band spun off to launch his solo career, few would have predicted that he would be one of the defining stars of the era. Gary Numan's 'Are Friends Electric?' became a number one single in the UK in 1979 and the follow-ups 'Cars' and 'We Are So Fragile' fared even better. To critics, Numan was a ridiculous figure, dressed in his black shirt like a wimpy Oswald Mosely, pulling Bowie-like poses, always on the edge of a sneer. The songs were gauche science fiction anthems inspired by authors like Phillip K Dick ('Are Friends Electric?' was inspired by his novelette *Do Androids Dream Of Electric Sheep?* later filmed as *Blade Runner*) and – particularly – JG Ballard. 'Cars' was explicitly inspired by Ballard's fable of automobiles and eroticism *Crash*, as indeed was The Normal's 'Warm Leatherette'. Numan was a phenomenon, attracting hordes of kids far too young to remember or care about Bowie or Kraftwerk, drawn to this self-styled remote New Man, an asexual post-human, devoid of emotions, a prophet of a crueler and less human future. For Kraftwerk, the imagery of the Man Machine – also the title of their 1978 album – was ironic and, unusually for Germans, they had their tongues stuck firmly in their cheeks. But Numan had absolutely no sense of irony or cynicism about what he did.

Numan's influence was enormous. At the time, he opened the door to a whole new wave of electronic pop – represented by the re-imagined Human League, Heaven 17, Soft Cell, Orchestral Manoeuvres In The Dark, Depeche Mode, Yazoo – that was to dominate UK and international charts for most of the 1980s. But his longer term influence on a more diverse range of artists like Detroit techno pioneer Juan Atkins as well as the Prodigy, Beck, Blur and Smashing Pumpkins can clearly be seen and they all acknowledge their debt to him.

Ironically, with Numan's career somewhat revived thanks in part to the patronage of some of these bands, he has expressed his admiration for Trent Reznor, naming him as one of his favourite musicians ever in an article in *Mojo* magazine in 2002: 'He has such a good ear for atmosphere...' Numan said. 'I'm not going to go do down as one of the greatest musicians of our time... I wish I could be as half as good a musician as him.'

The explosion of synth-pop in the late '70s and early '80s quickly produced a thriving underground of electronic bands who were anything but pop. Daniel Miller, the man behind The Normal, soon found his career as the boss of Mute Records overtaking his career as a sort of Phil Spector of electronic music. Mute very quickly became the first stop for young synth-wielding hopefuls eager to emulate the success of Depeche Mode and their offshoot Yazoo, who had both been snapped up by Miller. He also grabbed Spanish/German duo DAF, whose electro-bass heavy disco was to foreshadow the industrial bands of the late '80s as well as sounding occasionally like Nine Inch Nails.

'It was a way of shaking the foundations of the music business but in a more intelligent way than punk rock,' Reznor told *Details* magazine. 'When that fizzled out, it started melding with disco and you got bands like Front 242 and Ministry. NIN focuses on noisy electronic music. It's menacing but a far cry from Throbbing Gristle.'

This heavier sound was to find its way across the Atlantic. In Canada, the relatively successful Images In Vogue had based their sound on the British synth-pop acts but drummer cEvin Key (*né* Kevin Compton) wanted to use what he had learned about electronic music to create something much rawer and angrier. A fan of both Kraftwerk and Throbbing Gristle, Key was aware of the new school of extreme electronic music like SPK, Legendary Pink Dots and Portion Control filtering over from Europe. He claimed that after hearing them he got rid of his entire record collection and started again. Leaving Images In Vogue he experimented with sound collages, found sounds and tape samples. In 1983 Skinny Puppy released their first album *To A Baser Nature* featuring former bandmate Joe Vizvary, though it was on their 1984 album *Remission* that the band found their style, sound and line-up. Paranoia-soaked jackhammer beats, a wash of spoken samples like constant white noise and tortured vocals screaming about oppression, vivisection and fascism, Skinny Puppy were no threat to Gary Numan but soon built up a hardcore following of disillusioned punks and electronic fans hungry for something heavier than Erasure. Meanwhile, in Chicago, a duo called Ministry who had been around in a different form since 1980 released their debut album *With Sympathy* on major label Arista. This was still essentially a pop album and the contrast between it and the more abrasive follow-up *Twitch* was very marked, but it was their 1988 album *The*

Land Of Rape And Honey that defined their style. Loud, heavy and ugly, it was almost like a heavy metal album. That year Skinny Puppy and Ministry went out on tour together and completely changed the face of music.

Although a fan of both bands, Trent Reznor was close enough in age to be considered a contemporary. He toured supporting Skinny Puppy and collaborated on several Ministry side projects including The Revolting Cocks and 1,000 Homo DJs.

Although they were a well established band before Reznor had even written a song, it was in the wake of *Pretty Hate Machine* that Ministry enjoyed their first major commercial success with their 1992 album *Psalm 69*. As well as taking Ministry out of the industrial 'ghetto' to mainstream chart success, it was also one of the most brutal and uncompromising albums to do so.

'I don't really know what happened,' Ministry's second-in-command Paul Barker told me. 'We took entirely too long to finish that record and perhaps the difference is that all of a sudden we had a power behind us – we had management after years of being self managed – where we could get more money for recording. That gave us freedom and the ability to not have to finalise decisions too quickly. It let us work out tons and tons of material, and not necessarily have to finish it. We were absolutely self-indulgent.'

Behind a veil of samples, spoken word and backward masking – to bait the fundamentalist no-necks – was a potent, speed-freak hard rock album. The power guitars by Mike Scaccia and Louis Svitek and the crunching machine drums and the rapid-fire collage of noise bubbling away under every track was a new direction: while *The Mind Is A Terrible Thing To Taste* still betrayed Ministry's goth/electro roots, this was unquestionably a prime metal record. It was also their biggest seller, going platinum in the US.

'We played at Lollapalooza that year and there was great fall-out from that. Sleazy [Peter Christopherson – ex-Throbbing Gristle, now of Coil, occasional collaborator with Trent Reznor] did some great videos and that helped. We were happier that our music on that album was heavier than heavy metal. There was no guitar solos, no wanking and all this shit. We're coming from a punk rock aesthetic... I mean, we love heavy metal, we love heavy music, but we weren't into that aesthetic at all,' says Barker.

Metal was changing and becoming less of a 'ghetto'; in the '80s, metal fans were listening to all sorts of slushy big-hair-and-bandana bands like Poison churning out dreadful power ballads while ignoring bands like, for example, The Rollins Band whose music had much more to do with the spirit of hard rock. By the early '90s the boundaries between metal, hardcore, punk, rap, industrial and funk were being dissolved by a new breed; metal bands playing rap, indie bands playing metal. *Psalm 69* rode this wave.

Everyone from Nine Inch Nails through to Fear Factory was touched by this dark, angry cyberpunk slew. You can still hear Ministry's influence in any number of bands today from Static X – who cover Ministry live – to Slipknot, who, consciously or not, tap into that same well of negativity.

'It's mind boggling. The reason that *Psalm 69* was so commercially successful was because of heavy metal fans. We don't know where that came from,' says Barker. 'Incredibly flattering that people see Ministry in other people's music because I hear other people in us. Once you have a template it's easy to copy. Are there bands that sound like us? I don't know, I guess so. There's bands that sound like Led Zeppelin or The Beatles too. I'm not interested in that. I'm not interested in commercial success, I'm interested in something novel. Something new.'

Reznor claims, 'I like Ministry, who were – more so than they are now – industrial. They pretty much established industrial music in America. They definitely put the anger and aggression element into electronic music. I mean, the first electronic music that I got into wasn't stuff like Throbbing Gristle – it was more like Human League and Devo and other less experimental things that made their way into Pennsylvania, which is where I was living at the time. Then you had the people who developed electronic personalities because their music was electronic – Gary Numan, Kraftwerk – very emotionless. There wasn't any humanity in it. Today, you have people who just want to follow the technology rather than innovate with it. The people who arrange Paula Abdul or Madonna – they just buy the gear, read the manual and make the sounds it tells them they can make. That's why every dance club hit sounds the same, they're all programming the sounds by the book.'

Reznor has never hidden the fact that these bands influenced him. In fact, in the early days he was positively evangelical about them, hoping that the success of *Pretty Hate Machine* would spread the word about his antecedents. As he told *Thrasher* magazine: 'I didn't get into music to make a lot of money or to be this big. But now that it's kind of happened, I think well, okay, how can I take advantage of this position? I'm thinking of the fuckin' kid in Nebraska in the cornfield that just heard about Nine Inch Nails and then bought the record. And it doesn't sound like the Pearl Jam record... It might open his eyes and maybe he'll think "This is really cool. I'll go buy a Ministry album. I'll go buy a Skinny Puppy record." It's not that I'm on a great mission to do that even. But I grew up in the middle of nowhere and a lot of my input when I was a kid – when I was forming my self opinion of who I am and what the world is about – music played a big part in that.'

4 Pretty Hate Machine

'I just wanted to put out a record that was honest with how I felt, something like Pink Floyd's *The Wall* or the first Smiths album or a Cure album. Records I'd put on a different periods in my life that wouldn't make me feel quite so bummed out and alone.'

– *Trent Reznor, 1991*

Setting to work on the album that eventually became *Pretty Hate Machine*, Trent Reznor – now officially working under the name Nine Inch Nails – did not quite have a clear idea of what he wanted to do.

'I don't know if you've ever tried to think of band names, but usually you think you have a great one and you look at it the next day and it's stupid. I had about 200 of those. Nine Inch Nails lasted the two week test, looked great in print, and could be abbreviated easily. It really doesn't have any literal meaning. It seemed kind of frightening. Tough and manly! It's a curse trying to come up with band names,' he said at the time.

He had a vision of music that would link with a lot of things he liked from the vibrant hard-edged industrial rock sweeping underground circles. Industrial music was angry, often political (usually on the left though there were artists such as Boyd Rice, leader of the influential band Non who flirted with fascist imagery and ideas). Slightly self-deprecating about 'Down In It' and modest – at least publicly – about what he hoped to achieve, Trent was at this time, in late-'80s Cleveland, much clearer about what he didn't want than what he did. As he told *Alternative Press*: 'I didn't want to come across as an industrial, snarling, Satan-singing entity. That's not what

63

Nine Inch Nails is. I try to juxtapose some sort of life or sincerity onto a tougher musical edge that normally wouldn't fit together. You wouldn't hear Ministry going through what I go through. It's not intended to be in the Skinny Puppy vein – snarling and griping that the world sucks. It's not about politics or grandiose statements. It's more introspective. Internal decay and collapse happened to be my motivation at the time.'

Like some boho novelist cranking out his masterpiece in the garrett while holding down a soul-destroying day job, Reznor spent nearly two years working very late at night in his apartment or during the hours that the studio was deserted, piecing together the music that would eventually result in his debut album. He painstakingly taught himself to use MIDI (Musical Instrument Digital Interface), a music-industry-standard communications protocol that lets MIDI instruments and sequencers (or computers running sequencer software) talk to each other to play and record music. In the '80s, MIDI – along with other digital music and recording processes – was still in its infancy. Trent was one of the first people to realise the liberating power that new technology would offer the creative artist. The early-'80s generation of synth-pop and early industrial bands were empowered by low-cost synthesisers and sequencers, though occasionally they would be forced to pay through the nose to use instruments like the Fairlight – one of the first digital samplers – which were usually only affordable to major studios and bands.

'Right from the beginning I was composing on computer and sequencer. I can't imagine composing on say a guitar or a conventional instrument. The idea is foreign to me,' he told a fanzine writer in 1990.

It was this approach that led to Reznor's reputation as a tyrant, a 'control freak' and a musical dictator. But he himself enjoyed this way of working. If he had an idea, he was able to sketch it out really quickly without involving other musicians, having to teach them the parts and struggling against any ideas that they would inevitably bring. He once claimed that he could go from the idea in his head to complete demo within an hour. The beauty of the new technology is that it allowed would-be auteurs like Reznor to work this way; in the past, the sort of producers who used the studio as an instrument such as Phil Spector, Joe Meek and Shadow Morton were limited by the sheer expense and the fact that they had to employ musicians to play the parts. Although Reznor was a trained musician and could read music, learning MIDI allowed him a real hands-on approach to writing and arranging music. It was visceral rather than cerebral. It also gave him the advantage that when he actually did come to assemble a band he could play them the tapes and tell them that that was exactly how he wanted it done. This was to be essentially the pattern for the way he would continue to work for the next decade.

Reznor made tentative approaches to labels without actually having a band. He was certain that gigging around Cleveland was pointless.

'You had all these bands who thought that the way that it happened was that you'd be playing in a bar and somebody would come along from a label and discover them. Which is absurd, particularly in Cleveland,' he said.

Reznor maintained control over everything, still uncomfortable at the prospect of having anyone from outside sticking their nose into his work. But his confidence was growing all the time.

'At the very beginning, during the summer of 1988, we were just going to put a 12" out on some European label, figuring that if we can make enough money to do that, see what happens. Maybe a year or two later after we get better idea of what the band is going to be like, we would approach a bigger label, major or decent-sized independent. At that time, I didn't know; Nine Inch Nails was three songs. I wasn't sure what direction it was going to go. I didn't want to get involved in a label where it was, "Hey, that's good, but let's smooth it out here and there, make that pop" or whatever. I got approached by a bunch of smaller independent labels. We sent out about ten tapes and got them all back with deals. Eventually, we realised that we didn't have to put out a 12" on a nothing label. I had my shit together by then,' he told *Alternative Press*.

Reznor assembled a live band towards the middle of the year that included Richard Patrick (brother of actor Robert Patrick who played the T-1000 cyborg in *Terminator 2* as well as John Doggett in *The X-Files*), Chris Vrenna and Lee Mars to play two shows with Skinny Puppy at the 9.30 Club in Washington, DC, and Irving Plaza in New York. The set list included songs that would later form *Pretty Hate Machine*: 'Sanctified', 'Maybe Just Once', 'The Only Time', 'That's What I Get', 'Ringfinger (Twist)' and 'Down In It'. The event was captured by an audience member with a tape recorder and later surfaced as a bootleg entitled *Show Up Or Throw Up*. Although the sound quality is awful, it's clear that Nine Inch Nails at this time was still quite a way away from perfecting the sound. The songs sound conventional and almost feeble, Reznor sounds unsure and the band sounds midway between a poor hardcore punk band and a ham-fisted synth-pop group.

'It was scary opening up for Skinny Puppy, and we were a tenth as intense as we are now,' he said two years after the event. 'I realised it was not what I wanted to do. So I got rid of those guys, and wrote the rest of the album, and redid everything, and put a new band together this past summer.'

Holed up in the increasingly squalid home he and Vrenna shared, the album finally started to take the form he wanted.

An article in *Alternative Press* gives us some flavour of what life was like during the recording of the album: 'He rents a run-down half-house with Vrenna "in the ghetto" of Cleveland, Ohio that's littered with empty beer bottles, plates and glasses, peanut butter jars, pizza and cookie boxes, clothes, shoes. An open refrigerator door reveals more full and empty beer bottles and pizza boxes. Reznor...says that when he needs clothes, he walks out and picks something up off the floor. A phone message lies on the kitchen tile near the answering machine. When it's pointed out, Vrenna shrugs and says it's been there since December. When we go to find a quiet place to do the interview away from Vrenna's and a friend's Nintendo game (clearly the only thing they have spent money on in this house is stereo and

VCR equipment), the best bet appears to be Vrenna's room. Before plopping himself on the unmade bed, Reznor is kind enough to add the clothes and shoes stacked on the desk chair to the pile below it so I, too, can sit down. It soon becomes obvious that at the Reznor residence, quiet is relative. The music from the upstairs neighbors is loud, omnipresent and unceasing.

"We get harassed because we don't look totally normal," Reznor says of his Cleveland neighbors. "Somebody up the street says they're going to get us because we're hippies. We get insulted pretty regularly".'

Following the Skinny Puppy shows, label interest started to really pick up. Skinny Puppy's label Nettwerk and Ministry's Wax Trax! - both heavily associated with the burgeoning industrial scene - both expressed an interest. Following the New York gig Reznor was approached by a representative from TVT Records.

TVT - short for TeeVee Toons - is now one of America's biggest independent labels with artists ranging from Snoop Dogg and Naughty By Nature to Sevendust as well as movie soundtracks like *Traffic*, but was then a small and relatively unknown concern. The charismatic founder and CEO Steve Gottlieb made a pile of money licensing an album called *Television's Greatest Hits*, which included theme songs from well-loved TV shows like *Mission Impossible*, *The Twilight Zone*, *Batman*, *The Flintstones*, *I Love Lucy*, *Star Trek*, *Mr Ed*, *Popeye*, *The Jetsons* and *Gilligan's Island*. The album caught a wave of baby boomer nostalgia and sold millions, earning a fortune for the company and allowing it to expand. Subsequent volumes of such albums (TV themes, commercials, cartoons etc) have been the company's cash cow ever since. Gottlieb, angry that the first album never registered in the *Billboard* Top 100 because of the stranglehold of, at that time, six major labels, soon established himself as a sort of buccaneer capitalist, building his company up by the bootstraps, resisting bids from the majors to muscle in on his company and remaining defiantly outside the cartel of the majors. The flamboyant former attorney gained a reputation as a sharp practitioner, able to get a dollar and ten cents change out of a dollar, and signed artists to long contracts, longer, in fact, than most careers could be reasonably expected to last. Nice guys finish last, they say, and that is particularly true of the music industry. Gottleib certainly had no intention of finishing last.

Reznor and Gottlieb were two mavericks, though in their own very different ways. Trent inked a deal with TVT Records. It was one of those things that seemed so right at the time.

Trent was by this time managed by John Malm, an acquaintance from his stint in The Exotic Birds, who managed a few local Cleveland bands. Malm had auditioned Reznor to play synth with another band that he was managing at the time and although Reznor never got the gig – it was apparent that he wasn't wholly committed to being part of somebody else's project – Malm was impressed by the demo that he gave him.

Some of the original Nine Inch Nails demos have cropped up as bootlegs over the years and it is interesting to contrast them with the album that was eventually released. House music and techno, coming from the clubs of Chicago and Detroit, had taken Europe by storm in 1986 and 87 – the so-called Summer of Love – and as is often the case with music of black origin in America, only enjoyed a small cult following at home. The hipper kids in most American cities, particularly at that time, tended to have Anglophile tendencies, seeking out music that was written about in the British music papers like *NME, Sounds* and *Melody Maker*. At that time most of the press had gone overboard on acid house, proclaiming it to be the end of rock 'n' roll.

Reznor certainly seems to have taken some of this on board because the music on the demos recorded in 1988 sounds more heavily influenced by the stark, minimal techno sound than the tracks that were actually released. Songs like 'Down In It' and 'Head Like A Hole' are much lighter and poppier, almost like Depeche Mode; the official versions were retooled into far heavier and more abrasive tracks.

Of course, they are inferior in every way to the songs as they finally appeared, but they do postulate an interesting 'what if?'

Reznor, of course, later claimed to hate house: 'I assure you there will be absolutely no fucking House, *ever*. I hate House.'

Gottlieb went to Cleveland to see Reznor perform a showcase and recognised his immense talent but wanted the essential sound that Reznor had captured at home to be retooled by more experienced producers. In retrospect, it seems that Gottlieb actually liked the demos pretty much as they were – all, of course, Reznor's own work – and was later to be disappointed that the finished album turned out in any way different. Three producers/production teams worked on *Pretty Hate Machine*.

Reznor's choice was Flood, a semi-legendary producer who is now well known for his collaborations with Reznor, U2 and Smashing Pumpkins. At the time, Flood's time was limited because he was about to begin work on Depeche Mode's new album, which would eventually be released as the classic *Violator*.

Born Mark Ellis the nickname Flood came about as a result of his habit of spilling tea over the mixing desk in the studio. Originally the bassist in the short-lived Jam-inspired Mod revival band The Lambrettas – who enjoyed a minor UK hit in 1979 with a cover of Leiber and Stoller's 'Poison Ivy' – started, like Reznor, as a general dogsbody in a London recording studio, before working as an assistant engineer on New Order's 1981 debut album *Movement* and subsequently engineering and producing Soft Cell, Psychic TV, Cabaret Voltaire and The Associates. His first high-profile productions were Nick Cave And the Bad Seeds' *The Firstborn Is Dead* and *Kicking Against The Pricks* and Erasure's *Wonderland* and *The Circus*. Reznor really wanted him to do the whole album.

Trent did preliminary work on the tracks before flying to Boston to work at Flood's studio Sigma Sound. But TVT had booked him studio time in London to work with another English producer, John Fryer, who had also worked with Depeche Mode as well as the ethereal Scottish duo The Cocteau Twins, then at their artistic zenith.

Fryer was also part of the studio collective who produced the seminal British acid house hit 'Pump Up The Volume' under the name M/A/R/R/S/. Essentially a studio collaboration between bands Colourbox and AR Kane, it featured Fryer along with Martyn Young (Colourbox), Steven Young (Colourbox), AR Kane, CJ Mackintosh and Dave Dorrell – all would become major figures on the UK's post-house ambient scene – and may have been instrumental in TVT choosing him for *Pretty Hate Machine.*

Speaking to *Sound*, a pro magazine aimed at the studio trade, Flood recalled: 'I first heard a set of demos for *Pretty Hate Machine* before he was even signed, and they just blew me away – by far the best set of demos I've ever heard. They were good strong songs, not pop songs; then, on top of that, someone had spent a lot of care and attention on how the songs were represented musically. To me, that was the best of both worlds. So I played the demos for the first album and thought, "Well, what do I have to do?" I was asked if I wanted to work on it, and I said "Totally!". Sometimes you hear something and you say, "Sorry, I've just got to do that – I don't even care if it's just one song."'

Trent and Flood hit it off immediately, finding that they had ideas in common and also that the English producer did not want to fundamentally alter the work that Reznor had written, arranged and performed on his own.

'There was a problem in the middle, the way "Head Like A Hole" dropped down,' said Flood, 'I think we changed the drum sounds, changed the feel, re-introduced backing vocals at the end. Encouragement was important: can we get anymore out of the vocal? Bring it in a little bit earlier? It was a mutual respect thing, rather than storming in there and saying, "Well, we need to change that and that." But really, 60-70 per cent was there before we got into the studio.'

Reznor told *Alternative Press*: 'Flood is the type of producer who says, "Well, I don't care about the status of the band I'm working with. I don't care about money," which is cool because we didn't have a huge budget to work with. We became good friends.'

Reznor then arrived in London to work with Fryer. When he was not in the studio, he was at a completely loose end. He did not know anyone and was too shy to go out on his own, perhaps to a club. Besides which, London was unfamiliar territory. Reznor had not travelled very widely and the bewildering metropolis, despite being a centre for some of the music that had influenced him greatly, was a dreadful and lonely place. During the month that he stayed there he dreaded weekends most of all when there was no work to be done in the studios because Fryer worked a conventional working week.

Reznor briefly considered relocating to London, which at the time seemed a lot more open-minded towards the music he wanted to do that the US. It was also, he noticed, easier to break big in the UK relatively quickly because it is a geographically small country unlike the US, which requires heroic commitment to touring. He went as far as putting an ad for musicians in *Melody Maker* and met several people that he describes as 'wannabes' rather than anyone who was actually going to be a worthwhile addition to the band as sideman or even collaborator.

Despite the negative feelings he took away from the John Fryer sessions, he was comparatively happy with the album.

'I'm pleased with the way it came out,' Reznor told *Spin* at the time, 'although working with a bunch of people was a roundabout, backwards way of doing a record. In an ideal situation, if I had musicians who I thought were competent and who I could collaborate with on an equal level, things would be easier. I could write songs faster and it would probably be more exciting. It would be nice to have input from people you respect. When there's somebody you just don't see eye-to-eye with, it's more of a hassle than anything. The way I write, there isn't anybody to bounce ideas off of. It's not like a band, where you've got so-and-so on guitar and a bass player and the whole four-piece format. I approached it knowing my tools and my limitations. I'm a shitty guitar player, but that's my style and that's where it's going to be. Same with bass and whatever else. The vocals were one take. I tried to create a very minimal feel. I think something

71

that sets NIN apart from other groups of its ilk is that as much as I try not to do it, I still end up writing in a pop song vein. Also, I'm not coming from the same point of view as they are. I'm not saying it's better, it's just different. What I'm doing is taking a song and arranging it, rather than building up a groove and chanting over it.'

Adrian Sherwood and Keith LeBlanc were also drafted in to remix 'Down In It' and *Pretty Hate Machine* (later working on the singles 'Head Like A Hole' and 'Sin'). Sherwood had worked with Ministry, Einstürzende Neubauten, Skinny Puppy and German band KMFDM (an industrial outfit signed to Wax Trax! whose name meant – according to the rumour mill – Kill Mother Fucking Depeche Mode though actually it is Kein Mitleid Für Die Mehrheit, meaning No Mercy For The Masses. They would later find undeserved notoriety in the wake of the Columbine High School shootings in 1999). As part of the influential group Tackhead, along with Keith LeBlanc, Skip McDonald and Doug Wimbish – three musicians who formed the backline of Sugarhill Records house band in the late '70s, playing on early hip-hop hits like Sugarhill Gang's 'Rapper's Delight' – whose explorations of ultra-heavy dub reggae, left-field funk and proto-industrial rock continues to crop up as a major influence in many areas of music. Sherwood, one of the first artists to really blur the line between DJ, producer, musician and remixer, may have been inspirational to Reznor's approach to music in that there seems to be no definitive version of a track that he records. It will only be like a snapshot of a particular moment in its evolution that appears on a given album or EP, though in fact earlier versions exist and the track may be remixed again, perhaps years after its initial release.

Reznor said to *Alternative Press*: 'I've always wanted to work with him in some context. He's expensive, so I just wanted to do a 12" with him – let him take one of my songs, fuck with it, and do whatever he wants to do. I called him up and he listened to it, and he was into doing it. That's when we were doing the deal with TVT. He did that first. I recorded it all in Cleveland myself, then Keith LeBlanc did some pre-production in New York. And then Adrian mixed it in London without me. So I never met him face to face. We just talked on the phone. Then he just sent it back and I heard it. I had no idea what to expect. It was radically different from my version. I didn't want to put that on the album, but the forces that be... The original version may show up somewhere. I think he's great at what he does. I think he tends to smother who he's working with. But I can't complain. My only complaint is that my version could have shown up somewhere. It's much more rap-hip-hoppy. It's real tiny. More emotional, not as linear. They could have complemented each other very well.'

Relations with TVT began to show the first cracks as successive versions of the album were knocked back and forth between label and artist. TVT apparently had big reservations about the entire album – Gottlieb at one point describing it as an 'abortion' – thinking that it was not as poppy as the demos that Reznor had already submitted, while Reznor was unhappy at having producer John Fryer foisted, as he saw it, upon him, despite the fact that Gottlieb had apparently never heard of anyone – Fryer, Flood, Sherwood/LeBlanc – who worked on the album.

Speaking to *Industrial Nation* magazine, Reznor said: 'When [Gottlieb] finally heard it, he hated it. After two weeks of silence, he called me up and says, "I think your record is an abortion. I think you'll be lucky if you sell 20,000 copies of it. You ruined it by making sounds not friendly to the radio. These are good songs, but you've ruined them." Oh, to hear that at a stage when I didn't know what I had created... I was too close to it. At that point, I felt like I had fucked up. I spent a couple of days thinking about it, and I thought, well, I made this record and I like it. Sorry he didn't like it, but fuck him, that's the record.'

The rift would grow when TVT substituted a Sherwood remix of 'Down In It' for Reznor's original and preferred version. Ironically, for all their reservations about how commercial the album would be, initial reactions from industrial fans was that it was a sell-out pop album with a few industrial flourishes, something that Reznor actually agreed with.

'[*Pretty Hate Machine*] is not pure anything. If I hear, say a Skinny Puppy record, it has a very unique sound, it defines a certain musical territory. You can say without a shadow of a doubt, "That's an industrial album." It's real noisy, it's unintelligible (for the most part), it's dance-oriented – none of which is bad – I mean Puppy is definitely an influence on me. While I didn't want to end up as the Vanilla Ice of industrial, I did want to toss a few more things into the mix. I wanted to take what I liked from industrial music. What I don't like about industrial is that not much of it is among my all-time favorite music. I don't listen to it over and over again. I mean lyrically a lot of it is vacuous and they're basically communicating one emotion which is snarling ferociousness. What I wanted to do was take that anger part of it, (real anger, not poser anger) and add other emotions, vulnerabilities, frailty and to put some effort into the lyrics, instead of chanting the same thing over and over again. So, it starts to depend on how you look at it. Am I taking a pop song and arranging it in an industrial fashion to fool people into thinking we're an industrial band, or are we an industrial band that pays more attention to lyrics and, by bastardizing the genre a little bit, turned more people on to it. We've sold more records than the average industrial band, and while I don't care much about numbers, perhaps that's because we've given people more to grab on to. A problem I have with Skinny Puppy, for instance, is that while they do something well – all the anger and the snarling and the meanness – I don't want to hear that for a whole album with nothing else, after a while it really starts to bore me. Give it up!'

Perhaps Reznor was over-defensive of the record that was personal to him. Speaking four years later to *Spin* he said: 'The most bizarre thing is how intimate that record was when I made it,' says Reznor. 'I was so embarrassed when someone would hear it. It was my journal and then to think that a million people bought that thing. It's giving yourself away and that's a creepy feeling.'

Halo 1 – Reznor refers to all single, album and video releases by the codification Halo, regardless of format or label – the single

'Down In It' was released in September 1989 on CD and 12" vinyl. It contained the album version (labelled 'Skin') along with two remixes ('Singe' and 'Shred'). The album *Pretty Hate Machine* followed a month later. The Skin mix was the version that appeared on the album, the other two were respectively a brief dub mix and a full blown extended experimental heavy dun reworking, Sherwood's trademark sound.

Reznor was dissatisfied with the version of track, telling *Anti Matter*: 'The 12" single "Down In It", which is produced by Adrian Sherwood and the most industrial sounding song on the album, was finished before the album. I think this track is the closest to predictable industrial music, the rest of the album is not so predictable which is what my goal was, and I feel I have reached it. Sherwood, I didn't work with him. He mixed it, but he mixed it in London and I talked to him on the phone. So I didn't get a chance to rip off all his great tricks. And Flood, we only worked briefly together, and John Fryer had nothing to offer me.'

A video for the single was shot by Chicago's H Gun (aka Eric Zimmerman) and Benjamin Stokes, who had shot clips for Ministry offshoot The Revolting Cocks and KMFDM. It was a simple enough idea and one that was already pretty clichéd: Trent and the other members of Nine Inch Nails are chased through an empty urban landscape by a gang of assailants. This is intercut with footage of Reznor in front of a neon crucifix. One scene at the finalé featured Reznor lying apparently dead, filmed from above with the camera tied to a helium balloon. Inevitably, the balloon slipped its tether...

As Trent told *Convulsion*, a UK fanzine: 'We got a call from my manager saying, this is the most unbelievable story, you will not believe what happened... The camera landed 200 miles [340km] away in a farmers field somewhere. He finds it and takes it to the police thinking that it's a surveillance camera for marijuana, they develop the film and think that it's some sort of snuff film of a murder, give it to the FBI and have pathologists looking at the body saying, yeah he's rotting (I had corn starch on me, right) he's been decomposing for three weeks. You could see the other members of the band walking away and they had these weird outfits on and they thought it was some kind of gang slaying. When the camera went up they could see it was Chicago so they went to the Chicago Police Department and they went to all the art schools and asked if this was anybodies work that you might know and traced it down to one of our video directors who went to one of the art schools, then there was talk that I would have to appear and talk to prove that I was alive, stupid, but funny.'

The video made its debut on sensation tabloid TV true crime show *Hard Copy*. Whether this was actually a publicity stunt to generate some controversy is now unclear as nobody is talking, but it was to be Reznor's first brush with censorship: MTV's censors threw one of their periodic fits of the vapours and demanded that the final scene be excised before they would show it. As MTV's importance to the Nine Inch Nails demographic was huge, they were forced to comply. As a taster for the album, it was hardly The Sex Pistols on Bill Grundy, but did at least generate a modicum of pre-release publicity. It was also the start of a fruitful collaboration with Zimmerman and Stokes, whose video for 'Head Like A Hole' – a barrage of imagery creating a sort of techno-psychedelic effect – was to capture some of the blood-curling mania that Reznor would project live.

Packaged in a black sleeve with a picture of turbine blades, photographed and solarised so that they actually appeared to be a section of vertebrae and rendered in contrasting pink and blue to add a quasi-organic effect, *Pretty Hate Machine* looked like a cyberpunk record. Not yet employing the distinctive NIN logo with the second N reversed cyrillic alphabet style, the overall impression conveyed by the stark minimalism of the sleeve design by Gary Talpas (who would work on subsequent Nine Inch Nails releases as well as Nothing Records artists Marilyn Manson and Tweak) was that it was a release on an arty English label like Mute, 4AD or Factory Records, whose own house style was a straight steal from European classical label ECM.

He spoke to the fanzine *Anti Matter* about the title: 'I thought...[it] was a good way to describe the music as a whole, meaning machine-generated music. It is electronic, which is derived from keyboards, which are machines. There is a lot of hate, anger and emotion in both the lyrics and music, the album is a "pretty hate machine".'

Initial sales were not encouraging. The album garnered some favourable reviews in fanzines as well as bigger magazines like the influential *College Music Journal*, which noted perceptively that they could be a breakthrough band: 'The Cleveland-based outfit strikes into truly uncharted territory: dance/ethereal/industrial/pop/rock, with more emotional (read: real) singing than 1,000 Nitzer Ebbs could muster. Head Nail Trent Reznor has penned some dark, bitter songs that are the staple of the genre... Rather than sinking into the muck of self-pity, Reznor creates catchy, ironic, static-y melodies... With Reznor's heartfelt and nasal vox (kinda like The Cure's Robert Smith with a head cold) leading the way, Nine Inch Nails could be the first hard-edged techno-pop group to find its way to mass appeal as well as critical acclaim.'

Others like the reviewer in techno-fetishist magazine *Black Ice* were even less restrained: 'Nine Inch Nails is a cultural virus loosed on the electronic datastreams, a revolutionary killer file in the guise of a blanded out pop version of Ministry, Foetus or any number of Birthday Party mopers. Nine Inch Nails make the sort of music that will stealthily enter the belly of the corporate rock 'n' roll beast unobserved and just when it thinks it has sucked in another dumb slave band to churn out mecha-pop to feed its profit hungry machinery, BAM! It gets it right in the fat guts. Nine Inch Nails are a perfect cyborg unit, man and machine in perfect harmony like the Terminator, a relentless killer machine with the soul of a man. This is what Nine Inch Nails have over their competition whether it's desperate futurists like Sigue Sigue Sputnik (whatever happened to?) or the bland and dopey electro disco, soma for the masses. This could be the spirit of punk renewed for one last spasm on the dancefloor.'

Reznor had little time to bask in this low-level adulation. His immediate task was to assemble a touring band that could reproduce the sound and feel of the album live.

'I'm not in the position to offer somebody 1,000 dollars a week to rehearse,' Reznor told *Spin*. 'So I took some young guys who were malleable, who would basically do what I want them to do but expand on it. The only context I've worked with them in so far is, "Here are the songs, here are your parts, learn them." When I start to do the next record, it'll be up in the air as to what happens. I don't see it becoming a democracy, ever.'

As he told *Thrasher* magazine, he wanted to 'mold them into whatever I wanted to use them for, instead of polished, great musicians who would come in with an attitude of "It should be like this..." The music wasn't created with a guitar part, drum part thing in mind. Live, there are just some things that just can't be played evenly. I just got some guys that I knew around here, who had the right *attitude*.'

Using the same line-up as had played on the two Skinny Puppy dates, Reznor played two dates in December 1989 in New Jersey and Boston before going out on the road as support to The Jesus And Mary Chain between January and April 1990. Those dates in turn were followed by a short headlining tour taking in more club shows.

Reznor, accomplished in the studio and rightly proud of his debut, hid his nervousness about touring behind a mask of sarcasm: 'I look forward to [touring] because you reach a point where you cannot look at a computer anymore. I'll look forward to rehearsing in a no heating environment, with people you don't like, singing songs you're sick of... I can't wait for that, y'know?'

5 The Long Hard Road To The Downward Spiral

'Head like a hole/Black as your soul/I'd rather die/Than give you control.'

- Nine Inch Nails, 'Head Like A Hole'

The band that Reznor went out on the road with at the end of January 1990 with The Jesus And Mary Chain was Chris Vrenna on drums, ex-Exotic Bird guitarist Richard Patrick (currently with Filter) and new keyboardist David Hames. Reznor played occasional keyboards but found himself in the unusual position of being upfront, the focus of everyone's attention. For a shy retiring kid from a small Pennsylvania town, this would be the making or breaking of him.

As bootlegs of those early shows prove, he had still to fully develop as a live performer. He may have felt disheartened too by the fact that album sales remained sluggish: with Gottlieb's remarks still ringing in his ears, it seemed that he would soon be heading back to obscurity in Cleveland. Yet for all that he may have been racked by self doubt, he still had a strong self belief. He *had* made a great record. Never a fan of the press, at least reviews showed that. And the fan reaction was growing. A hardcore section of the kids who came along to those Jesus And Mary Chain and later Peter Murphy shows went away as converts. Some, admittedly, were actually disappointed when they bought the album to find that it was not as abrasive and unapproachable as the songs were when played live: a lot of initial criticism of Trent Reznor from these kids was that the album was actually too radio friendly, too commercial, too much of a pop album.

The musical climate at the start of 1990 was bewildering. In Britain, micro-scenes like Madchester were the big stories in the music press. Inspired by acid house, which had a major impact in their home city of Manchester, two bands The Stone Roses and The Happy Mondays were creating big waves by fusing elements of that club culture with their slightly more retro sound. In the case of the Roses this was '60s pop and The Mondays seemed to be inspired by '70s funk. House DJs remixed their tracks, most notably Andrew Weatherall's reworking of The Happy Mondays' 'Hallelujah', inadvertently sparking off a crossover between two hitherto disparate scenes. Primal Scream's 'Loaded' – a remix by Weatherall using samples from their more traditional ballad 'I'm Losing More Than I'll Ever Have' from their second album *Sonic Flower Groove* as well as snatches of found sounds like guitar breaks from The Meters – was a dazzling example of what was possible. Independent rock music was revitalised. Unfortunately, it began a wave of retro music, mostly stuck in a psychedelic groove that English music has yet to grow out of.

'I hate them all,' Trent told *Guitar* magazine. 'I don't know if I'm getting more selective, or fickle, or if there's just no substance whatsoever to those groups. And with regard to that whole Manchester dance bullshit scene, it just seems like a bunch of follow-the-leader people who can't write songs – bands who have no talent, whose only merit is that they were in a club and at some point were seen by somebody in the English press. I find it all boring. Much the same way that house music doesn't interest me either.'

In the US however, despite a strong alternative sector spearheaded by Sonic Youth, Dinosaur Jr and Pixies with the Seattle scene kicking into full gear following the release of Nirvana's debut *Bleach* in 1989, mainstream rock was still dominated by embarrassing and awful 'big hair' bands like Poison, Warrant, Extreme and Bon Jovi. The idea that somebody like Reznor could be a major star when he lacked a curly bouffant, a set composed of excruciating power ballads and a bevvy of half-naked rock chicks on his album cover seemed to be totally absurd. Like all revolutions, the change that was to come would be swift and brutal and fortune would favour the bold.

Fault lines were appearing and rock music began to fragment. The influence of MTV cannot be over-estimated: when Reznor was growing up, kids listened to what was on the radio or on mainstream TV or what was available at their local Wal-Mart. But the advent of MTV – carried on cable and satellite – and its imitators brought a whole new world to these small towns. Initially MTV's agenda was anglo bands whose videos they could play for free. Despite the fact that the likes of Michael Jackson and Madonna dominated the channel, many left field artists who could not have gotten a look in on mainstream rock radio started to break through via heavy rotation on MTV. This helped to chip away at the monolithic corporate rock edifice; suddenly kids in small towns like Mercer were hip to bands who were not stadium rock drones like Ratt and Skid Row. This process, to some extent, has been accelerated by the spread of access to the world-wide web.

In 1990, both The Jesus And Mary Chain and Peter Murphy were bands on the way down. The Mary Chain, one of the most vital and era defining bands of the 1980s, made their reputation with shambolic feedback-drenched performances that occasionally ended in rioting. They used to goad their audience mercilessly, but were also able to play stunning numinous Stooges-meets-Beach Boys style punk, recording two solid classic albums in *Psychocandy* and *Badlands*. By 1990 they were starting to tread water. What had been revolutionary the previous decade now seemed stale. Reznor had, as he later said, little problem in blowing them off the stage. That went doubly so for Peter Murphy, former singer with Bauhaus, whose solo career – like the solo careers of most singers from such cult bands – was a disappointment to the bulk of the people who had been fans of his original band, though uncritically lapped up by blinkered devotees with the fervour of Moonies meeting their revered leader. Along with Siouxsie And The Banshees, Murphy was largely responsible for the subculture known as goth, which amazingly persists into the present day like some strange cargo cult. It was during the shows in March 1990 when they supported him that Reznor started to abuse the audience.

At one frustrating gig the stage was littered with half empty beer bottles and pizzas from the road crew's buffet. Reznor recalls that the black-clad goth audience just stood and sullenly stared. He started to throw the pizza and beer into the crowd. It got a reaction.

As he told *Alternative Press*: 'Our show just got much more anger-oriented, or just fucking frustration-oriented, rather than "We really want to do a fine job for everybody out there." Fuck you! Like our music, or we're going to fucking spill beer on you and insult you. When we do, they love you more, and then that makes you have less respect for them. It just fuels itself to where you just turn into something else. It's a weird thing. It wasn't hard to be hard, it was just hard, because it felt better being that way. It went from "Let's play these songs and try to be sincere," to explosions and screaming out. We won over the people we wanted to win over, but some of the vampire crowd were not gonna ever go for anything except their god, Mister Cheekbones.'

Murphy, in another interview, accused Reznor of ripping off early Bauhaus, miming to backing tapes and destroying his band's gear by covering it in flour.

'I remember being very impressed by their record. It seemed to be very similar to one aspect that Bauhaus had done; that was five years ago, still it was a little *déjà vu* in moments. However, the audience were almost battered into submission by the time we came on. Part of Trent's act was to throw and goad his band into throwing flour. My band were a little bit pissed off about this and the damage they were doing to their equipment. Trent was saying this is a part of our act and we have to carry on. Trent basically used backing tracks a lot of the time to make it credible; although the band was playing, the backing tracks laid the foundation of the sound. The band was just a visual device to make it look like there was a band entity. But actually it's just Trent. The band was just bit part players in the overall scheme of things; it was very theatrical in that sense. This is part of the very manipulative way that he works, which is clever in a way, thought out and planned.'

In fact, what Nine Inch Nails did was to cover themselves in cornstarch to resemble corpses. An old goth trick employed to best effect by the legendary Fields Of The Nephilim, who used enough to supply a medium-sized bakery.

As he told *Mondo* magazine: 'When we started out and needed to get press photos taken, we knew we didn't want to pose like pretty boys. We got this photographer Jeffrey Silverthorne from Ohio who was doing these really neat pictures of people covered in cornstarch. They're photographed really high contrast so they look almost corpse-like. The picture on the inside of the record was done this way. Most of his work is of nudes. There's something really disturbing about them. Very eerie. So, after working with him, before we did our first show, I just came out with this box of cornstarch and doused everybody. I said "Fuck it, let's just try it and see what happens." We looked so creepy and stupid, but we seemed to pull it off. It looks really great under the lights, grungey, a sort of anti-Bon Jovi and the whole glamour thing. That just escalated into the silliness of the tour... Certain things like that just seem to develop when you're on the road, out of the insanity of it all. You're always tired and hungover. Our shows are incredibly exhausting, I mean I'm not a big partier, we drank once in a while, but I had to cut all that out, 'cause if I drank the night before, the next day I just couldn't do as good a show. But, towards the end of the tour – the West Coast dates – it just started getting progressively more ridiculous, ya know – how can we outdo the night before? We were breaking things on stage and stuff like that. It got to the point where it was a complete situation of chaos. One night I was in a 7-11 before the show and I saw this big thing of chocolate syrup and I got this idea. During a certain point in the show, I always molest the guitar player in some fashion. I said to him "Rich, tonight I've got a surprise for you, don't worry it'll be cool." He's like: "What is it? What is it!? You're going to make me look like an idiot and my brother's going to be there." The point in the show is when things lighten up a bit, there's a break from the violent intensity. I pulled out two things of chocolate syrup and start pouring them over his head. It looked cooler than I could have possibly imagined – it was just amazing. It totally dripped all over his guitar, everywhere. The roadies are saying [deep gruffy voice]: "Fuck this, this isn't in my contract" (cleaning chocolate syrup off of strings and guitar parts). So, of course this had to go even farther. The next night in LA there was this wall of security guys in front of the stage so that I couldn't see the audience and the audience couldn't see me. At one point I just stopped the show and said, "What the fuck are you doing? Does anyone here wanna see these fuckin' guys?" Well, at the end of the show, I found out that there was this big hump in the dance floor that they were trying to keep people from walking onto. So I apologised to them and we became "good friends." The next night (at the same place) the security guys bring out 6–10 heavy naked girls and my road manager starts covering them in whipped cream. It was totally bizarre and silly.'

And although Reznor used tapes and samples, this was actually only a small part of their sound, recreating things that it was impossible to reproduce live. Reznor was unapologetic about this, telling *Keyboard* magazine in 1993: 'The dilemma that I faced was: I didn't want to have three guys onstage, faking everything, with a tape machine running. However, I also didn't want a seven-piece rock band where every cool bit of electronic-ness was converted into people approximating it live on other instruments. I don't use electronics as a cop-out: "I couldn't get a drummer, so I just programmed it", or, "I couldn't play this part good enough, so I programmed it". It's not that kind of thing at all. I program because I like the way it sounds. I like quantization. I enjoy the sound of it. I like using those elements of perfection amidst randomness. And live, I didn't want that element to be brushed under the table by a big live band. So we used four tracks of tape and four musicians: I'd play guitar on some songs and sing, plus a keyboard player, a guitar player, and a drummer. At the time, there were no digital four-track devices that were affordable to us, so we just used a four-track cassette deck – high-speed Tascam special. one track would be a click that the drummer would play to; he'd wear headphones onstage. One track would be bass because 90 percent of the bass was synth, and I wouldn't want a real guy playing bass, simulating that, nor would I want to see a keyboard player tapping 16th notes with his head down. And the other two tracks were stereo miscellaneous. Maybe it would be a percussion loop. Maybe it would be some sequency-sounding keyboard part, stuff like that. And all the drums, vocals, main keyboard parts, and guitars were being played live. I don't feel we have to justify why we used tape onstage – I've always admitted that – but the point was, that was the best way to get the stuff across live. That was the best way to maintain what was good about the electronic side of it. I didn't want to take sequencers and shit out live: "excuse me ladies and gentlemen, while I get on my back and get under the keyboard rig and figure out what MIDI cable isn't plugged in." I mean, we had enough problems with the one piece of gear that can fuck us up: the tape deck. We had a lot of problems with that. The only MIDI onstage was from triggers on the drum kit. The keyboard player just had an [E-mu] Emax; he'd load a disk for each song.'

Murphy, whose prominence dwindled as Reznor's grew, allegedly at one point tried to have Nine Inch Nails thrown off the tour.

What became apparent, however, was that the audience seemed to respond best when Trent abused them. This 'treat 'em mean, keep 'em keen' approach was to serve him well onstage from that point on.

As we have already seen, extreme performance was the hallmark of industrial music from the start. Trent just capitalised on this.

Nine Inch Nails are sometimes – wrongly – lumped alongside goth bands like Sisters Of Mercy. Reznor's biggest contribution to the goth genre, however, is Marilyn Manson. Although performers like Murphy may have indirectly influenced him, the Weimar vampyre act was looking ridiculous almost as soon as Bauhaus released their debut single 'Dark Entries' in 1979. Goth was a genre that attracted mostly women – perhaps because it is rock's only overtly romantic movement to have lasted – while industrial was almost wholly a male preserve, so much so that Ministry gigs used to stink like locker rooms. Reznor, shrewdly, managed to incorporate enough of a whiff of goth into his persona to ensure a certain sex appeal that Al Jourgensen, Skinny Puppy, Front 242 and The Young Gods lacked.

Outside of the concert arena, as we have seen, the club scene was becoming a more important arena for artists plugging their records. Alternative discos, where they played anything but house, hi-NRG or pop, were springing up across America in college towns and major cities as well as the sort of small town where bands seldom play but where 'outsider' kids want to congregate. Nine Inch Nails' second single, 'Head Like A Hole', started to spread in these clubs. It was good to dance to, commercial enough to be memorable and a good listen. Its obvious appeal was reaching out to kids who would perhaps have to wait years for Nine Inch Nails to play anywhere near them. The underground buzz was soon picked up by radio – mostly college stations initially – and then by the big franchises.

The video was striking and also involved a 'visual remix' by Flood, something very pioneering, particularly as the concept of 'desktop video' was still years away.

It was a time of experimentation in their live shows. They tried performing standing still. At one gig they all performed so drunk that they could hardly stand, falling into drum kits and amps; many people apparently left saying it was the best gig they had ever seen!

The squalor of Reznor and Vrenna's Cleveland home was replaced by the squalor of life on the road which, at the level Nine Inch Nails were at, was far from glamorous. Reznor, by his own admission, was drunk every night that they were on the road. The band were forced to share motel rooms as well as travelling together, which builds up the inescapable intimacy that both binds band members together and forces them to live in a permanent stew of psychological contempt. It's often said that if a band can survive each other after three or four years on the road and not hate and despise each other enough to cancel going into a recording studio or out on the road again, they will be together forever. Although Reznor was the acknowledged leader and his band members were mere hired hands, it is telling that even after their professional relationship was terminated after touring, they chose to work with Reznor again on subsequent projects. The message to Reznor from audience and band must have been that the more you abuse them, the more they love you!

Ministry's Al Jourgensen hooked up with Reznor before he signed to TVT; Wax Trax!, the Chicago label that grew from a record shop to being the imprint most associated with industrial music, had actually considered signing Nine Inch Nails. In the first half of 1990, Jourgensen and Trent went into the studio together, Al producing a Nine Inch Nails cover of Queen's 'Get Down Make Love', which later appeared on the b-side of 'Sin'. Trent also recorded vocals for one of Jourgensen's many side projects including 1,000 Homo DJs (the name came from WaxTrax! Records founder Jim Nash, who told Al that only 1,000 homo DJs would hear his music). Trent recorded the vocals to the 1,000 Homo DJs cover of Black Sabbath's 'Supernaut'. Al had released a previous single under this name in 1988. The line-up on the 1990 12" single of 'Supernaut' backed with 'Hey Asshole' was given as Buck Satan - Guitar, Bass, Vox on Supernaut; Officer Agro - Drums; Ike Krull - Guitar; Wee Willie Reefer - Drums; Viva Nova - Chick Vox; with Count Ringworm - whiney vox. Trent was Ike Krull.

Upon discovering that he had lent his vocals to this project, TVT issued a flood of writs. Jourgensen claimed that he rerecorded the track with his own voice, though allegedly he distorted Trent's voice electronically so that it was unrecognizable. The original version cropped up on a compilation album a few years afterwards, though ironically by that time TVT had actually bought Wax Trax! and its back catalogue.

'The version of "Supernaut" that eventually came out is not me singing. The one that we originally did had me singing the lead, but because my record label in America TVT, which is the shittiest label in the entire planet, totally shit their pants about it and made a big hassle about it. Basically, it was me and Al hanging out in a studio together, totally drunk, so after two months of my label fighting with Wax Trax! I called him up and said, redo it save yourself the hassle,' Reznor told Brit fanzine *Convulsion*.

Reznor also sang on another Jourgensen side project, the 'comedy' industrial band The Revolting Cocks, and it was suggested that Jourgensen may be the producer of choice for the follow-up to *Pretty Hate Machine*. But even as the album picked up momentum, Reznor had sworn that whatever he did after *Pretty Hate Machine*, it would not be released on TVT.

Trent appeared on one track of Jourgensen's Revolting Cocks project, adding vocals to 'Stainless Steel Provider' and being credited as an 'Additional Cock' on the album.

Reznor had started thinking about the follow-up as early as 1990, though the set list for the shows that Nine Inch Nails played never strayed far from the ten tracks on *Pretty Hate Machine* plus occasional B-sides. The format of the band was not conducive to improvisation, so the set – even the order of the songs – remained static for the 18 months that the band toured.

Reznor continued touring throughout 1990, playing the Hate 90 dates in the summer and autumn and then some winter dates with James Woolley replacing Lee Mars. Woolley played with Nine Inch Nails during Lollapalooza the following year and was there for part of the Self Destruct tour. He was replaced by Charlie Clouser in 1995, who remains a close collaborator at the time of writing.

The Hate 90 tour took in a show in Melbourne, Florida. Before going onstage a young music journalist from a local glossy magazine called *25th Parallel* approached Reznor. He recalls: 'When I first saw Trent he was sulking in the corner during the soundcheck as his dreadlocked tour manager Sean Beavan hovered protectively over him. Once we started talking, he thawed and became affable. But I was just another journalist. Talking to me was as good a way as any for him to kill time before a show in a city where he knew no one. The next time Trent Reznor came to town, I was his opening act.'

The journalist Brian Warner was soon to play a major role in the life of Trent under his more famous alias Marilyn Manson.

As Manson recalls, the opportunity to play with this rising band came around the same year: 'I had gotten a call from Bob Slade, a punk-rock DJ in Miami with a Monkees-style bowl haircut. We didn't have a manager at the time, so I was mishandling our business affairs.

"Listen," he said in his nasal, obnoxious radio voice. "We need you guys to open up for Nine Inch Nails at Club Nu." Club Nu was a guido bar in Miami that we all hated. Though we only had seven songs... I agreed. It was too good an opportunity to pass up just because we sucked. Before the show, Nancy [his then girlfriend] handed me a tab of acid... I stuck it under my tongue without a second thought-until afterwards. On stage, I wore a short, orange dress and dragged Nancy around by her usual leash and collar. For some reason, I didn't freak out on the acid: Nancy did. She cried and screamed throughout the show, begging me to beat her harder and harder until welts rose up on her pale, anemic back. I was frightened by what I saw myself doing, but excited too, mainly because the crowd seemed to be getting so much enjoyment out of our psychedelic sadomasochistic drama. After the show, which I don't even think Trent Reznor watched, I ran into him backstage. "Remember me?" I asked, trying to pretend like I wasn't tripping though my ultradilated eyes probably gave it away. "I interviewed you for *25th Parallel*." He politely pretended he remembered me, and I gave him a tape and scurried away before I could say anything too stupid. Crazed on drugs and still under the spell of Nancy, I stumbled to a backstage hospitality area – most likely Nine Inch Nails's dressing room – where I found her waiting for me. We had sex, and I saw the devil in her eyes again.'

Manson and Reznor would keep in touch this time, though the fruits of their professional association were some three years in the future.

As Reznor's confidence onstage grew, he actually started to enjoy performing, even although he was cast in the role of some sort of male dominatrix. As he told *Mondo* magazine: 'I'm incredibly pleased with the success of our live shows, which I was very concerned about when we started – how the music would go over live with a new band. Well, the crowd response has been really great. There's people stage diving and people just doing whatever they want to do, which some people may interpret as violent or out of control. We've had some problems with the security people. At the beginning of every show I have to give a speech where I say, "Look, people are going to be having fun out there. They're not hurting each other, so don't stop them. No one is out there to hurt anybody. We're about fun and letting people get it out of their systems." You have to understand where security people are at, you know, little brains, big muscles, small dicks. This is basically their chance to get tough and beat people up. We've played shows where someone incredibly harmless jumps up on stage for a minute and jumps back off and security will grab 'em and just start beatin' on 'em while carrying them off the stage. We stop the show and say, "hey, the only people who are getting hurt are the ones you're beating up on, you're causing the problem." And then articles come out saying that we don't allow stage diving. It's not us. Like on the upcoming Lollapalooza tour, we're going to be in these big venues. I'd rather be in clubs where people can do whatever they want. This music releases a lot of energy so you should have the freedom to do what you have to do – stand on your chair and scream, jump up on stage with me, whatever, I don't care. The big challenge on this tour is going to be trying to create that feeling with a) lots of people who've never seen our shows, b) giant daytime venues. That's my challenge for the next months.'

Lollapalooza was the brainchild of Jane's Addiction vocalist Perry Farrell, inspired by a visit to Europe, playing at festivals like Glastonbury, Reading and Roskilde where a comparatively broad swathe of contemporary music – rap, alternative, dance, metal – were all together on the same bill. Farrell wanted to create something like Glastonbury in the US, a festival that would not only have the best of a wide variety of different kinds of music, but would also have a strong social and political message. The first Lollapalooza was set for

1991, a touring show that would cross the United States, giving people who might not otherwise have gone a chance to see a bill that included Jane's Addiction, Ice-T, Living Colour, Siouxsie And The Banshees, The Butthole Surfers and Nine Inch Nails.

'The whole idea of playing outside for us is a totally foreign idea because we are a totally, indoors, controlled environment, dark band and initially when we were asked to do this, our reservations were trying to translate to a big venue and the outside, in the daylight and not have the things we were accustomed to and then we tried to change that into a challenge to make it, to try to adapt the set to work in an outdoor, hostile environment. I really don't like playing big venues. I much prefer clubs where people can interact. It's very impersonal when people are miles away from people.'

One reviewer described Trent and his band, covered in flour with smoke billowing around them as 'looking like a bunch of dead guys at a cook-out'. Despite his reservations, Reznor is generally acknowledged to have been the star of the 1991 festival.

'Even if there wasn't one band I wanted to see, as a consumer I would go see this. Potentially have a lot of fun,' he told MTV.

There was drama aplenty, like the date in Phoenix when the band stormed offstage after only a few minutes: 'Well, we were officially the first casualty of the Lollapalooza tour here in Phoenix, Arizona. I guess what happened is a lot of our equipment in the back was sitting in the sun, baking in the desert heat, and since we are a electronic-based kind of band, when the main part of your sound becomes ruined and melted, which I think is what happened, it was cutting out and becoming a nightmare and that complemented with the incompetence on the part of the crew led to a disastrous embarrassing situation.'

But the tour and the coverage it received helped boost sales of *Pretty Hate Machine* even further; more interestingly, Nine Inch Nails t-shirts outsold everyone else's. By now the NIN logo was a strong identifiable trademark, something as important to a new generation of kids as KISS merchandise had been during Reznor's youth.

By the middle of the tour Trent was talking seriously about a follow-up. Talking to *Guitar* magazine, he said: 'I have worked by myself, to the point where I need some other input. I've had experience with bands and group decisions, and all the compromising that involves, which is why I've been a one-man band for so long. But the problem there is getting each instrumental part to have its own individual identity. That's what slows the whole process down to a crawl. [The next album will be] much more guitar-oriented. It's going to be a lot more live and a lot more raw and harder – a lot uglier. I think our fans are in for a shock. And if we lose them all? Hey, I can't say I don't care. Because I do. But I'm not going to tailor my music to what I think those people are going to like next. I don't think in terms of radio and MTV.'

Not exactly great news for Steve Gottlieb and the folks back at TVT.

While on the tour, Reznor also received the news that Guns N' Roses wanted Nine Inch Nails to be the opening act on their forthcoming European tour.

Trent told *Convulsion*: 'It was shocking to me, so I figured it would shock a lot of people, especially those who think we are a total synth band. Axl started showing up at a lot of gigs and said that he liked us and we sort of became friends and said "If you guys ever want to open for us, let me know." We said "Maybe in Europe or something?"'

Problems with the label were further exacerbated by what Trent perceived as their reticence to promote the album in the UK and Europe. Originally, the UK licensee Island Records had planned to release *Pretty Hate Machine* to coincide with the band's visit and had set up a lot of publicity, hoping that TVT would split some of the cost. TVT refused until the band landed the Guns N' Roses opening slot.

By the time they arrived in Europe, *Pretty Hate Machine* had sold 400,000 copies. For a band like the Black Crowes, for example, that was 'piss in a bucket, for us its good!' said Reznor.

The connection with Guns N' Roses is a strange one. Formed in 1985 in Los Angeles, Guns N' Roses seemed to typify everything that was stifling and traditional about rock 'n' roll in the '80s. They were the ultimate 'big hair' band, white trash heroes, big with the unsophisticated small towners that Reznor detested. Yet there was another side to Guns N' Roses, one that was inspired by punk, that was soaked with raw energy. Singer Axl Rose was not comfortable as the icon of the mullet hairdo and pick-up truck driving set and desperately wanted to make Guns N' Roses a more innovative band. It's telling that during the band's long silence (at the time of writing the album *Chinese Democracy*, originally promised for 1998, still shows no sign of being released anytime soon) there were rumours that Rose had scrapped the band's traditional sound and was experimenting with electronic music. Guitarist Robin Finck, a Nine Inch Nails member, would join and leave Guns N' Roses before any music was released and Chris Vrenna was briefly associated with them as a drum programmer.

In 1991 they were probably the biggest rock 'n' roll band in the world, blissfully unaware of an album being recorded by Nirvana called *Nevermind* that would change everything.

The Nine Inch Nails sets were a disaster. Like the legendary Suicide supports with The Clash in the '70s – New York electronic art duo confront rock reactionaries – the hostility of the two worlds colliding was a sight to behold. Almost as soon as Trent walked onstage at Wembley, London, England in August 1991, the booing from the crowd was loud enough to drown the intro to 'Now I'm Nothing'.

'It's a strange place for a band like us to be in,' Trent told *Rockbeat* magazine. 'Especially since we're trying to use electronics and give them some merit, which is something the average Guns N' Roses fan isn't used to. Whether you're playing a guitar or a keyboard, the bottom line is that they're both tools that are there for you to use. I think what we're doing is just as intense and as real as any so-called "real" rock band.'

Despite the hostility, there was a sizeable contingent of fans who had actually gone along to see Nine Inch Nails. You could pick them out of the crowd of curly permed or 'mullet' sporting 30-plus men in skin tight leopard skin print jeans and fringed leather jackets: the Nine Inch Nails fans were the ones with shaved heads, full length leather coats and gas masks! The next show in Mannheim, Germany was worse.

Speaking to Lorraine Ali at *Spin* magazine a few years after the event, Reznor said: 'People were just starting to hear of us over there 'cause our record just came out. Our American label did not license the music over there until about two years after it came out. I'd kind of gone into it, like, "Well, we did Lollapalooza and that worked out okay and in the big picture it benefited us and, well, what's the difference?" Well, it was a big difference. It was the worst of situations. It was us, Skid Row, Guns N' Roses. I like Guns N' Roses for what they do. Skid Row, however, is the epitome of what I don't like about spandex rock. Poseur toughness, bullshit. I hate them. So we open up. First song, people are, like, "Yeah, there's a band onstage," and they're slowly realizing that we're not Skid Row. Second song, "Okay, these guys are not Skid Row and I think I hear a synthesiser." Third song, "We definitely hear a synthesiser – this is bullshit. These guys suck, they're faggots, let's kick their ass." There is something about the feeling of standing in front of 65,000 people giving you the finger... An intense terror took over. In a word, it sucks. I decided just to make it the worst half hour of this crowd's life. The point when it actually became humorous was when I saw a sausage flying up onstage at the show in Germany. A link sausage. But we got off the stage with our lives. Another sad moment at that date was toward the end of the set I actually saw one poor fucker with a Nine Inch Nails shirt, holding it up. Seconds later, I just saw a scuffling and no more Nine Inch Nails shirt. We did somehow sell eight T-shirts that night. Eight out of 65,000. That's not a bad ratio. It also made me realise that I'm not trying to be all things to all people.'

Axl Rose – photographed wearing a Nine Inch Nails t-shirt (one of the eight?) on several occasions – was undaunted and asked Trent to support them on their forthcoming US dates. Battered from the constant touring, with the TVT situation coming to a head, Trent turned him down. After their initial reluctance to push *Pretty Hate Machine* as sales started to really take off, the record company then, as Reznor saw it, started to exploit it ruthlessly.

'I decided that there's no way I could make another record for these people because I have to deal with things like them putting my music in bad movies and buying advertising time during David Letterman for a record that's two years old,' Reznor told *Chaos Control*. 'I'm the one that had to answer to my fans for that, and it's not me doing it and I have no control over it. It was a really bad situation and personally we hated each other.'

He was angry that decisions had been made by the label, such as releasing 'Head Like A Hole' on a CD with so many remixes that its running time was actually longer than that of *Pretty Hate Machine*. With the ideas for the next recordings germinating in his mind, fertilised with the righteous anger he felt towards Gottlieb, Reznor played his last live show at the London Astoria Theatre in September 1991. Stupidly, he was put on a bill for an MTV show along with The Wonder Stuff and EMF, in its way even more bizarre than Guns N' Roses. Press reaction was scathing. The British weeklies were sympathetic to the glorified pub-rock of The Wonder Stuff or the seemingly modern rave-friendly EMF at the expense of Nine Inch Nails.

Reznor told *Alternative Press*: 'We weren't easily categorizable as to what was happening in England at the time, the Manchester scene. The Stone Roses were God and EMF was Jesus Christ, plus the press didn't invent the trend that we were supposedly following. They're into dictating what's cool in America later – "Here comes rave and house" – but surprise them with something they're unfamiliar with and you catch them with their pants down. Plus, everyone was attacking me because the stage shows were "some theatrical thing".'

Drained, drunk and drenched in sweat, he told people at the aftershow party to expect a new record 'real soon', that he couldn't wait to get back on the road, about his move from Cleveland to Los Angeles and about other people he planned to work with.

Reznor was briefly involved with industrial 'supergroup' Pigface, formed by former Killing Joke/Ministry drummers Martin Atkins and Bill Rieflin. He recorded a song called 'Suck' for their album *Gub*.

Those involved in Pigface read like a who's who of alternative music at that time: David Yow of the Jesus Lizard, Alex Paterson of The Orb, Dean Ween of Ween, Dead Kennedy Jello Biafra, Chicago industrial pioneer Flour, Becky from Lunachicks, Caspar Brotzmann from Gwar, Genesis P Orridge, Leslie Rankine of Silverfish, Revolting Cocks man Chris Connelly, Youth from Killing Joke/The Orb, Black Francis of Pixies, Chris Vrenna, Mary Byker from Gaye Bykers On Acid, Danny Carey from Tool, Paul Barker from Ministry and Steve Albini of Big Black/Rapeman fame. Reznor hated working with Albini – who was producing the session – although later drafted him in to work on *The Fragile*. Trent also contributed to rhythm/noise track 'Bushmaster' and played some live shows on their 1991 tour.

Then he disappeared from sight and would not resurface for nearly two years.

6 The Sound Of Silence

'One ultra-fast chunk of death.'

– Trent Reznor's description of Broken

By most modern rock 'n' roll standards, the break between *Pretty Hate Machine* and *Broken* was not really an inordinately long one. There are bands whose gaps between albums have become legendary: The Stone Roses, for example, took over five years to make and release a follow-up to their debut; Tool retreated from public view for six years before coming back with *Lateralus* in 2001; Guns N' Roses last released an album in 1994 and have been promising a follow-up ever since. There are bands like the incredible My Bloody Valentine who release a classic album, such as their 1990 record *Loveless*, but just never get around to releasing a follow-up.

Usually the reasons are to do with conflicts between artist and label, drug problems or downright laziness – there is sometimes a hint of 'the dog ate it' about the excuses that artists come up with – and after a long gap it can be hard to pick up on the momentum that the previous release generated.

The relationship with TVT was now beyond repair and Reznor was determined not to write a note of music that could be used by the label. Like many artists, Trent was disillusioned that the label only seemed to be interested in squeezing a profit from him, though few labels have ever tried to pretend that they are Medici-like patrons of the arts, uninterested in anything other than a wonderful piece of art, regardless of its commercial value. There's also some evidence that while TVT, a small company without the margins and room for movement of a major label, behaved over-cautiously with Reznor's music, CEO Steve Gottlieb did take a personal interest in Trent and his music, accompanying him on the trip to London – Trent's first foreign trip – to record with John Fryer. And in fairness to TVT, a major label would hardly have lavished Reznor as an unknown artist with the long-term commitment necessary to break the album. Often if an album is felt to have 'underperformed' in its first weeks of release, planned promotional activity is cancelled and the record is left to flounder. Most young bands who sign with major labels have horror stories to tell.

Throughout 1991 and 1992, Reznor was under pressure from TVT to deliver new material for a follow-up. Unknown to Gottlieb, Reznor and producer Flood were recording in Miami's South Beach Studios under a different name.

Speaking to *Alternative Press* he said: 'I tried doing an album that I actually just wrote on guitar rather than my tried-and-true method of a drum machine and keyboards. So with the exception of "Happiness In Slavery", all songs were written on guitar. I was gonna make it totally stripped down to guitar, bass and drums but as I started it I realised I could easily fall into another trap. What might sound interesting to me – because I'm not used to it – may sound like a garage band to the world. So we just took the three instruments and sampled 'em, fucked with 'em, processed them. It's kind of overboard, we did go crazy. It's kind of dense, too dense. It's over analyzed – every song has 20 different melodies that you won't hear the first five or ten times you listen, or maybe never.'

The songs that were to be eventually released as *Broken* (and the remix version *Fixed*) were as uncompromising and unappealing as Reznor could possibly make them. There was none of the approachability, the lightness of touch that he demonstrated on *Pretty Hate Machine*. It was, as he later described it, a big 'fuck you!' though as well as being aimed at Gottlieb, it was also directed at the sneery industrial snobs who dismissed him as a pop sell out.

'My whole life became my career, essentially,' Reznor told *Rolling Stone*. 'And then I was faced with the fact that my career could easily have been over because the people that controlled it are fucking assholes. It's a horrible feeling. On one hand, Nine Inch Nails had a platinum album. On the other hand, I thought it was over because I was not doing another album for Gottlieb. And I was told litigation [to get off the label] would have taken two years. That's where a lot of the rage on *Broken* came from.'

It was a difficult process. As well as financing the sessions out of his own pocket and working in secret, even from the rest of the Nine Inch Nails touring band, the sessions were charged with emotion. As well as hate for Gottlieb, there was also a lot of bitterness directed towards a former girlfriend. There was also the frustration that after three tracks Flood had other commitments.

He told *Alternative Press*: 'Flood was working on Depeche Mode's record and my life alone was totally frustrating so why don't we make something that's not right, that doesn't sound right? I'm really proud of the stuff he and I did together but I don't ever, ever want to do that again. On a couple of songs I was really embarrassed about the lyrics so I wouldn't sing them right. I didn't realise that I was doing it until I'd sing it muffled, then he'd say "Do it again." Like the song "Last," I can't listen to it anymore. For some of them I was in the studio crying because I couldn't get it together in a goddamn month, and "We're doing it today! I suck!" It's mixed that way because that's the way I felt. It's a pretty true statement about how things were then. Now I've got to move on.'

Although it contained only six songs and at just over half an hour would qualify as an EP rather than a full length follow-up to *Pretty Hate Machine*, *Broken* is as intense a listening experience as anything several times its length. Guitar heavy, but almost atonal, tuneless, a constant barrage of samples sizzling away throughout every track, this album has absolutely no concessions whatsoever. Like, for example, Miles Davis's *Bitches Brew*, Tool's *Lateralus* or Captain Beefheart's *Trout Mask Replica*, it is an album that is hard to listen to but is ultimately very rewarding for the listener that perseveres with it. It also seemed calculated to confuse and repel anyone who thought they loved Nine Inch Nails after hearing *Pretty Hate Machine* and being captivated by its pop side.

The opening track 'Wish' positively brims with loathing and is obviously directed at Gottlieb: 'This is the first day of my last days/I built it up now I take it apart/Climbed up real high now fall down real far/No need for me to stay/The last thing left I just threw it away/I put my faith in God and my trust in you/Now there's nothing more fucked up I could do/Wish there was something real/Wish there was something true/Wish there was something real in this world full of you/I'm the one without a soul/I'm the one with this big fucking hole/No new tale to tell/Twenty-six years on my way to hell/Gotta listen to your big time hard line/Bad luck fist fuck/Don't think you're having all the fun/You know me/I hate everyone.'

'Last' was equally full of self loathing and frustration: 'Gave up trying to figure out my head/Got lost along the way/Worn out from giving it up my soul/I pissed it all away still stings these shattered nerves/Pigs, we get what pigs deserve.'

And 'Happiness In Slavery' was little more than another extended middle finger to Gottlieb, though a smarter and more satirical one than the screaming tantrum of 'Wish': 'Slave screams/He thinks he knows what he wants/Slave screams/Thinks he has something to say/Slave screams/He hears but doesn't want to listen/Slave screams / He's being beat into submission/Don't open your eyes/You won't like what you see/The devils of truth steal the souls of the free/ Don't open your eyes/Take it from me/I have found you can find happiness is slavery.'

One humourous Nine Inch Nails website suggested that *Broken* was Trent's alternative to battering Gottlieb to death with a golf club!

Every track on *Broken* seems to be about his loathing for the music industry. 'Happiness In Slavery', ironically, was recorded before Reznor was aware that he was about to be sold on by Gottlieb, like a human chattel.

Interscope Records was a label formed by veteran producer Jimmy Iovine, whose work had included producing Tom Petty, The

Pretenders, U2 and Patti Smith. Iovine had a distribution deal with Warner Brothers and, like TVT, was hungry to acquire new artists. Iovine was interested in Nine Inch Nails and signed a deal with Gottlieb to license Reznor's music from him. Interscope would release his records and take over all of the promotional activities as well as dealing directly with Reznor. TVT's imprint would still appear on releases and they would take a percentage of the royalties. As far as Gottlieb was concerned, this was a deal that worked out well for everyone. That wasn't exactly how Trent saw things at first.

Initially furious that the deal had taken place, he was persuaded by Iovine that he would be free to record and released as he pleased without any interference from the label. As a compromise, future releases would carry his own imprint Nothing Records. Initially Nothing Records was merely a shell company (Nothing was part of TVT was part of Interscope was part of Warner Brothers) but it gave Reznor another opportunity, to develop other artists that he liked.

Ironically, the money that TVT received was used to expand the label. When Wax Trax!, the home of Ministry and all their side projects including the disputed 1,000 Homo DJs recording with Reznor's vocals, filed for Chapter 11 bankruptcy in 1992, Gottlieb was able to snap up the label and its back catalogue, reissuing everything under the TVT imprint. A Best Of compilation called *Black Box* included the track with Reznor's original vocals as they had been recorded, before Jourgensen was forced to a) rerecord it using his own voice or b) electronically distort Reznor's voice so as to be unrecognizable.

Broken was released on TVT/Interscope in 1992. Its existence came as a big surprise to everyone, not least Iovine who was prepared for at least a year's wait before he would see new material. As well as the six tracks recorded with Flood, the package included a cover version of an early Adam And The Ants song 'Physical' and 'Suck', his contribution to the Pigface project. Neither of the two bonus tracks were listed on the album information. Although there were no singles from *Broken*, promo CDs of 'Happiness In Slavery' include remixes by

Adrian Sherwood. And a 'clean' version of 'Wish' was rerecorded as a radio-only promo without the words 'fist fuck'.

The formats were perplexing: it was released on CD with the six main tracks, with a mini-CD with the unlisted bonus tracks. Some record store owners took the mini-CD out of the package and sold it separately. The second pressing was released as a single CD.

'I really had to rediscover how to write music because I hadn't done it in so long,' he told *Alternative Press*. 'I'm not the kind of guy that writes songs on the tour bus. The only way I can do it is to sit down and think. I have mixed feelings about what's on the EP. Some of it I really like and some of it...it's reflective of that time when I did it. I don't think I owe anybody an apology for not putting any music out though because what we've been doing is touring. I could write an album about riding in a bus and puking after a show somewhere, but that's what Bon Jovi's for.'

Critical reactions to the album were mixed. A lot of reviewers who had liked *Pretty Hate Machine* detested *Broken*: this split would also be true of fans. But equally many liked it, though their praise was still reticent.

Q magazine's Peter Kane wrote: 'As a follow-up to last time's *Pretty Hate Machine* he's channelled his angst into this mini-album that, along with Ministry's recent *Psalm 69,* can be considered some sort of landmark in the bleak wastes of industrial metal. From the opening "Pinion", beats are hammered home with the gleeful force of a dentist's drill while layers of rabid guitars and Reznor's spiteful voice pile on the nihilistic agony all the way through to "Happiness In Slavery" and "Gave Up". It's an undeniably ugly noise all right, but one where the mastery of dynamics is never less than compelling. Cult status guaranteed.'

CMJ also appreciated it: 'The explosive nature of *Broken* is a direct reflection of Reznor's volatile emotional state, and what better way to represent hostility and paranoia than with distorted guitars and jackhammer percussion. Having grown increasingly disenchanted with relationships, and flat out furious with the corporate music industry, Reznor has used his music to lash out at all the ex-girlfriends, journalists, publicists, groupies and money-grabbing executives he feels have tainted his life.'

The sleeve notes quoted 'Happiness In Slavery' followed by 'No thanks: You know who you fucking are.' It also bore the mysterious 'Warning: Not for use in mono devices.' According to Reznor: 'Without getting too far in detail, a scientific property of sound is its "phase". When recording music in stereo, you're supposed to be aware of it's phase. If not, certain parts of the sound will disappear when its played in mono. So, we discovered that by messing around with the phase, we could make elements of the music stand out rather oddly. Certain songs on *Broken* we mixed out of phase (because we felt like it) BUT... The songs don't sound right on mono devices (like some radios or TVs). Has anyone heard "Happiness In Slavery" on the radio? I heard it on KROQ in LA and the snare drum was gone through most of the song (and yes, it kind of destroys the groove!). So, basically, that's what that means.'

Broken was also followed by the video for 'Happiness In Slavery'; if the 'snuff' movie/*Hard Copy* controversy over the video for 'Down In It' was the taster of things to come, then this was to be the main course.

Directed by Original Video's Jonathan Reiss, 'Happiness In Slavery' is a sadomasochistic fantasy. The black-and-white mini-film features a naked male actor who is prodded, pinched and eventually pulverised into ground meat by a brutal machine to which he willingly sacrifices himself.

'Some people derive pleasure from pain and the character in this video is there willingly; he gets something out of this. For him, the ultimate ecstasy is worth the ultimate sacrifice,' Reiss told *Billboard* magazine.

The actor in the film is Bob Flanagan. Bob, born in 1952 in New York City, grew up with cystic fibrosis (a genetically inherited, nearly always fatal disease) and has lived longer than any other person with CF. The physical pain of his childhood suffering was principally alleviated by masturbation and sexual experimentation, wherein pain and pleasure became inextricably linked, resulting in his lifelong practice of extreme masochism. Flanagan came to prominence through his performances – detailed in 'underground' source-book and magazine *Re/Search*'s piece 'Bob Flanagan: Supermasochist' and Kirby Dick's 1997 documentary *SICK: The Life And Death Of Bob Flanagan, Supermasochist*. Before his death in 1996, he was the author of several books of poetry and prose including *The Wedding Of Everything, Slave Sonnets*, and the infamous *Fuck Journal*, which was destroyed by its printer in India out of fear of reprisals by customs agents.

It was an example of Reznor delving further into the underground, this time connecting with the sexual outlaws. It was calculated to shock: there was no way that it could be edited to appear on MTV – or any other mainstream TV network – and any public showing would seem to court the possibility of legal censorship from the police. For Reznor, it was a step beyond the comparatively cosy body horror of David Cronenberg.

'These were the most appropriate visuals for the song,' Reznor told *Billboard*, though it was obvious that what he was doing was testing the limits of his own artistic freedom. By his own admission, the video was 'money flushed down the toilet': 'When I signed to Interscope, I made it clear I wanted artistic control over what I do. Granted, this is an extreme example. I see music video as an art form that could have turned out to be pretty cool,' he adds. 'But due to the powers at MTV, it turned into nothing but a business of three-minute commercials for the public to be told what to buy and what to like. A lot of people won't see this video but we've gotten as far as we have with no support from radio or MTV and we're as big as I want us to be.'

As he later told *Rolling Stone*: 'It wasn't a conscious decision to make the most vulgar thing we could do to get press, which it could be easily be attacked as being. But it was a chance for me to finally be able to do something I wanted without having to ask someone who has no fucking idea. The question came up "how far can we take this?" I said: "Let's just take it as far as we think right. Forget that it's a music video, forget that it's basically a promotional clip, forget standards and censorship." Fortunately or unfortunately, depending on how you look at it, it's unplayable.'

Cleverly, the video did generate a great deal of controversy: MTV may not have played it within the normal programming, but news reports all featured tantalizing extracts. There was blanket news coverage in the music press as well as further afield. It became like one of those great 'banned' movies such as *The Exorcist* or *A Clockwork Orange* (not shown in the UK for over a quarter of a century) that everyone just has to see to be hipper than the herd.

It was not just a matter of taste: the video actually contravened Federal Communications Commission guidelines: the few stations that did broadcast the video had to digitally blot out the genitalia in every shot. The broadcast result was literally unwatchable. To have actually seen it uncut and uncensored became a mark of cool for 'insiders'.

Reznor was paving the way for artists fighting back against increasing corporate control over their music. Like Prince, who famously appeared at an awards ceremony with the word 'slave' written on his face, Reznor felt that he had been used and was striking back by being unyielding.

Oddly there is actually some evidence that *Broken* was musically a big influence on Prince. Speaking to *Musician* magazine in 1994 Reznor said: 'Prince was in the studio here the first day I came in, and somebody said, "Hey, Prince likes your stuff, he had your *Broken* CD in the car and he later actually told his people to mix their tracks harder and it might have been due to hearing *Broken*." I thought they were kidding, 'cause this is a guy whose work I respect immensely. Figured it might just be cool to say "hi" if I ran into him around the studio. Then I find myself at one end of a big long hallway and he's at the other end walking towards me. So I simply said "hi" and waited for him to make eye contact. He just turned away.

That strikes a wrong chord in my Midwestern upbringing regarding simple human decency. I don't mean to sound judgmental, but I've no great desire to meet Bowie now, because in my mind, I'd rather think of him as this cool guy.'

Perhaps 'Happiness In Slavery' was a factor in the statement Prince painted on his face.

Reznor's unyielding stance was a gamble that paid off. 'Wish' was awarded a Grammy for Best Metal Performance With Vocals. Although the multiple categories were starting to become ludicrous (look out for Best Country And Western/Rap Crossover By An Artist With Only One Arm in the near future) it was still important to win from an industry point of view.

'The best thing about it was that it's the only song to ever win a Grammy that says "fist fuck" in the lyrics,' Reznor said sardonically.

Reznor started to receive more and more mainstream attention. Douglas Coupland's brilliant novel *Generation X* had just been published and was already a runaway cult success. Coupland's story is of three young Americans who, following their 'mid 20s breakdowns', have gathered in California to while away their lives in 'McJobs' and to tell each other pointlessly superficial fictions from which they try to extract 'delicate insights'. Deeply nihilistic, the threesome have become so immersed in 'knee jerk irony', pop culture references and a landscape where every space has been colonised by corporate culture. The book was especially important in defining the lives of a generation born after 1960. Generation X – a punk band featuring Billy Idol named after a '60s 'pulp sociology' book – was a term loaded with irony and pessimism, like the 'blank' generation of punk and the 'lost' generation of the '20s and '30s.

Generation X, wrote London's *City Limits*, '[a]re those for whom the '60s, and even punk, are but a dim memory or a faded page in a history book – or more likely, something on late night TV – though the present is just a bore. Their icons are less likely to be iconoclasts or innovators. They would prefer, for example, to watch every episode of *Gilligan's Island* than read Trollope, they would prefer Trini Lopez to

Bob Dylan. These are people who grew up reading biographies of writers and musicians but never actually reading their books or hearing their music. Where in the past the hipster would be defined by radical ideas, or books or writing – however trite – the Xer defines his or her individuality by hoarding TV trivia. Generation X grew up post-modern. They can't actually say what they mean, but they could quote from somebody that says what they mean. An Xer could never say "I love you" and keep a straight face. Instead they would say "In the words of a kitschy valentine card, 'I love you'." It's like real life except in quotation marks. Trapped in this painful irony on top of irony, as far as genuine heroes go, only Trent Reznor, leader of the nihilistic Nine Inch Nails could be considered their foremost icon.'

Although the mainstream media lined up to bash anyone over 30 over the head for their apathy or perceived lack of political commitment or their cynicism, the real reason for their jaundiced take on modern life was the fact that all the supposedly 'idealistic' hippies of the previous generation had landed themselves jobs at the top of the corporate ladders and were proceeding to fleece everyone blind. What was the point of being rebellious when your rebellion would be sold back to you in a bid to sell Levis or Coke?

Reznor's status as 'generation X icon' resulted in some bizarre occurrences such as a TV commercial for a soft drink that employed a lookalike playing an almost-recognizable Nine Inch Nails song. As he told *Plasm* magazine: 'I had 100 people say "Why did you do that Gatorade commercial?" I was like, "What are you talking about?" I hadn't seen it. I finally got a copy. It was "Down In It". The beat's a little bit different. The singing has got a little bit of distortion, exactly the same kind of thing as my voice. So I looked into how we can sue these fuckheads. I don't want money. I just don't want them using my song. Well, they changed it a little bit. I remember hearing a commercial and I thought, "Joe Jackson, I thought he was cool, and now he's done a fuckin' commercial for something shitty." It was that song "Stepping Out". Something almost exactly like that, but it wasn't him singing. I remember in an interview he said, "They approached me to do this commercial, and I said "absolutely no way". And they said, "Well, we're just going to get someone who sounds like you to do it." Well, fuck you. And they did it. And everyone in the world thought it was him.'

Less controversial than the 'Happiness In Slavery' video was the clip for 'Pinion', directed by Eric Goodie and Serge Becker, also inevitably banned by MTV because it showed scenes involving a toilet and a man undergoing total rubber restriction in an S&M playroom.

Peter 'Sleazy' Christopherson, formerly of Throbbing Gristle and later Psychic TV and Coil, directed a video for 'Wish' that showed Nine Inch Nails performing in what looked like a mental hospital with the increasingly violent inmates going on a rampage and attacking the band.

Christopherson came from a wealthy background - something that has been used against him by disgruntled former collaborators - and, as well as working with early industrial pioneers Throbbing Gristle, he was a member of the Hipgnosis team, whose surreal cover acts from bands such as Pink Floyd was legendary. Throbbing Gristle, interestingly, were not only one of the first bands to make and sell videos, but the company that they set up was one of the first to make and sell commercial video cassettes for home use anywhere in the world.

Christopherson is highly thought of as a director of commercial videos and has worked with Rage Against The Machine, Erasure and The The as well as making videos for Nine Inch Nails and Ministry. He and Reznor embarked on an ambitious project; to shoot and release a film around *Broken* that would be released and sold in lieu of the fact that there would be no live shows around the record.

Whatever Interscope thought privately, they seemed happy enough to indulge Trent. The label would later become embroiled in controversy over the content of their music, with Charlton Heston threatening to sever his allegiance to Warner Brothers if the parent company did not sever its relationship with Interscope. The association between Interscope and Death Row Records - whose artists included Snoop Doggy Dogg and Tupac Shakur - would also do them few favours as far as the establishment was concerned.

The real importance at this time of the Interscope deal, the Grammy and the video controversy is that it whetted people's appetites for the next full length Nine Inch Nails album. And although Nothing Records - run by Reznor and manager John Malm and initially based in Cleveland - was just a name to put on future Nine Inch Nails releases, both had plans to sign other artists to the label.

Often when bands get their own label imprint, their signings are at best tax write-offs for the parent label: the imprints release deadbeat albums by friends, relatives and local bands that they may love but who have limited commercial potential. But destiny had other plans for Nothing Records.

Towards the end of the year, Reznor released a second EP of remixes under the title *Fixed*. These included reworkings by Coil and Jim Thirlwell of Foetus and came packaged in the same sleeve except with the colour scheme in reverse.

This would become something of a tradition for Reznor, releasing remix albums of songs from *The Downward Spiral* and *The Fragile*. At the same time, Reznor was working on remixes for thrash metal band Megadeth and two for Queen ('Stone Cold Crazy' and 'Tie Your Mother Down') released on Hollywood records.

Reznor decided to move to New Orleans permanently, though after a property deal fell through he ended up moving to Los Angeles. He wanted a property where he could set up a recording studio to work on his next album. It had to be sufficiently isolated but large enough to accommodate the gear and any collaborators like Flood and Vrenna who were there to work with him. He found a house to rent in the Hollywood Hills, a ranch-style bungalow on Cielo Drive. It was a beautiful, picturesque location, the real super-rich Los Angeles populated by movie executives, actresses and musicians. The house he rented at 10050 Cielo Drive, Beverly Hills, had had some famous tenants in the past. Actress Candice Bergen had lived there in the late '60s with then boyfriend Terry Melcher, a well-known record producer and son of 1950s icon of white apple pie American virginity Doris Day. After they moved out, the maverick Polish film director Roman Polanski and his beautiful young wife actress Sharon Tate moved in.

One sultry night in August 1969, while the heavily pregnant Sharon and her friends were turning in for the night, a group of hippies broke in. One of them, a rangy giant Texan with an acid gleam in his eye told them 'I am the devil here to do the devil's work'. He was accompanied by two dead-eyed hippie girls. In the space of an hour Sharon watched as her friends Abagail Folger, Jay Sebring and Voytek Frykowski were slaughtered in front of her. Then they killed Sharon, ripping the unborn baby boy from her womb. She was alive to see this. Then they wrote in her blood the words 'Pig' and 'Helter Skelter' on the walls and on the door.

Trent had moved into the house made famous by the Charles Manson murders. If people found *Broken* dark and depressing, then the next one was gonna be a doozy!

7 Down The Helter Skelter

'You should all turn around and face your children and start
following them and listening to them. The music speaks to you
every day, but you are too deaf, dumb and blind to even listen
to the music. You are too deaf, dumb and blind to stop what
you are doing. You point and you ridicule.'

– Charles Manson

With the songs to form the backbone of *The Downward Spiral* taking
root in his mind, Reznor intended to hole up in LA using a home
studio, armed with state-of-the-art technology, access to samples,
with the assistance of Chris Vrenna, who lived with him on Cielo Drive
for most of the year it took to make. He was adamant that he wanted
to break away from the conventional verse-chorus format.

He and Vrenna had fallen out after the intense period sharing a
house and touring in Nine Inch Nails. Vrenna did not, in fact, play
drums on the Lollapalooza, touring instead as KMFDM's drummer for
the Money tour: 'For several months, due to mental problems I was
having, Trent and I went through a phase of friendship where we just
hated each other. We just needed a break. It's tough for us because
he's the boss. It's kind of like we wear different hats. It's "you're
my boss" when he's in work mode, and "Chris, I need you to sample
this" etc and then work gets done and it's like...change hats and
"OK let's go and get a pizza and have a few beers." It's just trying to
keep the communication open all the time. So we do tick each other
off and get irritated.'

And although Trent and Flood had, by his own admission,
'burned' each other out during the recording of *Broken*, that

relationship too was salvaged enough for Flood to come in and work on *The Downward Spiral*.

Although Reznor has a reputation for feuding he has a less publicised side of making up afterwards.

Reznor had been listening to a lot of David Bowie and the influence of *Hunky Dory*, the 1971 album where he attempted to redefine the way that songs were written, had percolated through.

He told Australia's *Hot Metal* magazine: 'I hate retro thinking and I hate trends towards bringing back stuff that's dead and gone, but at the same time it really impressed me how much depth was in those albums in comparison with today's music. It's a very general and unfair statement, but it seems like the music industry is such a big corporate business now that a lot of albums just seem like products – one or two good tracks with a bunch of filler and general crap. My challenge was to try and make a record that's more of an album and less a collection of songs.'

He had been making notes since Lollapalooza, jotting down ideas for themes – mostly personal issues – that he wanted to address. While it was not exactly a concept album it was to have a thematic link. As he told *RayGun* magazine: 'It is personal experiences, but it's wrapped up in the highly pretentious idea of a record with some sort of theme or flow to 'em, and it was meant to be. I just tried to make a record as a big hour-long chunk of music rather than a bunch of three minute pop songs that just happened to be on the same record. I don't think many people are doing them that much these days. It's become a kind of a dated '70s concept, but some of the records that influenced me a lot on this album, like [David Bowie's] *Low* and even *The Wall* – I'm sure I'm ripping off Pink Floyd, in fact, I know I am ripping them off. There's records, although they may appear dated today, that try to do things that are more exciting to me than, "Here's my video track and here's my dance song and here's my power ballad." All that kind of disposability. It was just me bored, trying to come up with something that I kind of wanted to set the parameters to work within, to focus more.'

But that may have been justification after the event: *The Downward Spiral* was a long and painful album to make. Trent was suffering from writer's block and some of the luxury of having his own studio really served to distract him. The first months were spent messing around, familiarizing himself with the gear but also forcing himself to write again. The stresses of the past three years – the heavy touring, the TVT situation and the emotionally draining *Broken* – had taken their toll. He had no real idea of how he wanted it to sound. There were ideas but mostly very general broad strokes and big concepts. The really heroic part – the mark of a true professional – was filling in the details, writing songs when you are NOT gripped by inspiration, digging around and finding it.

As he told *Keyboard* magazine: 'I didn't have a definite idea of how it should sound. I mean, I had a theme lyrically and vibe-wise, but musically I wanted to put more emphasis on textures and mood, and not rely on the same bag of tricks. I had to develop a whole new palette of sounds to work with. Another thing that delayed this record was me learning how to write again, deciding what I wanted to do. I didn't want to make another *Broken*. I didn't want to box Nine Inch Nails into: "Make every song harder than the last one, meaner, tougher." I think that's a trap. That's not really what Nine Inch Nails is about. And I didn't want to go completely back to the *Pretty Hate Machine* style: percolating synth stuff. But I realised that when I sat down and started noodling around with ideas, I was much more inspired to sit at a keyboard than I was with a guitar. I wanted to fine-tune my engineering skills; That's one thing we've always lacked in the Nine Inch Nails inner circle. I figured if I had a studio around, I'd inevitably figure out how to do it. And also, for the first time, we had the resources to do something right, so we ended up buying a big console and a couple of Studer machines because it was cheaper than renting, in the long run.

'We moved out here [to LA] on 4 July 1992. What we thought would take X amount of time to get a studio set up, ended up taking three times as long. As much as I enjoy equipment, fucking around with stuff, systems, and all that, there came a point when the whole focus was just to get the damn thing working and then learn it. Eventually I realised, "Okay, I'm sick of being in this room, now it's time to write an album." So I started writing, and by Christmas I had about four songs that I thought were decent.'

Vrenna recalled in *Spin* magazine: 'We had three studios set up in our house. We had the big one, where a lot of times he was writing in there, or if we were tracking, we'd all be in there. But I had a B-studio set up out in the back house, which is the guest house where I lived. There was only three bedrooms in the main house and one bedroom in the guest house. So he took one of the bedrooms in the main house, and the other two we filled them up with guitar amps and mikes. And I took the one bedroom in the guest house, this way we all had our little space. So I would do most of my sampling out back.'

Over the course of *The Downward Spiral*, Vrenna and Reznor sampled dialogue or sound effects from nearly 3000 movies rented or bought on video. Watching two or three a day in their entirety, they harvested a wealth of ambient noise.

'I think I've done all the horror and sci-fi movies. Just everything. You find great little ambiances in things. We never sample for spoken stuff, but movies are just trying to recreate some sort of space, whether it be outer-space or a creepy hallway. They're recreating that falsely on film. But if you don't watch them, and you just listen to them, they don't sound like anything. They sound like just weird things. But there was other kinds of sampling too. Trent one day wanted bees. You want what? "I want bees." "Okay." So I found bee samples, swarms of bees, and the sounds of buzzing. Off I went.'

While it was clear that this was not going to be a rerun of *Broken*, it certainly was not going to be another accessible *Pretty Hate Machine*.

At the time, Reznor was ambivalent about his reasons for living and working in Sharon Tate's house. He claimed in interviews that he did not know that the house was the same one.

'It's a coincidence,' he told *Rolling Stone*. 'When I found out what it was, it was even cooler. But it's a cool house anyway and on top of that has a very interesting story behind it. The whole thing of living out here, I didn't even think of it. I didn't go on a press campaign saying "I live in Sharon Tate's house, and I'm really spooky."'

But Trent was drawn to horror movies and extreme material about murders and mayhem. As he told Canadian music website Much Music, 'I don't know the psychology of why someone enjoys horror movies or likes being scared, or enjoys films or music that might be considered depressing. I'm not sure what draws people to that – I am drawn to it; I'm intrigued by extremity in those departments, I don't know why. I mean, I've tried to figure it out – maybe it's because I grew up in a place where...there wasn't anything – there was no culture, there was no influence, and so what you got, you go through magazines, and what might be on TV or – there was no art cinemas, there was no college radios, there was no underground book stores or any sort of thing like that, so...maybe my desire to just...escape led me to searching for extreme. I don't know.'

Given his familiarity with the 'extreme' end of the underground and his growing professional relationship with Peter Christopherson of Coil, this actually seems unlikely. While a member of Throbbing Gristle, Christopherson and Genesis P Orridge had flirted with Manson imagery: at an early gig at the Rat Club in the Pindar of Wakefield pub near King's Cross, they showed a 16mm film called *After Cease To Exist*. It featured a castration sequence and the voice of a convicted Canadian killer recorded from a TV documentary with Throbbing Gristle providing an improvised soundtrack. 'Cease To Exist' was a song written by Manson and included on the album *Lie*. It was also recorded by The Beach Boys on their *20/20* album and used as the b-side of the 1969 single 'Bluebirds Over The Mountain'. They did, however change the title to 'Never Learn Not To Love' and the chorus from 'cease to exist' to 'cease to resist'. Previous performances had involved looping songs from Charles Manson's album *Lie* over the PA. As a member – albeit briefly – of Psychic TV, Christopherson and partner John Balance were involved in the sessions to record 'Roman P', a song relating to the Manson murders, in which all the members were photographed wearing Charles Manson t-shirts standing in a room mocked up to look like the murder scene at Cielo Drive.

But given Reznor's familiarity with the fetish/industrial underground in general – as demonstrated by the inclusion of Bob Flanagan in the 'Happiness In Slavery' video, the address Cielo Drive *must* have meant something to him before renting the house.

The first night that he slept in the house he admits that he was terrified, hearing noises everywhere, doors banging. It is a quiet area, deceptively so for LA. As one of the killers said of her journey up the hill to murder the inhabitants: 'It was so quiet that you could hear the rattle of ice in cocktail glasses all the way down the canyon.'

Although he never actively exploited it, the location for the recording of *The Downward Spiral* seems likely to have been very deliberately chosen. Knowing where it was recorded had to add some sort of atmosphere of malevolence to the album before the listener had even removed it from the jewel case.

Manson's cachet as an anti-establishment outlaw figure was rising in the post-punk climate. Artists as diverse as Evan Dando of The Lemonheads and Axl Rose of Guns N' Roses were dropping hints that they admired the cult leader by covering his songs and wearing Manson t-shirts onstage. With so few symbols retaining the power to shock, Manson was still enough to send a chill through the heart of Americans who remembered the appalling scene at the Tate house in early August of 1969.

'I'm not personally infatuated with serial killers. I find them mildly interesting at best. I have a curiosity about that, but by no means do I wish to glamorise them. From living in that house I've met every person in the world you can imagine who's obsessed with that whole thing and it's given me more of a perspective on it,' Trent told *Vox* magazine's Bob McCabe in 1995.

Two years later, he admitted to *Rolling Stone* that he had in fact chosen the location for the bad vibes but regretted this after a meeting with Sharon Tate's sister Doris: 'There's a part of me that is intrigued by that. For example, I loved the Hannibal Lecter character in *The Silence Of The Lambs*. The last person I want to see get hurt in that story is him. And I think, "Why do I look at him as a hero figure?" Because you respect him. Because he represents everything you wish you could be in a lawless, moralless society. I allow myself to think, "Yeah, if I could kill people without reprimand, maybe I would, you know?" I hate myself for thinking that, but there's an appeal to the idea, because it is a true freedom. Is it wrong? Yeah. But is there an appeal to that? Yeah. It's the ultimate taboo.

'My awakening about all that stuff came from meeting Sharon Tate's sister. It was a random thing, just a brief encounter. And she said: "Are you exploiting my sister's death by living in her house?" For the first time the whole thing kind of slapped me in the face. I said, "No, it's just sort of my own interest in American folklore. I'm in this place where a weird part of history occurred." I guess it never really struck me before, but it did then. She lost her sister from a senseless, ignorant situation that I don't want to support. When she was talking to me, I realised for the first time, "What if it was my sister?" I thought, "Fuck Charlie Manson". I don't want to be looked at as a guy who supports serial-killer bullshit. I went home and cried that night. It made me see there's another side to things, you know? It's one thing to go around with your dick swinging in the wind, acting like it doesn't matter. But when you understand the repercussions that are felt...that's what sobered me up: realizing that what balances out the appeal of the lawlessness and the lack of morality and the whole thing is the other end of it, the victims who don't deserve that.'

Nevertheless, at the time they were recording in the house, Vrenna and Reznor nicknamed the studio 'le pig', alluding to the word 'pig' scrawled on the wall in Sharon Tate's blood by killer Susan Atkins. One of the strongest tracks on the album was also 'March Of The Pigs', though Reznor denied that there was any connection between this and Manson.

He told *Musician* magazine: 'I had the song "Piggy" written long before it was ever known that I would be in that house. "March of the Pigs" has nothing to do with the Tate murders or anything like that,

I'm not going to say what it is about, but it's not about that. Ya, the name of the studio being "Pig", that was a definite bad taste kind of joke about being there. You know, it was written on the front door at one time, you know, I'll admit to that.'

Interestingly, although the original house was demolished not long after Reznor's departure he took the door as a souvenir, which he installed in his next home in New Orleans. When I questioned him about the matter of taste involved in this he said: 'It's a door. It opens and closes.'

Actually 'March Of The Pigs' is about Reznor's increasingly jaundiced view of the media and the cult of celebrity that he was being sucked into.

'I want a little bit/I want a piece of it/I think he's losing it/I wanna watch it come down/Don't like the look of it/Don't like the taste of it/Don't like the smell of it/I wanna watch it come down/All the pigs are all lined up/I give you all that you want/Take the skin and peel it back/Now doesn't it make you feel better?'

One interpretation of this line is about the media looking for the 'truth' and in the process tearing their subject apart, to make their readers 'feel better' about their own lives. A less charitable one is that it's about Reznor's fans. Talking about one show he said it was: '[T]he first time I've seen a crowd roaring in front of me, they seemed to be like pigs fighting over a piece of rotten apple...'

He would regularly introduce the song live by screaming 'You fucking pigs!' at the audience.

Although Reznor always made an effort to go and meet fans who waited for him after shows, trying not to behave badly in front of them and disillusion them in the way that Prince had him when he snubbed him, there was a part of him that was starting to find the adulation oppressive. He told *Musician* magazine: 'I don't know what kind of mail a mainstream rock band gets but we get about one letter out of 1,000 that says, "Your music is the only thing that keeps me going." And then, "I totally relate to what you're saying, however..." Insert horrible situation: "My parents beat me, I'm gonna run away;

I'm a drug addict; I've tried to kill myself...and if you get this please just call me and respond...you don't know how much it would mean...that would keep me going." I didn't know what to do. I could call this person up, but I'm inevitably going to let them down. I can't talk to you 100 times a day. And if I write a little note, you get one back the next day and another the day after...the world fucked them and then I did too, by inaction. I felt shitty about this for four or five days, and after talking to some people I thought the best thing was not to, because I did exchange letters with a woman once and she wanted tickets and she showed up with this, "Hi, we're engaged to be married" scenario. I try to make a point of not being a dick to anyone who comes up to me, and believe me there are many times when you don't want someone on your bus fucking with you. I always try to think about if I were meeting someone I respected.'

By this time Reznor was a 'star'. He was on the cover of magazines like *Spin* and *Rolling Stone*. He appeared regularly on MTV. He got recognised on the street. People wanted his opinion about seemingly trivial and profoundly important matters. He was a celebrity: 'I don't actually remember the point where I realised this. I guess a lot of bands probably know personally the first fans that come to your shows. Even out of the first 1,000 or so there are familiar faces. Then when you sell 100,000 records or more you realise that more and more people know who you are. Suddenly you don't have to queue up to get into clubs anymore.'

The expectations for *The Downward Spiral* were almost crippling. *Pretty Hate Machine* and *Broken* had - in a sense - been produced in secret. Nobody was expecting either of them. But the constant pressure from fans, admirers and other bands asking when the new album was out, how it was going, what it would be like, what the songs would be, what colour the cover would be, started to take their toll.

Between July and Christmas he had four songs, but the album was more of a struggle to make than he realised it would be. The original intention had been to make the album quickly. Reznor cited the example of Nirvana, who had gone into the studio and made

Nevermind in two weeks. The process was different for him and soon his new record company Interscope were expressing 'concern' at the time that the album seemed to be taking to make.

Another insight into Reznor's life at this time comes from Marilyn Manson. In The *Long Hard Road Out Of Hell* he recalls: 'I went by the record store where I used to work and bought Nine Inch Nails' *Broken*, which had come out that day. I was thinking that I hadn't heard from Trent in a while because every now and then he would call just to say hi and keep in touch. As I was listening to it, I got a call from Trent's manager asking for a copy of our demo tape. (These kinds of coincidences always happen to me, and have led me to believe that everything happens for a purpose.) I didn't know why he wanted a copy of our demo tape. Maybe he just wanted to listen to it.

'A few days later I got a phone call: "Hey, it's Trent."

'And I'm like "Hey what's going on."

'And he said "Well, you'll never believe where I'm at. I'm living at the Sharon Tate house." It was funny because when I first met him told him that one of my dreams was to record "My Monkey", our revision of a Charles Manson song, at the house where Sharon Tate had lived. I liked the irony of it. And lo and behold, Trent was there now. He said, "why don't you come out? We're shooting a video for one of my songs and I want you to play guitar in it." I told him "Well I don't really play guitar." But I went out there anyway and pretended to play guitar in a video that was never actually released. It was a song called "Gave Up". I didn't know Trent was starting a label. We just hung out and had a great time, and that's when we became really close and established our friendship.'

If Trent was reticent about his admiration for Charles Manson, Marilyn Manson was not, having assembled his name from those of America's greatest sex symbol and its greatest death icon. Sex and death. He also included bits of Charles Manson's song 'Mechanical Man' in 'My Monkey'. The storm over Manson was triggered by Guns N' Roses recording a cover of Manson's 'Look At Your Game Girl' on their 1993 covers album *The Spaghetti Incident*, something that

Marilyn actually takes some credit for: 'Trent took me to a U2 concert one night and backstage I met Axl Rose. He was very neurotic and was telling me all about his psychological problems, his split personalities, and I felt like, "This guy's a total fucking flake." Being the overzealous type, I started telling him about my band anyway. And I said, "You know we do this song 'My Monkey' and it's an adaptation of a Charles Manson song off his album *Lie*." And he's like, "I never heard of that before." I told him, "You should check out the album, it's cool." And lo and behold six months later Guns N' Roses put out *The Spaghetti Incident* and Axl Rose covers "Look At Your Game Girl" from the *Lie* album. Then he started getting all that heat from Sharon Tate's sister and everybody.'

During the time that he and Reznor hung out at the Tate house, the two became close through a mutual interest in the seedier side of LA life: 'I remember one night Trent ditched his girlfriend, a rich teenaged bitch who had become so obsessed with him that she tattooed his initials on her butt, and we went to a bar in LA called Smalls, where we met some girls that today I wouldn't even let take out my garbage. But at the time they seemed like people worth wasting my efforts trying to fuck because I didn't know any better. Actually, we weren't really interested in sex. We were more interested in having fun because we had this new friendship. So we invited these two terrible individuals back to his house, and I remember one of their names was Kelly, which I found interesting because, like her face, it could have belonged to a man or a woman. We went on to make a videotape which I've since lost. But it was known only as "Keity's Cornhole". You can imagine why. Well, what we did was we pulled a trick that I've become quite famous for. It is pouring a large glass of tequila for your adversary, or your victim, and then pouring a large glass of beer for yourself and pretending that yours is tequila also. You convince them to drink down their large glass until they vomit and pass out and are left to be tormented. A similar trick had been done to me when I was young. So the trick worked, as it always does, and Kelly and her friend were drunk and running around the lawn where Sharon Tate's friends had been murdered. They jumped in the pool and somehow I was convinced to join them. That's something I don't like to do because I don't know how to swim. So I was in the pool with this sea bass, I suppose you could call her. By smell she was some sort of porpoise fish-woman, and by sight she looked like a water behemoth. Trying to create some sort of entertainment for everybody, I said, "Why don't we play Guess Who's Touching You? We'll put a blindfold on you and try to figure out whose hands are on you." So Trent and I take this sea bass back into his living room. The other had since passed out and was hopefully drowning in her vomit. We blindfolded the sea creature. No, I think we just wrapped a towel around her head, which also covered up her face and made us both feel better. Not that her body was any greater than her face. It was all terrible. I grow ashamed of myself right now as we speak of this. So we started squeezing her nipples and prodding around her genitals and what have you. We were laughing because we were both drunk, though not nearly as drunk as she was. In the background a Ween album was playing, "Push the little daisies and make 'em come up..." as me and the young Trent Reznor poked our fingers into the birth cavity of a bizarre fish lady in search of some sort of caviar. But what we ended up finding was a mysterious nodule - maybe it was white fuzz or a piece of corn that she had on the outer region of her rectum. It horrified us and we looked at each other with disgust and shock. But we knew that we must continue with our debasement of this poor unsuspecting person. So I found a cigarette lighter, and I started to burn her pubic hair. Though it didn't hurt her, it didn't help things smell any better than they already did. Unfortunately, there isn't any real climax to this story other than I think that she wanted to cuddle with someone and we both ran. I have a feeling that Trent may have ended up cuddling with her because he has a soft spot for shitty women. Not that we all don't all have a penchant for taking ugly girls under our wings in the hopes that they'll be better in the morning. But they're always worse. So I went to sleep and hoped that it all would go away. The next day it did and we felt a lot closer to each other of course. He told me that he was starting his own label through Interscope Records called Nothing, and he wanted Marilyn Manson to be the first band on it. I thought it was the best label to be on because was so upset about his experiences with his old label, TVT, that one of his biggest goals was never to deceive or mistreat the artists on Nothing.'

Pressure was exerted, albeit gentle pressure, and Reznor admits that he made the mistake of ploughing away with the sole motivation of getting his album done regardless of how good it actually sounded. He was blocked and was flailing around for inspiration, though as with the songs on *Pretty Hate Machine* and *Broken*, the only place that he could find it was inside himself.

He later told *Spin*: 'I just wanted to kill myself. I hated music. I was like, "I just want to get back on the road because I hate sitting in a room trying to, trying to" - how do you say this? - "just scraping my fucking soul." Exploring areas of your brain that you don't want to go to, that's painful. You write something down and you go, "Fuck, I can't say that. I don't want people to know that." It's so naked and honest that you're scared to let it out. You're giving a part of your soul away, exposing part of yourself. I avoid that. I hate that feeling of sending a tape out to someone: "Here's my new song. I just cut my soul open. Check it out. Criticise it."'

Reznor wanted to finish the album and get the hell out of LA and back on the road.

'That's the stupidest fucking reason for doing an album I've ever heard,' legendary producer and American recordings boss Rick Rubin told Trent when they ran into each other. 'Don't do it. Don't do it until you make music that it's a crime not to let other people hear.'

Rubin - an inspirational communicator at the best of times - was to work with Reznor on a future project. The advice given in 1992 seemed to shake Reznor up out of his lethargy.

The Downward Spiral took almost a year of solid work, taking up most of 1993, with Reznor taking time out to work with his first signings to Nothing Records, Marilyn Manson. With Flood once again in the co-producer role and Chris Vrenna actually getting to play drums on the last track 'Hurt' - unusual for a member of the Nine Inch Nails! - as well as acting as Trent's assistant and buddy, other people were drafted in as the sessions progressed. Alan Moulder, another British producer whose credits included the infuriating and brilliant My Bloody Valentine arrived to helm some of the tracks while Steve Perkins, drummer with Jane's Addiction and Perry Farrell's post-Jane's band Porno For Pyros who Reznor had met on Lollapalooza, laid down the raw drum tracks that Reznor then sampled to construct the album's percussion loops. David Bowie/Tin Machine guitarist Adrian Belew, whose CV had included stints with Frank Zappa, Laurie Anderson and King Crimson played guitar on six tracks.

In keeping with Reznor's place at the leading edge of technology, *The Downward Spiral* was one of the first albums to be recorded entirely using state-of-the-art digital technology whereby sounds were recorded and stored on a computer hard disc. They could then be digitally altered - adding effects, reverb or taking such effects off and cleaning the sound up where necessary - rather than just putting the band in the studio, recording the instruments and mixing it together. As a pioneer of the technology, there were no established rules. As Alan Moulder told the Apple website: 'I first got into the audio manipulation side when working on *The Downward Spiral* with Nine Inch Nails. Trent had a four-channel Pro Tools 2 set up on which he was running Opcode's Studio Vision. I was so impressed with what he was doing that I bought the same set-up as soon as I got back. Although he is considered more of an artist, I think Trent Reznor is an absolute genius producer. I learned a lot from him.'

And Adrian Belew told *Ink* magazine: 'Most of [Trent's] stuff is done on the computer, Pro Tools, and so what he does is he turns everything into a loop. To give you a comparison, if I'm going to do a song, usually there's a space in the song where I may play a guitar solo for 35 seconds, or 36 bars. With Trent, everything has a continual loop, so you can play for a half an hour. He'll go back and edit just the part that he wants and take that and put in the loop.

He's brilliant with his manipulation of sounds. He probably has a reputation in the lifestyle press as being kind of a dark and foreboding kind of guy. He certainly wasn't that way to me.' Danny Lohner, soon to become a full time member of Nine Inch Nails, played on 'Big Man With A Gun' with Andy Kubiszewski, Trent's old Exotic Birds bandmate from Cleveland, playing drums on the title track. Kubiszewski would later become better known as the drummer in the Nine Inch Nails-inspired Stabbing Westward.

The flurry of writing and recording produced 16 songs and then some leftovers that would crop up on b-sides, or would be reworked as material for remixes for Nine Inch Nails as well as other artists. The songs were like frontline reports from the battlefield of Trent Reznor's psyche. That they were classic songs of negativity, angst, despair and hatred would come as no surprise; that he would be able to fill an hour long CD with this and sound even more pissed off and discontented than he had on *Pretty Hate Machine*, without necessarily treading the same ground, was definitely surprising.

Compared with *Pretty Hate Machine* and *Broken*, the resulting album was an epic. If they were respectively a novel and a novella, *The Downward Spiral* was a big fat blockbuster. Clocking in at 65 minutes, it fell just short of the running time of the first two albums combined.

As Trent had wanted, it was a dense album that was complete in itself, like *The Wall* or some other monolithic '70s concept album but worked less well as individual songs, though there were in fact some really strong ones like 'March Of The Pigs', the first single from the album and a perennial Nine Inch Nails crowd pleaser.

The whole climate of music had changed in the intervening period between moving to LA in 1992 and releasing the album in the early spring of 1994. Sonic Youth released a documentary about their European tour wittily entitled *1991: The Year Punk Broke*, though in a sense they were a year out. Mainstream America had ignored The Sex Pistols and The Clash, but suddenly it seemed as if they were experiencing their own delayed summer of punk. Bands like Nirvana,

Smashing Pumpkins, Hole, Alice In Chains, Pearl Jam and The Lemonheads were now massive. Although it was an alternative to both big hair metal and boy-band pop, the new grunge and post-grunge scene was actually really regressive. Like its successor in Britain, Britpop, it harked back to the '60s and '70s, it was a return to old values, anti-technology. If they used synthesisers, as Smashing Pumpkins did, for example, it would be in a self-consciously retro way. To Reznor it seemed like a step back. He particularly hated Pearl Jam.

Yet these artists, like Trent, delved into their own souls to create harrowing and personal songs that, like Nine Inch Nails, struck a chord with the so-called Generation Xers.

As he told *RIP* magazine: 'NIN doesn't have the mechanical structure, or isn't the kind of band that can ever be a Pearl Jam. It's appealing to a limited cross-section of people. Pearl Jam, to me, are a good band at what they are and they're also all things to all people. They've managed to be labelled alternative, their songs are already on classic rock stations, there's not one element or anything that they've ever done that would offend your grandmother, there's a cute guy in the band, it's teen-throb, it's alternative rock in theory, it's corporate rock. They're on every chart. They're everything to all people. And they're politically-fuckin' correct. They're standing up for the rights of the concertgoer – fighting some silly fight about ticket prices – which I don't think that many people give a shit about. And NIN is not that and never will be that, and it was never meant to be that. It's bigger now than I ever dreamed it would be and I went through a phase of really hating that fact. It is easier to go on tour in a van and play clubs opening for some band with no expectations and if you do good, then people go "why, man, these guys are really great. You blew the headliner off stage." It's cool to be in *Alternative Press*, and it's cool to be in *Option* magazine – they think you're cool 'cause nobody's ever heard of you. It's comfortable, it's nice to have that kind of support from the truly alternative fans who I think do have a bit more integrity than the people who are spoon-fed MTV videos all day. However, if it happens that you do start to sell more records, whether you've done anything consciously to sell out, or people just started to listen to you, there's nothing you can do to stop that. I could say "I'm never gonna make another video again, and I'm never gonna make an album, I'm gonna make an album of sheer noise, just to bum everybody out." But that's not being anymore true than if I sat down and said "I'm gonna write 15 'Head Like A Hole's' so that I can be Eddie Vedder." I'm not saying Eddie Vedder does that either.'

The event that overshadowed everything was the suicide of Kurt Cobain in April of that year following his much publicised battle against attempts by his management, his band, his wife Courtney Love and the media to cast him in the role of a bloated rock 'n' roll star. Racked by personal torments – his chronic low self-esteem, his spiralling heroin use, the taste of ashes that his success left in his mouth – when he splattered his brains against the wall of his Washington state home it was like a big bloody blot on the whole of rock 'n' roll.

Suddenly other artists who, like Cobain, had made a career out of making public their 'demons' found themselves on 'suicide watch'. One music paper ran a less than tasteful feature entitled 'Who's Next?'. Heading the list of potential rock 'n' roll suicides and casualties – including, prophetically, Richie Edwards of The Manic Street Preachers, Layne Staley of Alice In Chains and Scott Weiland of Stone Temple Pilots – was Trent Reznor.

Unlike Cobain, Trent steered clear of heroin, a creativity-killer and a substance that leaves the user chronically depressed when he or she stops using. Trent was more of a dabbler in psychedelic substances. But as well as Cobain's suicide, news reached him of a death much closer to home. Jeff Ward, original Nine Inch Nails tour drummer, a long time heroin user, had just died. As he told *Kerrang!*: 'I'm not anti-drugs at all. Drugs can be misused, but they can also be tools. I know my capacity for handling certain drugs, and I feel a little guilty in a way, because when we had Jeff Ward in Nine Inch Nails, he told me that he liked to get fucked up and party. He asked if I had a problem with that, and I said no. He was older than me, and I wasn't about to tell him not to smoke pot, or in his case heroin. Then he tried to hide, and I didn't realise how bad it was, and now he's dead. He killed himself – he didn't OD, but he couldn't get off it. I've been around that shit too much, with friends in LA going into rehab. There's nothing fuckin' cool about that, and heroin is inherently evil. The only thing I occasionally do is mushrooms. It's kind reassuring and educational in a way and it's natural. Chemical things frighten me, and I don't trust my brain enough. I went through heavier drug phases than I'm in right now, but it was stupid.'

Having finished the album to his satisfaction and played it in its entirety to friends, management and label, there were some reservations expressed as to how many copies would sell of a record that consisted of great pop songs rammed full of discordant noise with lyrics about sex, despair, suicide and insanity. It was hardly The Backstreet Boys.

Unlike TVT, Interscope at least seemed to be aware of what Trent was actually trying to achieve. Label boss Jimmy Iovine, a producer himself, claimed to be in awe of Reznor as a studio mechanic as well as as a musician and songwriter. They may have been impatient to hear results but stayed true to their word by neither interfering with the creative process nor messing around with the finished product.

There was also some speculation in the press as to whether there was any room for 'depressing' music after Cobain. But in fact the opposite was the case. While *The Downward Spiral* would have been well received in any case, the suicide of Kurt Cobain added some momentum to the record. Trent, to some extent, became the inheritor of Cobain's mantle as spokesman for a generation.

Reviews of the album were enthusiastic: '*The Downward Spiral* may be less accessible than *Pretty Hate Machine* but Reznor's pop savvy still resonates often enough to assure his record company that it still has another platinum platter on its hands. Fortunately, those who dig noise and distortion won't go wanting either. Reznor's unhinged persona is in your face from moment one. "Mr Self Destruct" barges in with a locomotive chug and stabbing guitars con

Line-up circa 1990 (l-r): Lee Mars, Chris Vienna, Trent Reznor, and Richard Patrick.

Keyboard player Lee Mars on vocals
at Lollapalooza, Chicago, IL, 1990.

Trent Reznor onstage, also at Lollapalooza.

Trent at the 2005 Coachella Valley Music Festival, Indio, CA.

Candid captured on April 7, 1995.

Trent covered in mud at
Woodstock '94, Saugerties, NY.

Reznor and NIN at the Shoreline Amphitheatre in Mountain View, CA, as David Bowie's opening act during the Outside Tour. October 21, 1995.

Bowie (left) joins Reznor onstage at the Shoreline.

Reznor in silhouette, Los Angeles, November 2003.

The Bridge School Benefit in Mountain View, CA, October 22, 2006.

NIN at KROQ's Almost Acoustic Christmas concert in Los Angeles, December 10, 2005.

Reznor and company at The Bridge Schoool Benefit in Mountain View, CA, October 21, 2006.

Reznor performing at Coachella in Indio, CA, May 1, 2005.

Reznor performing at Allstate Arena in Rosemont, IL, October 7, 2005.

Voodoo Music Experience in New Orleans, October 29, 2005.

At Coachella, May, 1, 2005.

Rocking at the Brixton Academy in London, July 14, 2005.

Voodoo Music Experience in Memphis, October 30, 2005.

Reznor at the Allstate Arena in Rosemont, IL, October 7, 2005.

Voodoo Music Experience in New Orleans, October 29, 2005.

Reznor and U2's Bono, Los Angeles, February 13, 2005.

ReAct Now: Music & Relief hurricane benefit concert in Los Angeles, September 10, 2005.

mucho warpage, building to an annihilating intensity. Reznor charges up "Piggy", a subdued slinky number with subtle use of black noise and chilling synth miasma, over which he intones, "Nothing can stop me now/because I don't care anymore". That may be Trent's manifesto, unless it's "Your God is dead and no one cares/If there is a hell I'll see you there".'

And the mainstream press as well as the music titles picked up on the album too. *Time* magazine carried an enthusiastic review: 'This is not music for the squeamish – or even the optimistic. Meshing the angry nihilism of punk and heavy metal with the synthetic sheen of techno, *The Downward Spiral* is a 14-song, 65-minute howl of somebody falling into the void. What keeps it from being just another nauseating exercise in shock rock is the intelligence and creative force behind its dire sound. On "March Of The Pigs", for example, layers of shifting static are suddenly broken by a lyrical piano riff that blooms like a flower through cracked pavement before the wall of noise crushes it again. Reznor maintains that the message of *The Downward Spiral* is ultimately uplifting. "I think the very act of wanting to discover and uncover unpleasantries is itself positive," he says. "The act of trying to rid yourself of these demons, to prepare yourself for the worst, is a positive thing." If only Kurt Cobain, who purveyed a similarly despairing view of the world, had looked at things that way.'

Even populist tabloids like *Entertainment Weekly* got in on the act: 'Reznor's pet topics (sex, power, S&M, hatred, transcendence) are all here, wrapped in hooks that hit your psyche with the force of a blow-torch.'

Public anticipation of the release ensured that the album would enter the *Billboard* charts at number two, before topping it the following week.

Billboard noted that: 'The success of Nine Inch Nails may be opening the door to mainstream acceptance for other once-underground industrial-styled acts... KROQ is one of 24 modern rock stations playing the NIN track "March Of The Pigs". APD Gene

Sandbloom says *The Downward Spiral* "is going to be huge in LA". The station also is one of five modern rock stations playing "Closer", a second track from the album. Those stations have even gone out of their way to edit the track, which contains explicit lyrics, to make it suitable for airplay.'

The story also noted that TVT - now home to KMFDM, My Life With The Thrill Kill Kult and Sister Machine Gun - was actually having difficulty getting its acts played on the radio because of the huge response to Nine Inch Nails: 'Right now we are up against Nine Inch Nails,' says TVT national director of promotion Jim McNeil. 'Even though programmers understand that there is a huge fan base for industrial, they only have one slot for it. They pigeonhole it into nighttime rotation, and often add it reluctantly. Their hands are forced because of the tremendous sales and phone response.'

Reznor must have thought of the old Mafia adage that revenge is a dish that men of taste and refinement savour when cold!

8 Now I'm Nothing

'We're just looking for interesting stuff. A lot of artists get their own labels and most of them fall by the wayside. But we're really taking things seriously; we'd like to be around in 10 or 20 years.'
- *John Malm, Nine Inch Nails manager*
and co-founder of Nothing Records

In the wake of the 1999 high school shootings in Columbine, Colorado, when Dylan Klebold and Eric Harris, two students, went on a rampage shooting dead 12 students and a teacher, Marilyn Manson became a national symbol of hatred for middle America. Desperate to explain why two teenagers would turn into mass murderers, commentators sought scapegoats in the usual places: violent films such as the recent hits *The Matrix* and *The Basketball Diaries*, video games such as *Doom* and *Mortal Kombat* and 'the gothic movement', the decades-too-late discovery by the media that some high school kids dress in black, listen to depressing music and try to look like vampires. Obscure industrial bands such as KMFDM, Filter (featuring ex-Nine Inch Nails man Richard Patrick) and Thrill Kill Kult turned on their TVs to discover that they were part of a sinister Satanist plot to brainwash the youth of America because they were included in Klobold and Harris's record collections.

But it was Manson that was singled out for special treatment: despite the fact that the two misfits had been the victims of bullying at the hands of the school's 'jocks' and had easy access to guns, it was the fact that they were fans of Marilyn Manson that seemed to be more of a motive for investigators. When Manson cancelled his Colorado show 'out of respect for the dead' (a statement by the promoter, not Manson) it was like an admission of complicity. His concerts were picketed by born-again Christian groups, there were calls for stricter censorship and, even in 2001, when he joined the bill for Ozzfest, there were calls for him not to be allowed to perform in Colorado. He even received death threats. In George Bush's home state of Texas, the Crime Prevention Resource Center, a spin off of the Fort Worth Chamber of Commerce's Code Blue Crime Prevention project, declared that school officials should closely monitor any students who were fans of Marilyn Manson or were attracted to 'gothic' fashions. The group suggested that student lockers be searched, and that officials even examine their art work and track which books they were checking out of the library.

Columbine, Manson said, 'is probably the only event since the Kennedy assassination to really shock America... It's grotesque that they used it as a toy to toss around to set up the election – the only thing Bush and Gore were talking about was violence in entertainment and gun control. I may have nihilism in my music, and it may not be pretty, but at the same time I don't think I behaved in such a disrespectful way as these other people.'

In his song 'The Nobodies' Manson sang: 'Some children died the other day/You should see the ratings' expressing his disgust at the capital made by the media and religious groups.

Manson made it easy for them. Like all of his band (Madonna Wayne Gacy, Daisy Berkowitz, Twiggy Ramirez) he took the surname of a notorious American mass murderer or serial killer, conjoined it with the Christian name of America's greatest screen sex icon. He was ordained into the Church of Satan (who do not, despite the name, literally believe in the existence of the devil) and was an unapologetic and intelligent critic of the conservative 'family values' lobby centred around right wing churchmen such as the presidential hopeful Pat Robertson.

Formed in 1989 by Tampa, Florida-based music critic Brian Warner, Marilyn Manson And The Spooky Kids built up a strong local following. The band's initial sound was jokey, goth metal with overtones of other 'dark side' bands such as horror-rockers White Zombie. Many critics immediately recognised Manson as a rallying flag for a new generation of goths, many too young to remember bands like The Sisters Of Mercy, The Mission and Fields Of The Nephilim.

Goth was a romantic tradition that flourished in the '80s in the wake of bands like Siouxsie And The Banshees, New Order, Joy Division and Bauhaus who had all emerged from the British punk rock scene but soon eschewed its minimalism and anti-intellectualism for a dreamier, almost psychedelic music heavily influenced by David Bowie and imagery informed by German expressionist cinema, Weimar cabaret, horror movies and a hint of Luciferianism. Manson, painfully thin and pale with long raven black hair was in the mould of Byronic goth pin-up boys like Peter Murphy of Bauhaus and Andrew Eldritch of The Sisters Of Mercy.

The relationship with Reznor was mutually advantageous to both parties. Signed to Nothing in 1994, work on *Portrait Of An American Family*, the breakthrough Marilyn Manson album, took place concurrently with the recording of *The Downward Spiral*. Although Manson was to be Nothing's most high profile signing – apart from Nine Inch Nails, of course – other acts on the roster displayed a sharp accumen for things that were cool if not commercial. And while it would have been easy to turn the label into an industrial 'boutique', that was something that both Reznor and manager John Malm avoided.

Explaining his criteria for signing bands to Nothing, Reznor told *Beat* magazine that he was basically looking for: 'Bands that I think are self-sufficient and have a strong vision and don't need a lot of hand-holding. I'm basing this on my own experience with Nine Inch Nails when we were on a shitty label in America, before Interscope, and we were constantly being fucked with. And I know what it's like to constantly have your art interfered with and if I see a band that primarily I like and I believe in, secondly I feel that have a unique enough vision that it could be destroyed by the idiocy of major labels and most of the people that work at them – most, not all – that would be somebody I'd go after.'

Many of the bands he sought out were fellow artists he had met on the way. Signings or one-off record deals included the leftfield post-techno band Autechre, Peter Christopherson's brilliant post-ambient band Coil, The Bowling Green, analogue revivalists Plaid, Plug, grebo rockers Pop Will Eat Itself, Prick featuring Kevin McMahon, ex of Lucky Pierre, from Reznor's Cleveland days, another War Records act the techno/jazz crew Squarepusher, 12 Rounds and Matt Johnson's The The, like Reznor seeking refuge from a Philistine record industry. But it would be fair to say that Manson overshadowed everyone else.

While Reznor was to be made uncomfortable with his association with Charles Manson, Marilyn Manson revelled in it. Hanging out and recording at the Tate house on Cielo Drive was a dream come true. But some of the spirits around the house may not have taken too kindly to his flirtation with the nasty little man with the staring black eyes who had ordered their grisly deaths: 'We were mixing the song "Wrapped In Plastic", which is about how the typical American family will wrap its couch in plastic and the question, "Will it keep the dirt out or will it keep the dirt in?" Sometimes the people who seem the most clean are really the dirtiest. We were using a computer because we had a lot of samples and sequencing. While we were working on that song the Charles Manson samples from "My Monkey" started appearing in the mix. All of a sudden, we'd hear in the song, "Why does a child reach up and kill his mom and dad?" And we couldn't figure out what was going on. The chorus of "Wrapped In Plastic" is, "Come into our home/Hope you stay?" And we're in the Sharon Tate house, just me and Sean Beavan [the record's assistant producer]. We totally got scared and we're like "We are done for the night." We came back the next day and it was fine. The Charles Manson samples weren't even on the tape anymore. There's no real logical or technological explanation for why they appeared. It was a truly supernatural moment that freaked me out.'

'And when the album was finally delivered to Interscope, they were actually concerned about the inclusion of a snatch of a Charles Manson song in one of the tracks. Trent was left to break the news to Marilyn: 'When our album was finished...we had the song "My Monkey" on it but I had this five-year-old kid Robert Pierce sing on it. That was the great irony: here's a kid that's singing a song that to him is an innocuous nursery rhyme but to everybody else is this horrible thing.

'After we turned the album in, I got this call from Trent and John Malm, who's Trent's manager and runs Nothing Records. And they're like, "Listen, are you willing to put out your album without the song 'My Monkey' on it?" I asked, "Why?!" And they said, "Well, Interscope is having problems because of the shit that Axl Rose has got. He's had to donate the proceeds of the song to the victims' families." I said, "Well I don't have a problem with that. Just explain to me what's going to happen." (The entire song wasn't Charles Manson's song. I just borrowed a few lyrics and the rest were my own.) In the end, Interscope insisted that we take the song off. I said, "No." So they told us they weren't going to put the album out. All of a sudden we went from being South Florida's brave new hope, from being the only band that will ever make it out of there, to being like an unsigned local band again. And it sucked. It was the most soul-destroying period in my life because we had an album done and everyone was expecting it to be in stores.'

Trent, mindful of his experiences with TVT, was determined that a fellow artist would not be shafted by his label the way that he felt he had been. In the contract that was drawn up with Interscope, there was a clause that allowed him to take an album on the Nothing imprint to another label if Interscope rejected it. Maverick – Madonna's label – was looking for acts to prove that it too was more than a vanity imprint. They had failed to sign Hole (Courtney Love famously described Madonna's interest in her as being 'like Dracula's interest in his next meal'.) and were seriously looking for talented alternative artists. And just to confuse matters, like Interscope, they were distributed through Warner Brothers.

They offered Manson a deal on the bizarre proviso that he had no swastikas tattooed on him! (Both Maverick boss Guy Oseary and Madonna manager Freddie DeMann were Jewish and mindful of Charles Manson's anti-Semitism and swastika tatoos). Before the Maverick deal went ahead, Interscope relented and offered to put the album out.

It was not that Iovine or Interscope themselves had a problem with the album; they were under increasing pressure from parent company Time-Warner whose shareholders were becoming more and more concerned at the censorious mood that was sweeping America at that time. In 1992, a Texas state trooper was killed by a teenager who was reportedly listening to rapper Tupac Shakur's '2Pacalypse Now', which included songs about killing police officers. Although, it was later determined that the killer didn't own the tape in question, then-Vice-President Dan Quayle, one of a long line of politicians who have sought to exploit popular culture as a political issue, demanded that the album be pulled from release. Interscope refused, but the flap focused attention on angry rappers and helped actor Charlton Heston lead his eventually successful campaign to force Time-Warner to drop its investment in Interscope.

Though no longer on the album, 'Cop Killer' remains Body Count's most famous and most controversial track ever. It was on the eponymous album, released by Interscope, of rapper Ice-T's hard rock band. Ice-T – who jammed onstage with Reznor during Lollapalooza 1991 – sang about killing a cop in retaliation for police brutality in the wake of the Rodney King videotape assault by LAPD officers. The song attracted the attention of law enforcement officers, politicians, Oliver North, Quayle and even President George Bush, Sr, who called the record 'sick'. When Charlton Heston read the lyrics of the song at a meeting of Time-Warner shareholders, 'I'm a cop killer, better you than me/Cop killer, fuck police brutality!/Cop killer, I know your family's grieving (FUCK 'EM!)/Cop killer, but tonight we get even, ha ha' and Heston's response was, 'catchy little number, don't you think' it eventually 'shamed' the parent company into reining in Interscope.

The 'Cop Killer' controversy was so huge that Ice-T decided to pull the song off the record.

Former Education Secretary William Bennett and C DeLores Tucker, president of the National Political Congress of Black Women, blamed the high death rates of black youth from gun and drug-related violence not on poverty or the easy availability of firearms, but on gangsta rap.

Eventually even Nine Inch Nails' 'Big Man With A Gun' was cited by Bennett and Tucker as being dangerous because of its violent imagery.

'They don't have any idea what they're talking about. They called Nine Inch Nails a rap band. I think my music's more disturbing than Tupac's – or at least I thought some of the themes of *The Downward Spiral* were more disturbing on a deeper level – you know, issues about suicide and hating yourself and God and people and everything else. But I know that's not why they singled me out. They singled me out because I said fuck in a song, and said, "I got a big gun and a big dick."' Reznor told *Rolling Stone*. But it was to be Manson that they were really to pursue in the coming years.

There were further problems with *Portrait Of An American Family*: 'I wanted to use a photo in the album's booklet of me naked on a couch when I was a kid. When you hold up something to people, usually what they see in it is what's inside them in the first place. And that's what happened because the lawyers at Interscope said, "First off, that picture's going to be considered child pornography, and not only will no stores carry the album but we're subject to legal retribution from it." They said if a judge were to look at it, the law states that if a photograph of a minor illicits sexual excitement then it is considered child pornography. I said, "That's exactly my point. This is a photograph that was taken by a guilty person? You're the person who's got a hard-on. Why aren't you punished?" That's still a point I'd like to make. People's morality is so ridiculous: If they get excited by it, then it's wrong. You see, we also had a John Wayne Gacy [notorious '80s serial killer] painting of a clown on the cover, and look at the other photograph on the inside. It's one of my favorite photographs and I've never gotten to use it. It's a picture of one of those dolls from the '60s and you pull a string on the back of it and the eyes get really big and they change colors. Around it is this like circle of wisdom teeth, and candy corns, and peppermints, and these Polaroid photographs of a completely mutilated girl. But it was something I had faked. It wasn't real but it looked very authentic. So they called again and said, "Listen. First of all we won't print this kind of photo, and second of all we couldn't do it because unless you provide us with a name and a written affidavit from the person in the photo we're gonna get arrested for distributing it." They still thought it was real, so I told them it was okay not to use it. In the end I thought it was cooler for them to think it was real. It's always been a game of not compromising but also knowing your limits and doing the best you can within those limits.'

Despite touring heavily with the album, garnering positive reviews in the metal press, there was a feeling in the Nothing/Manson camp that the album was under-promoted by the label, though by this time despite their success with releases by Nine Inch Nails and others, the label was under financial pressure because of the situation with Time-Warner.

Reznor was listed as executive producer while Alan Moulder and Nine Inch Nails associate Sean Beavan were also listed in the production credits. Compared with later releases, *Portrait...* was unsubtle. On 'Cake And Sodomy' Manson's scream of 'I am the god of fuck/I am the god of fuck' – a quote from Charles Manson – is almost liberating. Everything about Marilyn Manson seemed to owe more to *Famous Monsters Of Filmland* magazine than any real existing occult/Satanic underground, though while he was recording the album in LA, he did make contact with Anton Szander LaVey, founder of the Church of Satan. Originally he wrote to LaVey asking him to play theremin on *Portrait Of An American Family* – LaVey, as well as being America's great Satanist was also a talented organist and the only Musicians' Union registered theremin player at that time – though the two found a lot of common ground and eventually Manson was ordained as a Reverend in the Church of Satan. LaVey, who had once had an affair with Marilyn Monroe while playing organ in a strip joint where she worked, would call Marilyn Manson by his given name Brian because of the soft spot he felt for Monroe. He also had bad associations with Charles Manson: Susan Atkins, the killer of Sharon Tate, had once been a dancer in LaVey's Satanic Mass cabaret show.

'The day I became a Satanist also happened to be the day that all forces of Christianity and conservatism began mobilizing against me. Just after our meeting, I was told that the Delta Center, where we were to play in Salt Lake City, would not allow us on the bill with Nine Inch Nails. We were offered, for the first but not the last time, money not to play – in this case, $10,000 [£7,000]. Although we were removed from the bill, Trent Reznor brought me out as a guest, and I condensed my entire set to a single gesture, repeating "He loves me, he loves me not!" as I tore pages out of the *Book Of Mormon*.'

Stylistically similar to Marilyn Manson, though decidedly less cartoonish, Reznor would also be instrumental in recording and producing the debut album by Prick, the project fronted by Kevin McMahon. Following Reznor's departure from Lucky Pierre, McMahon crossed the Atlantic, spending a year in Paris, returning home to play a few shows, make some money and put out another single. But in 1988, now in San Francisco, McMahon set his sights higher, and began recording Lucky Pierre's EP, 'Communique'. He was already in the studio when Reznor came out to visit, so he asked them both to play on the record. Eventually, McMahon began to work on a new project, Prick. Reznor produced his early demos, he also produced, engineered and programmed four of the tracks on Prick's debut album. Although Prick initially signed to Interscope, when Reznor set up Nothing, Prick's debut came out under that imprint. Several Lucky Pierre songs would turn up on Prick's album ('Tough', 'Need To Get To Know', 'Other People' and 'Communique' included). Along with guitarist Chris Schleyer was drummer Andy Kubiszewski (another Reznor bandmate, late of Cleveland's Exotic Birds, who also played on *The Downward Spiral*).

Produced by Reznor with Alan Moulder and Richard Norris of The Grid, the album sounds less like Nine Inch Nails and more like some forgotten electronic gem from the late '70s. McMahon's voice veers between Gary Numanesque coldness, Bowiesque camp cabaret and Alex Chilton sneering.

The Prick release is interesting: McMahon had been hugely influential on both Reznor and Manson, yet somehow he never seemed to quite make that leap to the mainstream the way that Trent had done. When it was released in 1995, the album sold poorly and despite live shows buoyed up by the connection to Reznor, the appeal was limited.

Reznor's next project for Nothing, like Marilyn Manson, was to indirectly associate him with another controversy that would have social conservatives and even the liberal left screaming out for censorship.

Natural Born Killers was a script written by Quentin Tarantino before the overnight success he enjoyed with his 1990 film *Reservoir Dogs* and its follow-up *Pulp Fiction*. Two of Tarantino's scripts were to be filmed by other directors: Tony Scott would make *True Romance* and Oliver Stone, flush with the success of his paranoid *JFK*, was about to become embroiled in the ongoing debate about violence in the media.

Tarantino, in many ways, was doing in films what Trent Reznor was doing for music. Just as Reznor took several strands of extreme 'underground' culture and imported them into the mainstream, so Tarantino gleefully took elements of cult films, genre movies and video nasties and used them to revitalise the crime thriller, bringing it bang up to date for a new post-punk era. Like Reznor, Tarantino managed to offend everyone from traditional 'family values' Republicans to – particularly – feminists. The violence in Tarantino's movies and in Reznor's music was, in a sense, pornographic in that it delivered a fantasy that gave the impression of being 'real' though was in fact cartoonish, stylised and aestheticised to deliver something to shake up their respective audiences, to get them off.

Quentin Tarantino wrote the original draft for the film. Afterwards, Oliver Stone and a few others rewrote it making it less Tarantino-like. *Natural Born Killers*, starring Woody Harrelson, Juliette Lewis, Robert Downey Jr, Tommy Lee Jones and Tom Sizemore, was ostensibly a satire on the media's treatment of serial killers, building them up as superstars through TV shows like *Hard Copy* (where Reznor made his TV debut with the controversy over the video for 'Down in It'). Mickey and Mallory (Harrelson and Lewis) are a white trash couple, a modern day Bonnie and Clyde, who go on a killing spree across America pursued all the way by tabloid TV reporter Wayne Gayle (Robert Downey Jr) eager to sign them up for a ratings-whoring tabloid TV special called *American Maniacs*. Heavily stylised, Stone frequently switches not only from color to black-and-white, but from one film stock to another (18 different film formats were used to shoot *Natural Born Killers*). He uses a variety of odd angles and filters, animation, slow motion, fast motion, rear screen projection – it is laden with gimmicks. The soundtrack, then, had to fit with this film that resembled a rapid-fire collage of crude analogue video, monochrome film and heavily fantasised shots in too-bright technicolour that looked like a cheesy '50s Hollywood musical.

As Reznor told *Vox* magazine: 'Oliver approached me about doing the soundtrack. I got a call from his people to say he had used some Nine Inch Nails music in the film and would I like to see a screening of it to approve its use? I thought it was used tastefully for a change, which is unusual in Hollywood movie-making. I went to another screening the following week and Oliver asked if I wanted to put out a soundtrack on my label in the States. I agreed without realising what the soundtrack was going to be. I thought about it and had another meeting with him and agreed that it would be cool to make a record that followed the flow of the movie, to layer the music just like the movie did and use a lot of dialogue. I wanted to try to make something that's listenable to as a piece of music but also to call to mind the feel of the movie. He told me to go ahead and do it. So from that point on I had pretty much free rein to use whatever I wanted.'

By this time Reznor was touring with *The Downward Spiral* and had to work on the soundtrack while he was out on the road: 'We set the computers up in hotel rooms. It was a question of self discipline. Instead of having fun, I sat in front of a computer.'

Vrenna and Flood were both roped in to the sessions to produce the soundtrack as was Charlie Clouser, who made a brief appearance on *The Downward Spiral* but was to play an important part in Nine Inch Nails, both as a collaborator and as a member of the touring band. A former member of White Zombie, Clouser had quit and relocated to LA, playing sessions, mostly TV music and adverts. Reznor had heard about him through mutual friends and initially hired him to fix some drum tracks on *Portrait Of An American Family*. He was impressed enough to take him to South Beach Studios in Miami – where he and Flood had recorded much of the music on *Broken* – to make the soundtrack for *Natural Born Killers*.

As Clouser told *Scene* magazine: 'Nine Inch Nails were going on tour in Europe and this project had to be finished by the time Trent (Reznor) got back. Trent called me about three days before they left, saying, "Why don't you come with us on tour. We'll bring a Pro Tools system in the bus and we'll set it up in the motel." We had all of the original cuts of the music that were used in the movie and we had the edited version as the music editors had used it. The music editors on the movie were very creative in the way they would make compilations out of three or four songs and you wouldn't even notice things were changing. Basically, we were adding dialogue over a semi-edited soundtrack of songs. Trent didn't really have that much experience with that type of thing and I've done a lot of soundtrack work for television shows and things like that. I knew a little bit of the terminology of how film editors work and how cues are numbered and so forth. So, I was brought in to operate the computer and helped out because of my editing experience and a small background of film editing. I had worked with him in the past. I edited *The Downward Spiral* album, putting it all together into a finished piece. Also, I programmed sound effects for the "Happiness In Slavery" video.

They were sound effect overdubs and that was really the first thing that I ever did with Nails. I did that gig and a year went by, then I did *The Downward Spiral* and another year went by, and that's when I went to Europe with Nails and ended up joining the band. I replaced James Woolley, the old keyboard player. All that stuff had been worked out at the beginning of the Downward Spiral tour. When I joined, the tour was half over, so there was going to be no changing of anything. They had made a tape with the old keyboard player on one channel and all the rest of the band on the other during one of their concerts. I would just listen to that tape and isolate what the old guy had played and I had all the banks of sounds for his sampler so it was a simple matter of reverse engineering the whole thing.'

It was a new role for Trent. Although there were previously released Nine Inch Nails songs included on the soundtrack ('Something I Can Never Have' and 'A Warm Place'), Trent also wrote and recorded a new track, 'Burn', as well as commissioning new stuff from Dr Dre.

'With the "Dogg Pound" track they busted their asses to get it done but I didn't think it fitted very well anywhere. So I tried to place it where it wouldn't disrupt the flow – in other words at the end.'

The soundtrack was mostly composed of a disparate collection of artists – Diamanda Galás, Duane Eddy, Leonard Cohen – many remixed and reworked and cut up with dialogue from the film. The challenge was to fit the music to the film, something in which he succeeded brilliantly.

One particular scene, a hallucinatory dialogue in the desert when Mallory tells Mickey about her vision of him as a destroying angel cut to the Cowboy Junkies' quiet and trippy cover of Lou Reed's 'Sweet Jane' is a perfect marriage of film and music, as is Flood's remix of Patti Smith's intro to 'Rock 'n' Roll Nigger' (originally produced in 1978 by Interscope boss Jimmy Iovine) over a chase scene and a diner killing frenzy to Patsy Cline's 'Back In Baby's Arms'.

An army of lawyers were then employed to clear copyrights so that they could use the carefully chosen tracks that fitted with the film rather than being limited to the dross that some record company required them to use.

Released on Nothing, the controversy surrounding the film certainly did not hurt album sales. Ironically, arriving in cinemas within weeks of Tarantino's *Pulp Fiction*, both movies sparked the hand-wringing debate in the media about violence in film. But both in their way helped to redefine the movie soundtrack. In the past, soundtrack albums tended to be bought only by movie obsessives with a few – such as *A Clockwork Orange, 2001: A Space Odyssey* and *The Sound Of Music* – crossing over to the album charts. *Pulp Fiction* with its mix of obscure '70s funk, '60s instrumentals, contemporary alt.rock and dialogue from the movie became the biggest-selling soundtrack that year with *Natural Born Killers* almost neck and neck with it.

The down side of this is that ultimately it led record companies and film companies – increasingly part of one big mega-corporation – to use one as a marketing tool for the other resulting in films being loaded up with inappropriate duff pop and R&B tracks from the parent company. But *Natural Born Killers* was done with real imagination.

In its enthusiastic review of the soundtrack, *Q* magazine said: 'Our killers awoke before dawn. Crash of thunder. Mallory Knox (Juliette Lewis) is mad at her partner-in-slaughter, Mickey (Woody Harrelson). Acting weird, he reminds her that "this is the 1990's", that a man demands "choices, a little bit of variety". She is confused, mad at the psycho-hick delivery boy who delivered her from dead-end domestic abuse and promptly "married" her, cut palms clasped, on a bridge, so she lets rip at him. As she does so, the distressed synth-hum and delicate, haunted house piano of Nine Inch Nails' "Something I Can Never Have" swell up around her: "What you talkin' about, variety? Hostages? You wanna fuck some other women now? (Doooommmmmm-m-mm) Why'd you pick me up? Why d'you take me out of my fuckin' house and kill my parents with me? (Ding, ding, ding, da-ding ding) Ain't you committed to me? Where we fuckin' goin'?"

A rattlesnake rattles, Trent Reznor's haunted voice takes over: "I still recall the taste of your tears..." One day, all film soundtracks will sound this way.'

Reznor, looking to a future after Nine Inch Nails were no longer a touring band, was now desperate to not only produce and compile soundtracks, he wanted to score a movie from scratch.

'I'd really like to get into more film scoring. I think I'd be good at it. I also thought about doing a record of instrumental piano, like This Mortal Coil-type mood music, music you can put on when it's a rainy day. Or doing things like [PC shoot-'em-up game] Quake,' he told *Spin*.

In 2002 he was saying essentially the same thing, that he wanted to score films. But Hollywood was not exactly beating a path to his door. Nine Inch Nails tracks were included on soundtrack albums (including a cover of a Joy Division song for *The Crow*) but usually, as is the way of mainstream movies, were only used for a few seconds in the actual film itself. On the soundtrack to David Fincher's pseudo-intellectual serial killer film *Seven*, a remix of 'Closer' from *The Downward Spiral* was used on the closing credits. The remix had originally been done by Coil, yet the track that actually turned up was an uncredited remix of their remix that the film company for whatever reason had appended to the last few seconds. John Balance of Coil, rightly angered, said: 'Actually, it was based heavily on our precursor mix of "Closer". We don't receive a credit in the movie or video release which pisses us off even to this very day. The laserdisc *does* credit us in some way. I hate the way the film industry pisses all over the sources they derive their inspiration from.'

Reznor managed to escape implication in the controversy that followed the release of *Natural Born Killers*.

After the film was released, two 18 year olds, Sarah Edmondson and her boyfriend Benjamin Darras, went on a multi-state crime rampage in March of 1995, allegedly after dropping acid and watching *Natural Born Killers*. They shot and paralyzed a store clerk in Kentucky and Benjamin killed a man called William Savage in Mississippi. The bestselling author John Grisham, a personal friend of

Savage's, accused Stone of being irresponsible in making the film, and claimed filmmakers should be held accountable for their work when it incites violence. The lawsuit eventually took form though from the family of one of the victims using a 'product liability' claim in their lawsuit, alleging that Oliver Stone and Time-Warner had incited these two teenagers to commit murder because of *Natural Born Killers*. The case was dismissed in January 1997 on the grounds that the filmmakers and production company were protected by the First Amendment. However, in May of 1998, the Intermediate Louisiana Court of Appeals overturned the lower court decision, and thus the case returned to Amite, Louisiana, and moved forward. The attorneys for Byers's family have requested every single document related to the making of the film, as they attempt to prove that Oliver Stone purposefully meant to incite violence by the making of this still controversial film.

But Reznor was about to become the anti-John the Baptist to the Antichrist Superstar.

9 Route 666

'We think you could sell as many records as Ministry.'
                                    - Trent Reznor to Marilyn Manson

Between March of 1994 and November of 1995, Nine Inch Nails toured solidly, playing nearly 170 shows that took them across the US, to Europe and Australia. They played the ill-conceived Woodstock II festival as well as some low-key club dates at the end. Marilyn Manson accompanied them for the first leg, the aptly named Self Destruct tour.

Reznor involved himself in every aspect of the live show, right down to readjusting the lighting 'because it looks like a fucking Genesis show' he snapped, irritated at the way the hired professionals had made him look onstage. Unlike Manson, whose rubber-freak imagery was already strong, Reznor wanted theatricality without resorting to props.

'Probably because I don't bite heads off pigeons, I'm going to disappoint some people. But what we do is closer to Alice Cooper than Pearl Jam' he told *Rolling Stone*.

'If you go out with no production, wearing blue jeans and a flannel shirt, no-one's going to make fun of you, no-one's going to be challenged by that, really,' he told *RIP*. 'You're not opening yourself up to any degree of criticism. We decided to take in a pretty over-the-top production sense of an environment that might really help accentuate the mood of the music. Like when something's intense, when there're so many lights in your eyes it's hard to watch – in the sense of transforming the whole environment into something that can be oppressive...or seductive. That led to designing the sets.

I wanted to use the idea of raw wood and rubber, two textures against each other that you don't see in a normal rock set. In real life our guitar player wears more outrageous things than we do onstage, and he wanted to express himself, and fuck, we do what we want to do. Watching "Ziggy Stardust" tapes was more of an influence than Nirvana. We kind of wanted to put on a show not to be anti-fashionable, but because it's more really where we're coming from.'

Rumours about the on-the-road activities of Trent Reznor had circulated for a long while. He was said to lead the ultimate rock pig lifestyle of groupies, parties and insanity, getting up to things that would have made Led Zeppelin blush. With Manson in tow, he had an extra devil on his shoulder urging him on. He also had a faithful recorder, whose tell-all book *The Long Hard Road Out Of Hell* was to be a source of friction between the two.

The first gigs with the new line-up – Robin Finck, Danny Lohner, Chris Vrenna and James Woolley – were warm up shows in LA, San Francisco and Palo Alto. The show at LA's appropriately named Club Helter Skelter was limited to 500 people. Reznor let it be known that anyone from the record company showing up would not be allowed in! It was Reznor's first time onstage since the European shows with Guns N' Roses almost two and a half years before. It was also the first time that most people had heard the material from *The Downward Spiral*, live or otherwise. The setlist for the tour varied around 'Terrible Lie', 'Sin', 'March Of The Pigs', 'Something I Can Never Have', 'Closer', 'Reptile', 'Wish', 'Suck', 'The Only Time', 'Get Down Make Love', 'Down In It', 'Big Man With A Gun', 'Head Like A Hole', 'They Keep Calling Me', 'Help Me I Am In Hell' and 'Happiness In Slavery'.

Reviews from the rock press were positive. Jason Aarnop in *Kerrang!* wrote: 'Make no mistake, there are sonic devils at work here. Anyone still labouring under the delusion that Nine Inch Nails sound vaguely like Depeche Mode should take the shit out of their ears. This is hardcore stuff, bordering on total noise at several points. But one of the best things about this show is the dynamics... Some songs have been reworked for the live cauldron. "Reptile", for example – a quiet, alternative moment on *The Downward Spiral* – has a sickeningly heavy riff tonight, like 'Master Of Puppets' slowed down to a crawl. Surprisingly, we also get Reznor's take on Queen's "Get Down Make Love", the Joy Division tune "Dead Souls" (from *The Crow* soundtrack) and the lesser known "Suck", which was originally a Pigface song. After the last blast, "Happiness In Slavery", Trent Reznor does not introduce his new band, deliver a lovey-darling speech, or indeed say anything at all. He simply chucks a keyboard at the drum riser and leaves. The songs have been psycho-babbling all through the set, so there's no need to speak between them.'

The tour proper included The Jim Rose Circus Sideshow and Hole, as well as Marilyn Manson. History is still divided on who was the bigger freakshow.

The Jim Rose Circus Sideshow toured with Lollapalooza. It was a conscious attempt to build a travelling freakshow like the sort of 'carnies' that travelled the backwaters of America in a less 'politically correct' age. Jim Rose had a bizarre variety of acts ranging from The Enigma (the tattoo-puzzle guy) to Mr Lifto (who lifts weights with a chain attached to a hole in his penis). Rose and The Enigma appeared on an episode of *The X-Files*, and there was a Rose-esque freak show on *The Simpsons*. The acts included juggling with chainsaws, fat-lady Sumo wrestling and 'a young lady called BeBe The Circus Queen, who blows fire from her vagina'.

For the first time the tour experience involved going first class: Reznor had the tappings of a division one rock star and an army of lackeys to indulge him. An article from *Option* magazine gives us some insight into the backstage life on the tour.

'Backstage before the first San Francisco show, road manager Mark O'Shea types out the guest list on his portable Macintosh. He and a few others are cramped in a tiny room full of NIN gear boxes marked First Aid, Candles, Vinyl, PVC Clothes and Nylons And Such. Meanwhile, Reznor is in sound check, working through his current single, "March Of The Pigs". Every few minutes the music stops, and a Nine Inch Nails manager, roadie or bandmate bursts into the room with a request from the boss: "Trent wants a Throat Coat"; "Trent wants some Advil"; "Trent needs some water." When Reznor himself appears in the doorway and asks where the bathroom is, you almost expect those present to jump up and offer to go for him. All communication between Reznor and outsiders takes place through his handlers – including his decision to cancel an interview after keeping a writer waiting for two hours. "I'm sorry. Trent can't do the interview," O'Shea soberly announces. "He's in a bad mood. He thinks he's gonna suck tonight." O'Shea reschedules the interview for the next day, but Reznor cancels that one as well. Frequently his commitments are secondary to his whims, regardless of how others might be put out. Reznor later flies his regular makeup artist from New York to Los Angeles to prepare him for a photo shoot; the photographer waits in a studio full of rented equipment for three days, and the makeup woman cools her heels, but by the time Nine Inch Nails leaves LA, the pictures have not been taken.'

In his book *Freak Like Me*, Jim Rose recalled life on the road with Nine Inch Nails: 'Muncie, Indiana. I was sitting on a packing crate backstage at Ball State University, writing a set amid broken down, folded up basketball hoops. From the shadows of nets a dark figure approached.

'It was Trent Reznor. The master of Nine Inch Nails, the man who had bought the house where Sharon Tate was killed. The guy who invited us on this tour. The prince of destruction.

'I looked up, expecting to see someone in need of an exorcist. Instead I saw a guy with a shy smile and honest eyes, delicate features and inky black hair, who seemed so composed, so elegant, and so striking that he might have stepped out of a Renaissance painting.

'"Hey Jim," he said, extending his pale hand. "Happy you're here." He was neither cocky nor demented, but soft-spoken and completely relaxed.

'I, on the other hand, was freaking. Here we were an hour away from opening for NIN, perhaps the most outrageous band of the late 20th century. Trent was the main buzz of music magazines – and the celebrity ones too, all of which painted a picture of him as moody, brooding, sullen, tortured and slightly maniacal. Qualities I happen to like, and so apparently did the listening public, but that might have had more to do with his mesmerizing music. His following was huge: I've lived in towns with fewer residents than the people out there in Ball State's arena.

'My mouth flew open, and I heard my voice croak out, sounding even more hyper than usual. "You know, Trent," I said, gnawing on my thumbnail, "I'm scared to death. At Lollapalooza we played the second stage. These crowds are going to be our biggest audiences ever. I mean, Trent, before this we were just 'Sanford and Son'. Now we feel like 'The Jeffersons'."

'Just as I was saying "sons", an amoeba-like crowd surrounded Trent, engulfed him and swept him away. That brief encounter was the closest I'd get to him for days.

'We headed to our dressing room, which was brimming with catering trays, wine, cocktails and exotic beers. First-class all the way. This place even had a shower. And towels.'

Marilyn Manson describes Rose as the instigator of much of the tour madness, including a a contest to see which groupie could hold an enema the longest before ejecting into a bowl of Froot Loops. There was also a story about a fat goth girl who would lie naked while everyone took turns trying to spit into her anus, something so crude that even Manson declined to take part. For Manson himself, still regarded a little bit as Trent's 'Mini-Me', it was a chance to indulge rock 'n' roll behaviour on a grander scale. He was already big on sex and rock 'n' roll, but for the first time serious drugs – in fact, cocaine – were introduced to the mix: 'We had just played in Chicago, and one of the roadies called me and Twiggy into Trent's dressing room. He was there with someone else in the band. The room was destroyed. There was food everywhere. Shit was crushed into the floor. Dirty clothes were strewn all over. And everything was covered in flour because those guys used to pour flour all over themselves. In the middle of the wreckage there was a strange, gray-haired, pockmarked hippie who had bribed his way backstage with drugs and carved out something like 30 lines on a stainless steel counter in the bathroom. It was some ridiculous rock star amount of drugs, something insane like an ounce [28g]. He was like, "Do you want some?" and I was like "I've never done this before." And he said, "Try it." So we did, and we were wired out of our minds. We were doing lines like crazy. I was wearing rubber underwear that had been built only with an opening for your click; I wore them all the time on that tour. And there were these two girls who were hanging out backstage. One was a blond and one was a redhead, and they were both pretty cute. One was studying to be a psychiatrist, and the other one was just a slut. I remember being really high and really confused and still having my pants on because I never took them off until I went to bed. And I was fucking both of them in the back lounge with this underwear on like I was some kind of debased version of Superman. My skin never touched them. It was like wearing a body condom.'

Reznor too was not exactly unfamiliar with the world of non-prescribed pharmaceuticals. Talking to *Rock Sound* he said: 'I wouldn't say we took lots of drugs, but we took drugs. This is not a sob story, but becoming successful in a rock band and going on tour, you live in a very unreal environment. It is like a big party every night and it really starts to warp your personality. At some points when you had enough and don't want to deal with it, the easy option is just numb yourself out to what is going on. I think you can lose yourself in the process and I certainly did at one point. I think I have been an asshole, I think I have been too sensitive to people's feelings, completely insensitive to people's feelings; I have used people, I think I have been used – I have been trustworthy and foolhardy with that, and in other ways I don't trust anyone. It's been a forced course of self-awareness.'

Reznor gradually became enmeshed in the on-tour insanity himself with, by all accounts, Jim Rose acting as the sort of demonic ringmaster, procuring willing groupies for ever sicker and more depraved stunts. Recalling this a few years later, Trent told *Select* that he actually drew the line when The Enigma asked him to perform a trepanation on him - literally, boring a hole into his skull: 'No way! I'm not having a dead tattooed guy with a hole in his head and his rain fluid all over the studio,' he said at the time.

In the summer of 1994, Reznor arrived in Saugherties in upstate New York to take part in Woodstock II, 25 years on from the original festival of peace, love and good music.

The original festival was an event that got out of hand: the bill included everyone from Jimi Hendrix and The Who to Sha Na Na to Joan Baez and Country Joe And The Fish - the cream of '60s rock 'n' roll. Unfortunately for the organisers, when half a million people showed up and broke down the fences, it became a 'free' festival. On the second day torrential rain turned the site into a quagmire of mud. With limitless supplies of bad acid and dope but no food, the area was soon declared a disaster area. The myth of Woodstock - a potent one in the history of the counter-culture - was that half a million people had come together in a spirit of co-operation and - temporarily - built a model of a better society. Cynics may argue that the myth was largely a product of the movie, soundtrack album, posters and t-shirts that - unlike the festival - were not free and managed to recoup some of the losses made by the event itself.

Woodstock II had none of the idealism behind it. Every surface seemed to carry some corporate branding whether from MTV or Cola. At every step of the way somebody was out to fleece you, even to the extent that you were not allowed to actually spend real money on the site: you had to purchase 'Woodstock money', small plastic tokens accepted by all the concessions on the site. The bill included top flight bands like the Red Hot Chili Peppers, Green Day and Metallica, but it was hardly conducive to the supposed spirit of late-hippiedom.

History repeated itself when a deluge turned the site into a mudbath - the festival is less than affectionately remembered as Mudstock - and everything broke down. The Woodstock money proved useless and a 'black market' sprang up offering food, drink and drugs at rip-off prices. If the original Woodstock was a nation, then Mudstock was a nation too – Paraguay, Somalia or Lebanon, perhaps. One of the organisers was helicoptered off the site suffering from a nervous breakdown while miserable kids skated in the mud in front of the stage.

Perhaps in the midst of this chaos, it was inevitable that Nine Inch Nails would steal the day.

'I'm still cleaning the mud out of my ears,' Trent Reznor told the *New York Times*. 'I couldn't see. Every time I turned my head, my hair would slap mud in my eye. There was mud on the guitar strings. It wasn't conducive to technical greatness.'

He told *RIP*: 'We were right out by the big mud pit and watchin' everybody, I thought, "Well, this looks like a lot of fun." At that time there wasn't that many people that were muddy, but the people that were in the mud looked like they were having a great time and we thought "Fuck, y'know we kinda can't actually do that." But we didn't have showers backstage at the time either, so we went back and hung out backstage, and it was just a real nervous day. Then on the way to stage I pushed Danny, our guitar player, and he just fell face-first into the mud. Then he tackled me and it turned into a kind of all-male mud wrestling thing. It was actually really funny. After we did that, all nervousness kind of subsided.'

Broadcast on pay-per-view TV and then picked up by other stations after the news of the 'disaster', it was a bit of a watershed for Nine Inch Nails and their antagonistic relationship with MTV. The station was blanket-broadcasting the video for 'Closer'. Again speaking to *RIP* Reznor said: 'I don't think there's much of a danger in playing a NIN video right now. I think that we've been branded safe and acceptable and I don't think any programmer's gonna get fired for playing a NIN song, especially after the Woodstock thing. So, I mean, when we did Woodstock, I thought we would be, y'know, number 25 in the list of 50 bands that were playing there. When it kinda worked out that we've been getting a lot of attention from it, I never expected that. I don't exactly know why, 'cause I thought our performance was shitty.'

The 'Closer' video, directed by Mark Romanek, was less controversial than any previous Nine Inch Nails releases, though it was still rather grotesque – starting with a disembodied heart beating, then showing Reznor singing in front of animal carcasses – and rather David Lynch-like. Although Reznor had not changed and was not compromising to fit in with the demands of radio and TV and the industry in general, he no longer felt any need to shock for the sake of shock as he perhaps had done when 'Happiness in Slavery' was made. Romanek – whose credits included more mainstream artists like En Vogue, kd lang, Madonna and Lenny Kravitz – was like a Trojan Horse to get some of Reznor's extreme ideas onto MTV.

He later told *Spin*: 'I thought, fuck it, instead of the Super 8 video directors we've used in the past, underground people, let's go with Mr Fucking Gloss, Mark Romanek, who just did that Michael Jackson piece of shit. But he could do a beautiful shot, Stanley Kubrick-like in its attention to detail. So we decided to spend some money and go to ridiculous lengths to recreate works of artists that we liked, from Joel-Peter Witkin to Man Ray, the Brothers Quay, this hodgepodge of stuff. That video was great, it was cool-as-fuck looking. Right away, MTV said, "Can't have that, can't have that." Now okay, there was naked pussy. We knew that was going to get cut. And then we got complaints that people still found the video disturbing. "Well, why?" "Well, we don't know why, but it seems Satanic and evil." And then I thought, great, we did it.'

As the tour continued throughout 1994, Hole joined as the opening act in August 1994. Although she and Trent had never met before the tour, he had heard that Courtney Love was anxious to support the band and that she liked Nine Inch Nails. Trent had quite liked *Live Through This* and thought it would be a good addition to the bill. 'I thought, "What's the worst that could happen?" Famous last words...' he said.

The first night that she arrived on the tour Reznor says that he saw her passed out on a pool table, with her skirt hiked up around her thighs while people took photographs of her. Reznor says that he felt sorry for her and sad that people that supposedly loved her would let this happen to her. But her image as a messed-up rock chick junkie belied her harder side.

'What I didn't know then was her fierce competitiveness when she's opening for somebody – she's carrying the weight of alternative credibility on her back, and we're a New Wave faggot synth band that's easily dismissed. Even though my crowd doesn't give a shit about that.'

Courtney Love – aka the Widow Cobain – rather than disappear into a nunnery after the suicide of Kurt in April threw herself into touring and public appearances, having high profile affairs with Evan Dando from The Lemonheads, Smashing Pumpkins singer and pre-Kurt boyfriend Billy Corgan, Ministry's Al Jourgensen and movie stars Brad Pitt and Keanu Reeves. Any sympathy that people felt for her was very quickly dissipated: for Nirvana fans she became a hate figure and conspiracy theories surrounding her started to proliferate, fuelled by a private investigator that she had hired to find Kurt when he absconded from a drug rehabilitation centre, eager to cash in on the notoriety of his client. Despite a lack of any evidence, the rumour mill went into overdrive, whispering that Courtney had hired a hit-man to kill Kurt, stories given some credence by BBC 'spoof' documentary maker Nick Broomfield in his 1998 film *Kurt And Courtney*. Courtney's attempt to gag anyone who even investigated these rumours only added fuel to the fire. As News Editor at *NME* at the time I was personally in receipt of several threatening lawyer's letters stating Courtney's intention to sue anyone who started to investigate the allegations. It was, oddly, what first alerted me that there was a story there!

There were other rumours: Kurt had actually written all the songs on Hole's hit album *Live Through This* without credit and now that he was dead, so was Courtney's career. She had, then, something to prove by going out on the road. But given the judgmental nature of the mainstream media, there was no shortage of commentators who said that she was cashing in with unseemly haste.

But even before her highly publicised relationship with Kurt, Courtney was a rising star in her own right. Her ambition may have made her enemies along the way, but to say – as some actually did – that she was some sort of leech feeding off the talent of others is just plain wrong.

Courtney Love allegedly had a relationship with Manson's guitarist Twiggy Ramirez, though people kept on telling him that Courtney was using him just to get to Trent Reznor.

But apparently Courtney cemented her relationship as an ubergroupie of Nine Inch Nails by finally sleeping with Reznor during the tour.

According to Marilyn Manson, no friend to Courtney Love, 'All I'll say is that it seemed that Trent had picked Hole to be on the tour as a bit of a novelty. He seemed to dislike her greatly, and I think he wanted her on tour either to make a fool out of her or just to study her. But as the tour progressed I noticed that Trent and Courtney were hanging around a lot together, and it was a part of the tour where he wasn't talking to us too much. He had disappeared into his own world – or hers. Things started to get weird a month or so down the road as the tour was ending. Courtney showed up at Trent's bungalow door and doing some other stuff that I forgot about because I was drunk. But it was some sort of outburst that comes from a girl only if you fuck her. So I could tell that there was something going on that Trent wasn't telling us about, especially since he was stumbling around her hotel room at certain hours of the night that were very suspicious. Still to this day he won't admit to any of us what happened. So you can make your own judgment. What happened was that after the leg of the tour with Hole was over, for some reason we kept running into Courtney. Whenever she would pop up, it would cause great amounts of stress for Trent. He's a nonconfrontational person so rather than dealing with it he would let it torment him.'

'Yeah, I fucked Reznor,' Love told the press. 'But it wasn't that great an experience, I was slumming.'

'No, I didn't fuck Courtney Love,' Trent responded. 'She's a manipulator and a careerist.'

'Get back to me when you've stared horror in the face, farmboy,' she sneered at him.

'I think if there was an attraction on her part toward me, it was maybe because I showed compassion. The bottom line was, I thought I was around someone who was a victim and somebody who could use a friend, and what I was around was a very good manipulator and a careerist, someone not to be underestimated,' said Trent.

'Nine Inch Nails, huh-more like Three Inch Nails,' said Courtney.

But there were stories, not too fantastic, about Reznor and Love looking for a house together in New Orleans. There was even a story that she was carrying Trent's child, that she had lost it or had an abortion. She was, it was said, the one who was obsessed while Reznor just wanted to get on with his life. What pissed her off was that he had been the one who had dumped her, whereas Courtney, who is a 'user', felt her ego had been bruised.

Yet she did not always think that Reznor was a misogynist. In one interview she said that he was an honorary woman – about the highest compliment she could pay anyone.

'I know what she's saying, I think,' Reznor told *RIP*. 'The degree of vulnerability is probably what she's reading as being feminine because on every song there's an AC/DC macho-man perspective. But there's something creative. I don't mind an observation like that at all. It's unusually flattering for her to say something like that. She said that same thing to me, actually. She likened that to one of the reasons she liked the music because that was how Kurt used to write as well. At the time, I took that as a compliment.'

When Manson and Reznor fell out, Manson and Courtney apparently bonded at the 1998 MTV Awards, making jokes about how he kept one of Trent's testicles and Courtney had the other and he wouldn't talk to either of them until he got them both back. And Manson and Reznor made up after that to collaborate on a video that involved throwing pies at a Courtney Love lookalike!

On the tour, some of the shows were picketed by born-again Christians such as Fred Phelps of the Topeka, Kansas, virulently homophobic Westboro Baptist Church, a notorious figure who has picketed the gay community at hundreds of events nationwide. Often they carry signs proclaiming as does the headline of their website 'God hates fags!' and 'No fags in heaven'.

Despite the relentless touring, Reznor found some time to record and produce. In May 1995, the 11-song *Further Down The Spiral* was released featuring remixes of tracks from *The Downward Spiral*. Remixers included American Label head Rick Rubin (whose reworking of 'Piggy' included added instrumentation from Jane's Addiction/Red Hot Chili Peppers guitarist Dave Navarro), Foetus's Jim Thirwell, British leftfield ambient artist Aphex Twin, Coil and Nine Inch Nails themselves. As with *Fixed*, quality is variable, and it's evident Reznor had to clean up some of the remixes. (The UK import contains two different tracks, both remixed by Charlie Clouser.)

He also had some opportunities to work with long-time heroes.

'Gene Simmons himself called me up, and you're not going to say no to Gene Simmons if you're me,' Trent told *RIP* about his (unreleased) involvement in KISS tribute album *KISS My Ass*. 'He was my idol when I was 13 years old. On further inspection the dream list of bands that he recited to me over the phone got whittled down to about one out of 20 bands like Toad The Wet Sprocket and that kind of shit. Anyway, the song was going to be "Love Gun". I wanted to do "Parasite", but Anthrax was doing it. I was going to do a total gay disco version of "Love Gun" because I thought that would probably be most unlike the other bands, and they probably wouldn't like it. It would put them in an interesting position. I would have done it in the greatest sincerity, though.'

And at the start of 1995, David Bowie approached him to remix some tracks (he did 'The Heart's Filthy Lesson') as well as opening for Bowie on his Fall 1995 US tour. Although it was flattering to Trent to be approached by his hero, it was clear that Bowie actually needed him more than Trent needed Bowie. It had been five years since Bowie had last toured in the US and probably well over ten years since he had made a significant album (1984's *Loving The Alien*). Projects like Tin Machine, his band with Adrian Belew, were generally felt to be dreadful and sold badly. His film career had never quite taken off: despite high points like Nic Roeg's *The Man Who Fell To Earth* and Oshima's *Merry Christmas Mr Lawrence*, Bowie tended to be associated with high-profile flops like Julien Temple's *Absolute Beginners* and the embarrassing *Labyrinth*. Although far from creatively washed-up, or embarrassingly old, he struggled for a place in the modern rock world despite being its great prophet.

Reviewers noticed that Reznor seemed frustrated by the audiences he was playing to. The *Herald-Tribune* said: 'Reznor...seemed peeved that the audience wasn't sufficiently enthusiastic. This critic had seen a rowdier crowd at the Boston show, but didn't feel the Shoreline throng needed their pulse checked or anything. It could be that Reznor was used to audiences who were there mainly to see his show. It was clear Saturday that quite a few people at the big Mountain View tent wanted to see Bowie.

'When Bowie came on stage to the strains of "Warszawa" he was greeted warmly. Clad in a multi-layered Issey Miyake clothing event, Bowie intoned the lyrics from "Scary Monsters" in a style that was sort of goth Bing Crosby (one of Bowie's old duet partners). In the blink of an eye, the tune revved up with Reznor supplying backup vocals and a few keyboard wallops. Aiding and abetting on the tune was longtime Bowie sideman Carlos Alomar, as well as NIN band members Chris Vrenna, Robin Finck, Danny Lohner and James Woolley.

'Bowie and Reznor joined forces on NIN's "Reptile", as well as "Hallo Spaceboy" from Bowie's new album, *Outside*. The collaboration ended with the duo trading vocals on NIN's "Hurt". After that, the backdrop rose and Bowie's band kicked off his set.'

Bowie was unfavourably compared with Nine Inch Nails, ironically because of his insistence at playing new material rather than a nostalgia-laden 'greatest hits' set. MTV's *Alternative Nation* said: 'After Nine Inch Nails's initial assault, Trent broke out a sax and sat on a drum monitor to wail, and things got a little ambient and mellow. Then Lord Bowie breezed onstage for an initially low-key reading of the Bowie classic, "Scary Monsters" which soon broke into a more industrial, Nine Inch Nails-like interpretation. Although Reznor looked strangely boyish next to the elder Bowie, it was a match that was right on, musically. Watching the two trade macabre melodies on a handful of each other's tunes provided the one revelation this tour was striving for: Bowie as regal goth-rock progenitor; Reznor as black-clad keeper-of-the-glam. By the time the two duetted on "Hurt", the band had morphed from Nine Inch Nails to Bowie's back-up outfit. Bowie sounded great singing, "I hurt myself today to see if I still feel," but Nine Inch Nails would have twisted the song more wickedly than Bowie's backers did. After Trent waved farewell, the audience settled in for some stuff that legends are made of. But Bowie was on a mission to alienate, playing a bulk of material from his newly released, *Outside*. Sure, there were oldies: "Look Back In Anger", "Under Pressure" and rather obscure tracks reworked to further unrecognizability, like "Andy Warhol", "Joe The Lion" and "Teenage Wildlife". It was as if Bowie didn't keep his part of the bargain. This was a double-bill where the present joins hands with the past, where young maverick shakes hands with established icon and mentor. Nine Inch Nails did their part by puttin' on the hits; Bowie, on the other hand, stiffed everybody by denying the crowd his past. A wasted opportunity that, in the end, made Bowie look like an old fart.'

Immediately after the *Outside* dates with Bowie, Nine Inch Nails played a series of club dates at venues like Chicago's House Of Blues. The last appearance of that year took place in Santa Fe, Texas, when Reznor finally drew the curtains on *The Downward Spiral*. There were other projects demanding his attention – Marilyn Manson's *Antichrist Superstar*, a soundtrack project along the lines of *Natural Born Killers* with director David Lynch and, most importantly, the follow-up to *The Downward Spiral*. In interviews at the time Trent suggested that the album would be out 'soon' but never the most prolific of writers, 'soon' has a rather elastic definition.

10 Further Down The Spiral

'We're not a progeny of Nine Inch Nails'. I've always had a vision of where to take this band and Trent just made it happen more quickly. Trent is also a great producer and he was already exposed to the attentions of the media, which is exactly where I wanted us to be.'

– Marilyn Manson

After he left Pig or the former Tate residence on Cielo Drive, Trent took the door with him to his new home in the garden district of New Orleans. Only a thin layer of paint hid the stain where Susan Atkins had written 'Pig' in Sharon Tate's blood. New Orleans was like the next obvious home for Trent. He loved the city and its reputation as almost a separate country from the rest of the United States. At last he had both the kudos and the money to be left alone to record at home without any pressure being exerted on him to churn out albums. He had enough money to indulge his passion for toys – whether state-of-the-art gear for the studio or the black BMW he charged around the Big Easy in – and enough freedom to pick and choose his projects carefully. Although it did not signal a big sell out, a Nine Inch Nails tune – 'The Art Of Self Destruction, Part 2' from *Further Down The Spiral* – was shortlisted for a European Levis commercial. Reznor also allegedly kept a roadie on from his tour whose job was to ring around companies like sportswear manufacturers, record companies and video game companies and persuade them to send the band free merchandise.

Feeling increasingly at odds with the mainstream of popular music – 'I get irritated...' he told *Huh!* 'I mean, who the fuck is buying some of the shit that's on there? And a lot of it under the guise of being something that has some degree of conviction to it. That disgusts me. I just choose to work outside that. I do what I do. If it becomes popular, alright. It's my terms I did it on.' And despite earlier protests about his hatred of house, he developed an interest in the electronic club scene in the UK. Aphex Twin had remixed tracks on *Further Down The Spiral* and Nothing signings included US releases for artists on Sheffield's leftfield dance label Warp such as Squarepusher and Plaid.

The house he moved into in New Orleans' Garden District was a converted funeral parlour. 'I realised the press is gonna love this. First Sharon Tate's home, now a funeral parlour. I'm the spooky guy!' he said.

'We have lots of space. We're on Magazine Street in the Uptown area, and in addition to the A and B recording studios, we have the two live rooms, a full lounge, reception area, three bathrooms, a full kitchen, and even a laundry room in what used to be the embalming room. The Studio A control room was once the chapel. It's located in the center of the building, and is – no pun intended – as quiet as a tomb. The isolation is simply amazing. We raised the floor in there and moved in the gear. Studio B and the two live rooms were once viewing rooms for the dearly departed.'

The first projects in late 1995, early 1996 were sound effects for a *Doom*-style shoot-'em-up game called Quake, now one of the most popular cross platform games ever, and the next Marilyn Manson record.

Still close and still a bad influence, Marilyn Manson arrived in New Orleans after touring throughout 1995 with Danzig.

He recalls: 'On Trent Reznor's birthday, we were walking along the banks of the Mississippi River trying to figure out what to get for him, because he has everything and usually tosses gifts in a corner and never looks at them again, when I spotted a panhandler with one leg and hit upon the idea of obtaining his prosthetic limb as a present. As I was trying to convince him to part with it, a cute scrawny girl passed by, and I started talking to her. I asked if she knew the music of Nine

Inch Nails, and she said she did. Then she showed me a cut she had on her arm as if I would be able to relate.

'"It's Trent Reznor's birthday today," I told her. "Do you want to come and like create some kind of funny surprise?"

'She looked like she was ten, though she had to be much older. It turned out she was a stripper, and I thought about fucking her when we brought her back to the apartment to get changed for dinner. But she started talking about crack and alluding to prostitution, and scared me away. So we took her to Brennan's, one of the most expensive restaurants in the city. Trent assumed she was my date, and we didn't say a word about his birthday. After dinner, as Trent was talking, she nonchalantly climbed on the table, taking off all her clothes and outraging (yet titillating) the rich patrons of this high-class restaurant. She looked like Brooke Shields in *Pretty Baby*, and she succeeded in embarrassing everyone because she made us look like a ring of child pornographers. That got the shenanigans rolling, and we got drunk, we got high, and we talked to people we would never normally talk to unless we were drunk and high.'

Manson's second album *Smells Like Children* – also co-produced by Trent – spawned a hit single, Marilyn's cover of The Eurythmics' '80s electro hit 'Sweet Dreams (Are Made Of This)'. But the decision of Nothing not to release the single – they chose his version of the spooky Screaming Jay Hawkins horror-rock classic 'I Put A Spell On You' – seemed like a questionable one. Although Trent and Malm had bad experiences of the increasingly marketing-led record label sniffing a profit, Manson was actually desperate to have a hit and realised that even people who hated every other thing that he did would love 'Sweet Dreams'. It wasn't quite the big bust up it could have been but it created a certain tension between Manson, Reznor and Nothing. Also, relations within Marilyn Manson, the band, were becoming strained: there was tension between Manson and Daisy Berkowitz and Twiggy Ramirez stemming from their incessant touring.

The sessions began in the spirit of degenerate fun that the two were noted for. Reznor recalls: 'A lot of ridiculous stuff went down. The first rule was we all had to grow mustaches. My beard comes in this horrible colour of red for some reason. When we'd grown them, we all laughed, except for Twiggy. He's too fucking vain. There was a show coming he wanted to go to so he shaved. But we got to the point where we looked so stupid. You'd run into somebody and forget you had it on. Then you'd try to explain: "This is a joke." Manson and I joked about getting spotted at Tower Records, and instantly our records get returned. You know, "Those guys aren't cool anymore." I have some great photos of Manson in his Journey t-shirt. Pretty classic.'

The divide started to widen during the sessions for *Antichrist Superstar*. Manson had written 13 songs in a short burst of creativity after coming off tour and for the first time had a real vision of what his next album could be. But after five months holed up in New Orleans recording every day, they only had five completed songs and there were a lot of negative reactions to what they had.

'Everyone was telling me that it was weak and poorly executed and simply a repeat of what Trent had already done with *The Downward Spiral*. And maybe they were right. Maybe I had placed too much confidence in the concept of *Antichrist Superstar*.

'Maybe everyone was trying to save me from myself.

'But maybe they had never really taken the time to listen to and understand the idea. Maybe the album they had in mind for Marilyn Manson was not the one I had in mind. It seemed like Trent and I wanted to make different records. I saw *Antichrist Superstar* essentially as a pop album – albeit an intelligent, complex and dark one. I wanted to make something as classic as the records I had grown up on. Trent seemed to have his heart set on breaking new ground as a producer and recording something experimental, an ambition that often ran in opposition to the tunefulness, coherence and scope I insisted on. I had always relied on Trent's opinion in the studio, but what was I supposed to do now that our opinions differed? No matter what anyone said, I knew that *Antichrist Superstar* was not the same as *The Downward Spiral*, which was about Trent's descent into an inner, solipsistic world of self-torment and wretchedness. *Antichrist Superstar* was about using your power, not your misery, and watching that power destroy you and everyone else around you. What was happening to me now seemed to be some kind of perverse combination of both types of self-destruction. It had been nearly four months now, four months – and all we had to show for ourselves was five half-finished songs, sore nostrils and a hospital bill. Nobody seemed to realise that the band was falling apart.

'At the same time, Trent seemed to be growing more distant as a friend and as a producer each day, perhaps because we were taking up so much of his time on a project that he was rapidly losing faith in. He had said offhandedly in a conversation when we first started recording that it was impossible to make a great album without losing any friends, and I hadn't thought much about it at the time. Now it was all I could think about, because I was losing the three people who mattered to me most: Missi, Trent and Twiggy.'

Reznor, talking to *Spin* at a time when the chasm between the two was starting to become public, saw things differently: 'I've been friends with Brian for quite a long time, and I think he looked at me as a sounding board with an honest opinion. Not that it's always a great opinion, but at least it's no-bullshit. If something's bad, I'll say I think this is bad. On the *Portrait* album, they worked with a different producer, and they'd done this whole series of mixes. After it was done, he played it for me, and I listened and listened overnight. I went to him the next day and said, "I know you don't want to hear this, but I'm saying this as a fan, I don't think this is as good as it could be. Whatever was raw and good about the demos got lost in the polish." He thought about it and said, "You're right. I've been trying to convince myself that it's good, and it's not".'

The album eventually got made, and it was a classic, but the struggle was to take its toll.

'When he started on this record, Brian considered a lot of older producers who did more bombastic, over-the-top production. But he came back to me and said, "Would you like to do this with Dave Ogilvie?" (Dave and I had been working on some live David Bowie mixes.) So, we took the project on. Brian - er, Manson - has a pretty good idea of what he wants, and he's a really hard worker. And he's learned a lot from when I first met him. He's gone from not knowing how to get the sound he has in his head to pretty much having a grip on how the studio works. My role in this record was to create an environment where I kept the flow going. There were some internal problems with getting rid of the guitar player. There was such an animosity between the camps that, on one hand, I was playing counselor, using a lot of stuff I learned from working with (U2 producer) Flood. When I got a short fuse in the studio working on my own stuff, he'd say, "Go read a book. Go ride your bike." When you get stuck, know that you're stuck, don't try to break the wall down. And also, I was the organiser. When we started the whole thing, I said, from hearing the demos, let's get over the dread of saying "concept record." All these songs seem to fit into a story. I layed out what I thought the order would be before we recorded one note of music.'

Although Manson was depressed at the fact that he and Reznor were drifting apart, there was no actual animosity. It was more of a sense of sadness.

'I think that something had cracked between us. Perhaps it was because we both are strong personalities. Manson, from the very beginning to the very end, was and still is one big provocation but at some point he stopped sensing that very thin line separating being provocative from being ridiculous. In my opinion, he just started exaggerating, carrying things too far and he crossed some limits. I am particularly sorry it turned out that way cause there was a time when Manson was a very close person for me. Perhaps you know what it's like when you lose a friend,' he told *Metal Hammer* some years later. He also accepted some blame for the situation telling *Select*: 'I felt let down, betrayed. I still do. He was my best friend. I think both of us were in strange personality transitions and it just happened to spin out of control. I haven't talked to him in a while but, at the moment am I hurt? Yes. Betrayed? Yes. Is it all his fault? No.'

Reznor was also experiencing his own dark night of the soul. There was the comedown after the tour, which left him emotionally drained.

'The tour definitely contributed to that depression. I don't know if its the cause or the effect or what, but it ended up at a place with [sleep deprivation, alcohol and drugs] in excess. On top of that, and this is not a justification, more an explanation, it is a strange world to be dropped into. Every night's like your birthday party, you know, or New Year's Eve. The party's always for you and everyone treats you funny and everyone's trying to kiss your arse. It does tend to cater to numbing yourself as a way out of it. It's easier to deal with if you're to some degree fucked up. You have night after night after night after night of that altered reality that you exist in. And when the bus stops and you return to where your home is, there is an adjustment period of trying to find some degree of normality. What I don't suggest doing is starting a Marilyn Manson album which is what I did. Because those guys are like that all the time, even when they're not on tour. It just continues.'

There was also personal loss to contend with, with the death of his grandmother back in Mercer. Speaking to *NME*'s Stephen Dalton some time after the event, Reznor was candid about what he went through.

'The woman that raised me died and I just got into a fucking slump,' Trent says bluntly. 'Where maybe it was alright to flirt with the idea of depression before, it now developed into a black hole I couldn't get out of. I had to face myself and get to the heart of the matter, which was that I was depressed and I needed help.'

Anyone who heard Trent's doom-laden albums could have tipped him off that he was a tad miserable – or was it merely theatrical posturing?

'It was never theatrical, but it always came from me getting it out of my system. Expressing myself about being angry or distressed was a way I then could feel better in the process. But this time it prevented me from allowing myself to do that so it really got to be a struggle.'

So Trent tried therapy, grief counselling, chemical medication...

'I went on a brief stint of antidepressants, which taught me a lot about how little they really know what they do to you. But really the act of discovering there is something wrong with me, even though I didn't want to hear it, was some sort of comfort in the bigger picture because it provided an explanation for the way I felt. Somehow that gave me the power to feel like it wasn't completely my fault and I could try to understand it better. I really feel like I've come out of this a stronger person.'

But as with *The Downward Spiral*, Reznor was not exactly churning out a flood of songs. The only new Nine Inch Nails song he recorded in 1996 was to be 'The Perfect Drug' for the soundtrack to David Lynch's forthcoming film *Lost Highway*.

David Lynch had done as much as Throbbing Gristle, Cabaret Voltaire or Ministry to define 'industrial' culture. His independent hit *Eraserhead* – filmed at midnight over a five year period from 1972 to 1977 – was hugely influential on anyone who grew up alternative in the '70s and '80s. Set in a (possibly post-apocalypse) hellish monochrome world of filthy factories where time seems to have frozen in the 1950s, it is the story of a grotesque mutant baby, his hallucinating father and a fantasy world taking place behind radiators. The soundtrack involved industrial machine noises, a constant ambient hissing and clanking, a spacey electronic lullaby sung by a woman with hideous pustules on her face and half-heard snatches of Fats Waller records. Lynch, the closest there is to a true American auteur working in cinema today, has always had a hands on approach to the sound as well as the vision.

As he told *Cinefantastique*: 'Sound is 50 per cent at least – maybe 40 per cent in some scenes, 60 per cent in other. Sound and picture working together is what films are. It's many parts, and every part you try to get up to 100 per cent so that the whole thing can jump when all the parts are there – it's magical. So every single sound has to be supporting that scene and enlarging it. A room is, say, 9 by 12, but when you're introducing sound to it, you can create a space that's giant, hearing things outside the room or feeling certain things through a vent, and then there are abstract sounds that are like music – they give emotions and set different moods. Then music comes in. Transitions from sound effects to musical sound effects to music, or all things going at once, it's all letting the film talk to you.'

A David Lynch soundtrack is more than just a few pop songs slung into the mix at the behest of the marketing department.

In a *Rolling Stone* interview Reznor said: 'He was looking for somebody to provide some of the sound for *Lost Highway*, and a friend suggested he give me a call. I hadn't seen the film, but I'm a huge David Lynch fan – we used to hold up Nine Inch Nails shows just so we could watch the latest *Twin Peaks*. So we set up a weekend for him to come to my place in New Orleans. At first it was like the most high-pressure situation ever. It was literally one minute, "Hi, I'm David Lynch," and he's cooler than I even imagined he would be. Three minutes later, he's saying: "Well, let's go in the studio and get started." Then he'd describe a scene and say, "Here's what I want. Now, there's a police car chasing Fred down the highway, and I want you to picture this: There's a box, OK? And in this box there's snakes coming out; snakes whizzing past your face. So, what I want is the sound of in out of the box – but it's got to be like impending doom." And he hadn't brought any footage with him. He says, "OK, OK, go ahead. Give me that sound." He wasn't doing it to intimidate me. At the same time, I had to tell him, "David, I'm not a film-effects guy, I don't have ad clients, and I'm not used to being in this environment. I don't work that way, so respect that and understand that I just need a few moments to be alone, so that I know that when I suck, no one is knowing I'm sucking, and then I'll give you the good stuff." I'm thinking, "Boy, he must think I really suck now." But by the end it went cool.'

Unlike *Natural Born Killers* where Reznor had a free hand, Lynch had definite ideas about what sounds, what songs and what orchestration he wanted. Describing one scene, *Sight & Sound* wrote:

'It's night. A cabin in the desert is burning ferociously. But something isn't quite right. The spare, painfully melancholic strains of This Mortal Coil's version of Tim Buckley's "Song To A Siren" accompanies the conflagration. It could have been composed for the sequence. But now it's clear that the flames are retreating. The sequence has been shot in reverse, and the song is ending. The delicate voice of Elisabeth Fraser almost whispers its closing promise: "Here I am. Here I am. Waiting to hold you." The cabin now stands, completely intact, alone in the dark desert. A small light above the door glimmers like a distant beacon. There's a sudden chill in the editing room. Goose pimples and hairs rise to give their standing ovation.'

Lynch, for example, had wanted to use This Mortal Coil's 'Song To A Siren' in *Blue Velvet* but was unable to obtain the rights. It was at his insistence that the track was used, though Trent was also a fan (ironically, John Fryer, producer on *Pretty Hate Machine*, had been involved in This Mortal Coil). He also had other composers – notably his long time musical collaborator Angelo Badalamenti and ex-Bad Seeds/Magazine man Barry Adamson – working on the film. Reznor's contribution was really only to make the album.

'[Lynch] turned over all the music that was in the film and asked me to make a CD out of it. So I've done my best to make the CD a fair representation of the film, because this isn't *Mortal Kombat*, you know. This is David's movie. To the person who hates pop music who buys this David Lynch soundtrack, they will get what they want out of it. At the same time, I want it to have some degree of accessibility for the 13-14-year-old kid who buys it because I have a new song on it; or for the Smashing Pumpkins fan who buys it for that. Anyway, I think the whole thing flows, and that's my main contribution to that project.'

It also included the first new Nine Inch Nails song since the release of *The Downward Spiral*. As he told *RayGun* magazine: '"The Perfect Drug" lyrically and thematically was inspired by the film, but musically the way it happened to come out... It was one of those: One week. Write a song. Mix it. Done. I don't like to work that way. But I reached the stage where I was excited about it, yet it wasn't necessarily appropriate for the movie. And at the end of the day I am Nine Inch Nails and I have to do what's right for me. So I gave it to him and said, 'I don't know if this is the right thing for your film sonically, but this is the song I had to write right now and I had to be true to myself. And it's not in the film worth a shit. There's ten seconds of a bit of it buried somewhere, but it was just...I don't like being put in that "make a record commercial, add this Nine Inch Nails bullshit thing to it." Musically, I was on a whim going way out and it doesn't sound like Nine Inch Nails, I don't think. But it was what I had to do. I like it for what it is, but it's not my next major statement.'

The *Lost Highway* project, though, was to be the final nail in the coffin of Trent's relationship with Marilyn Manson. In 1994 while the film was in the planning stages and while Marilyn Manson were still on the first rung of the ladder, a girl called Jennifer Syme - an assistant to David Lynch - managed to wangle the band a meeting with Lynch and an offer to make the soundtrack to *Lost Highway*.

(In a bizarre twist, Jennifer Syme - the former girlfriend of Keanu Reeves who gained attention after she suffered a miscarriage with their child - died in Los Angeles in April 2001 when she reportedly lost control of her SUV and crashed into three parked cars, throwing her from the vehicle. Syme's mother, Maria St John, filed a lawsuit against Marilyn Manson claiming he gave her daughter 'various quantities of an illegal controlled substance' during a party at his home on the night of 1 April 2001.

'Words cannot express the pain that I feel over the loss of Jennifer Syme's life,' Manson said in a statement. 'After Jennifer was sent home safely with a designated driver, she later got behind the wheel of her own car for reasons known only to her. Her death is sad and tragic.' Syme worked as an assistant to David Lynch, appearing in Lynch's 1997 film *Lost Highway* as 'Junkie Girl'. Lynch later dedicated *Mulholland Drive* to her.)

With the album sessions for *Antichrist Superstar* stalled and the relationship between the band and producer David Ogilvie at their nadir, they received some unwelcome news about *Lost Highway*.

Twiggy and Manson met outside the studio. Manson recalls that Twiggy began: "'Remember how David Lynch wanted us to collaborate with him on the soundtrack for his movie?" he began.

"'For *Lost Highway*? Yeah."

"'Well, now he's in the studio with Trent, who's fucking doing the soundtrack himself."

"'I'm going to kill somebody," I fumed.

"'I would have already if I could," Twiggy spat, "but we're not allowed in the studio."

"'Aren't we supposed to be finishing our record?"

"'It only gets worse. Dave Ogilvie is fucking in there working with Trent.'"

Manson eventually barged into the studio and brazenly re-introduced himself to Lynch who said in his 'Jimmy Stewart from Mars' voice: 'Ready to go to work?' He had, effectively, gone over Reznor's head. Lynch, unaware of anything that was happening, had been keen to work with Manson and actually included Marilyn and Ramirez in the film in an orgy sequence towards the end.

Lynch in subsequent interviews made plain his preference for the music of Marilyn Manson, saying that if he had met him sooner he would have put much more of his music in the film.

Both the film and the album were well-received even though it is quite possible that no-one actually understood the moebius-strip plot. In their review of the soundtrack album *Kerrang!* said: 'Thankfully, Reznor has once again cast his own music in star roles. Prefaced by the 44-second "Videodrones: Questions", "The Perfect Drug" begins experimentally, like an out-take from 1994's *The Downward Spiral* album, then kicks loose with one of the catchiest choruses Reznor has spawned since *Pretty Hate Machine*. It ends stunningly in a storm of tribal drumming. "Driver Down" is credited simply to Trent Reznor. You may well wonder what difference there could possibly be between NIN and Reznor compositions, but "Driver Down's" instrumental insanity provides the answer. It begins with the most metallic section the singer has ever put his name to, before entering an indescribable cacophony involving yet more tribal percussion and piano. Hear it to believe it. That's NIN fans happy. Elsewhere, we have two exclusive tracks from Marilyn Manson. "Apple Of Sodom" sees the band in sinister, down-paced mode, brilliantly complementing the overall feel of the soundtrack. "I Put A Spell On You" is a cover of a 1956 tune by Screaming Jay Hawkins, once again subdued by Manson standards. The Smashing Pumpkins atmospheric "Eye" seems to herald their promised "cyber-future". Using electronic drums, the music sounds vaguely like early Erasure, with Billy Corgan's creepy voice the only Pumpkins mainstay. It's surprisingly good. The album's rock quota is completed by Rammstein. God knows how they landed slots on this album but they're clearly German, with macabre vocals over simplistic metal chugging. Seeing as David Lynch chose the utterly obscure Powermad for his *Wild At Heart* soundtrack, Rammstein's inclusion isn't so much of a shock. David Bowie's perky "I'm Deranged" is split into halves, which cleverly sandwich the whole album, while Lou Reed's cover of Doc Pomus' '60s classic "This Magic Moment" is less suitable. Besides Antonio Carlos Jobim's "Insensatez" (quality supermarket music), the album's remainder comes from soundtrack composers. Angelo Badalamenti co-wrote themes for *Twin Peaks* and *Blue Velvet* with Lynch. His material here ranges from insane sax warblings to *Pink Panther*-esque grooves. Barry Adamson's stuff is less memorable, but appropriately moody.'

'The Perfect Drug' was released as an EP with six remixes. Meat Beat Manifesto's Jack Dangers and The Orb's Alex Paterson and Andy Hughes deconstructed the original track to the extent that it actually became a new piece of music while Luke Vibert, Jonah Sharp of Spacetime Continuum, and Trent Reznor reworked it as 'progressive jungle', spacey acidic ambience and industrial drum and bass. The track itself may have been a fairly standard slab of Nine Inch Nails fodder, but the remixes were a clue as to where Reznor was heading.

By late 1996 *Antichrist Superstar* was finally completed and released. Contrary to the pessimistic reactions it had garnered during the recording phase, it was enthusiastically received by press and public, debuting at number three in the *Billboard* album charts and spawning that year's big anthem for the disillusioned outsider kids of America 'The Beautiful People'.

Many of the reviews were favourable to Manson at the expense of Reznor. *Rolling Stone* wrote: 'Musically, Marilyn Manson are the fun-house flip side to Nine Inch Nails's suffocating introspection. While Reznor emerges as a button-pushing nerd once the music subsides, you get the sense that Mr Manson – who wears body accoutrements that look like medieval prostheses and more melting makeup than Tammy Faye Bakker – actually kicks around the house in that gear. Manson's convincing freakishness is just one of many reasons why *Antichrist Superstar* is an alluringly nasty piece of work. The lurid grind of the mock-live opener, "Irresponsible Hate Anthem", sets a fine example for all the bad behavior to follow: "I am so all-American, I'd sell you suicide." In the catchy "1996", Manson recites a list of conflicting personal and political philosophies – "Anti-choice/Anti-girl ...anti-sober/Anti-whore" – and then offers himself as the simple solution. "Anti-people, now you've gone too far," he sings, "Here's your Antichrist superstar." The ever-present Alice Cooper influence is full-blown in "Tourniquet". It is also here that Manson divulges his idea of a perfectly seductive date – "She comes on like a crippled plaything". The suspense-filled "Beautiful People" offers enough ooh's and ah's to fuel an entire Hammer horror film. The song has a zombielike, repetitive quality, with ghostly electronic sounds that whoosh by like stale air blowing through ancient catacombs. Manson, in turn, hisses his lines, punctuating certain words with a shrill, insane pitch, others with a retching scream. In the morose death march "Cryptorchid", he even gets a little sentimental, recalling the sweet days of his youth: "When the boy is still a worm, it's hard to/Learn to count to the number seven".'

'Essential listening, regardless of how much input Reznor had,' said the increasingly influential Amazon.com.

Q magazine called it '...a near-death meisterwerk...goth to the point of seizure, its squealing riffs, Beelzebub vocals and monstrous sense of melodrama set new standards for saleable unpleasantness'.

Manson and Reznor stopped talking. The fall out seems to have been on Reznor's part with Manson making several attempts to get through to Trent. 'Can't we just start over?' he was overheard saying at an awards ceremony.

The next year saw him bonding with Reznor hate figures like Billy Corgan and Courtney Love. The next Manson album *Mechanical Animals* not only showed a heavy Smashing Pumpkins influence, but used Hole producer Michael Beinhorn, ditching as much of the sound that Reznor brought to the band as possible, and 'out-Bowie'ing Trent.

Publicly, Reznor did not acknowledge the schism, talking supportively about Manson, particularly as his stature as the boogie man of the American right started to grow. Trent saw Manson as an antidote to the anodyne rock muzak that was popular at the time. Talking to *Rolling Stone* he said: 'When I was growing up, rock 'n' roll helped give me my sense of identity, but I had to search for it. I remember I loved The Clash, but I was an outcast because you were supposed to like Journey. Before that, I loved KISS. The thing these bands gave me was invaluable – that whole spirit of rebellion. Rock 'n' roll should be about rebellion. It should piss your parents off, and it should offer some element of taboo. It should be dangerous, you know? But I'm not sure it really is dangerous anymore. Now, thanks to MTV and radio, rock 'n' roll gets pumped into your house every second of every day. Being a rock 'n' roll star has become as legitimate a career option as being an astronaut or a policeman or a fireman. That's why I applaud – even helped create – bands like Marilyn Manson. The shock-rock value. I think it's necessary. Death to Hootie And The Blowfish, you know. It's safe. It's legitimate. Look at Marilyn Manson: They have no qualms about taking that whole thing on. The scene needs that, you know? It doesn't need another Pearl Jam-rip-off band. It doesn't need the politically correct REMs telling us, "We don't eat meat." Fuck you to all that. We need someone who wants to say, "You know what? I jack off ten times a night, and I fuck groupies." It's not considered safe to say that now, but rock shouldn't be safe. I'm not saying I adhere wholeheartedly to all that in my own lifestyle, but I think that's the aesthetic we need right now. There needs to be some element of anarchy or something that dares to be different.'

Later, he would say that Marilyn Manson – the whole band – turned on him.

Some have suggested that the split was based in no small part of jealousy and insecurity. The music scene was changing. A new generation of rock 'n' roll bands were sweeping America. Korn's second album *Life Is Peachy*, released at the same time as *Antichrist Superstar*, seemed to tap into teenage angst and sizzling hormonal rage more effectively than any other band in history. And there were a whole bunch of them trudging across the US: Limp Bizkit, The Deftones, Papa Roach. Marilyn, rightly or wrongly, was perceived as part of this nu school while Reznor was now an established artist. In one of the ironies of the music business, suited executives in record companies, music radio and press who may themselves be in their '40s and '50s, have a tendency to decide that artists become somehow creatively redundant on their 30th birthday. There was certainly no love lost between Reznor and up and comers like Limp Bizkit.

Reznor attacked Durst in the pages of UK weekly *Kerrang!* magazine: 'It's one thing if you know your place but it's another thing when you think you're David Bowie after you've stayed up all night to write a song called "Break Stuff". I mean, Fred Durst probably spelt the word "break" wrong the first couple of times.'

Durst retaliated: 'Trent Reznor must think of me every day. I must take up 80 per cent of his life. It sucks for somebody to hate someone they don't even know for no reason.'

Ironically Durst – taken onto the board of Interscope records in 2000 – is now Reznor's boss, since Nine Inch Nails label Nothing is a subsidiary of Interscope. Durst got the last word on 'Hotdog', the opening track of his new album, parodying the dark lord of negativity's own words over a Nine Inch Nails sample from 'Closer': 'You want to fuck me like an animal, you want to burn me from the inside, you like to think I'm a perfect drug, just know that nothing you do will bring you closer to me,' Fred sneered.

As well as the personal trauma of his grandmother's death, there were some professional dilemmas too. An unknown songwriter claimed that he had been ripped off by Reznor. Mark Nicholas Onofrio filed a complaint in Los Angeles federal court claiming that Reznor used five of his songs on the *The Downward Spiral* and claiming that one other song, 'Burn' on the *Natural Born Killers* soundtrack bares an uncanny resemblance to another track he sent to Reznor. Onofrio reportedly claimed that he met Reznor in a chat-room online, asked if Reznor would listen to some of his work, and then mailed a demo to Reznor's house. The following year a federal judge threw out Onofrio's case against Reznor when the plaintiff couldn't produce the Federal Express receipt to show that he'd sent the demo tape.

Reznor, meanwhile, was talking up his next projects.

'There will be two records that will probably come out around the same time. One will be with people I had with me in the live band. We're playing and writing together in a group called Tapeworm. That one will be a bit more like what you think industrial music is like now. The new Nine Inch Nails will be more like a funk hip-hop record. It will piss a lot of people off, and it's going to change the world at the same time, I hope. That's all I can aspire to. That and staying ten steps ahead of Billy Corgan.' Tapeworm was a project started by Charlie Clouser involving his room mate Maynard James Keenan of Tool/A Perfect Circle as well as other collaborators including Danny Lohner, Phil Anselmo of Pantera and various members of Prong and Helmet. It would be the second half of 1999 before the long-awaited Nine Inch Nails album appeared, though it could hardly be described as a 'funk hip-hop record'. At the time of writing, there is no sign of the Tapeworm project even coming close to fruition.

11 Fragile - With Care

'This record will be huge or it will be a career stopper.'

- Trent Reznor

Despite any fears that Reznor was 'losing it' and despite the barking of younger pups at his heels, April 1997 saw him named as one of *Time* magazine's 25 most influential people in America.

'Among this year's 25 are good influences and dubious ones, public personalities and players so private you may not have known they were pulled up to the game board, much less that one of the pieces was you. They include the writer Henry Louis Gates Jr, whose thinking is influential; the chatterbox Rosie O'Donnell, whose cheer is influential; and the rock musician Trent Reznor; whose gloom is influential. (Funny world.) One way or another; these 25 are people to look out for.

'Trent Reznor - Industrial Rocker

'Trent Reznor is the anti-Bon Jovi. He is the lord of Industrial, an electronic-music form that with its tape loops and crushing drum machines, harks back to the dissonance of John Cage and sounds like capitalism collapsing. But Reznor, with his vulnerable vocals and accessible lyrics, led an Industrial revolution: he gave the gloomy genre a human heart. It's been said that he wrote the first Industrial love songs. It is a love that the Marquis de Sade would have found delectable. Reznor's...music is filthy, brutish stuff, oozing with aberrant sex, suicidal melancholy and violent misanthropy. But to the depressed, his music, veering away from the heartless core of Industrial, proffers pop's perpetual message of hope - or therapeutic Schadenfreude: there is worse pain in the world than yours. It is a lesson as old as Robert Johnson's blues. Reznor wields the muscular power of Industrial rock not with frat-boy swagger but with a brooding, self-deprecating intelligence.'

Spin magazine too put him at the head of their list of most important people in rock, saying: 'If anyone on the current alt landscape approached the status of both icon and auteur, it's Trent Reznor: natural-born chiller on the lost highway winding its way from Gothville, through the industrial park, and into the newfangled suburbs of electronica. He's the model action hero for the hypermodern universe (or, perhaps, alt-rock's Don Henley): a recording star who stays famous without actually, you know, releasing albums. Instead he makes singles, remixes, soundtracks, videos, even headlines. But mostly he makes scenes, lending his sensibility to David Lynch and David Bowie, getting toasted by Oliver Stone and quoted by Tori Amos, competing with Alanis Morissette for the most bleepable alt-rock single ("Closer") of the decade. And Reznor even has his own cartoon – oh wait, that's Marilyn Manson. The much-craved new Nine Inch Nails album, featuring production assistance by Alan Moulder (Smashing Pumpkins, Curve) is expected to arrive this fall.'

As he told *Guitar* magazine, he still felt that he had something to prove, but his whole situation had changed drastically since the days of *Pretty Hate Machine* that he couldn't tread water, but had to find ways to motivate himself to push forward: 'Success and money and things like that do change you, and anyone who says they don't is full of shit. But I do very much feel there's something to prove. And it's that I think honest music played well with integrity can and still matters. And as we're getting into a climate of shallowness – not that this is high art and everything else isn't – but I feel every time I turn the TV on I got something to prove. Not to sound like just another guy bitching about it; I can do that or I can put out music that I think is as good as I can make, and that the world needs to hear. It's not so much about selling more records this time around as much as in my heart and my soul I creatively owe it to people to show, "Hey, check out what I can do and what can happen here." And make things better. And quit bitching about stuff.'

The predicted album arrival date was, of course, wishful thinking. But despite the absence of a follow-up to *The Downward Spiral*, Reznor was prolific in the studio, acting as executive producer of a Nothing Record's release by ex-Judas Priest singer Ron Halford and producing remixes including an EP for David Bowie. Five different Reznor remixes of 'I'm Afraid Of Americans' – one of which featured guest rapper Ice Cube – surfaced on a six-track EP; the sixth remix was by UK drum and bass artist Photek. 'I've been a fan of Bowie's work for years and he's also a friend. When David asked me to do some remixes, I decided to use a collective approach... I wanted to throw some odd things in the mix and I have been planning to work with Ice Cube on some Nine Inch Nails material, so I asked him if he wanted to be involved. I am also a big fan of Photek's and I thought his mix for the same record would balance the EP out.'

Bowie's influence was permeating Reznor's approach to music. Once resolutely anti-house, he was now, like Bowie, delving into the UK jungle/drum and bass underground as well as other extreme shores of electronica.

As he said to *College Music Journal*: 'I think the whole industrial distorted thing is dead. I'm bored with it. All I listen to now is hip-hop. Erykah Badu's record is my favorite CD of the past year. The new wave of electronica also interests me. I was completely blown away by jungle. It's so not rock 'n' roll. Double-speed beats against half-speed reggae – what an interesting and cool style of music. I was pissed off, in a good way, that I never thought of it. Like I remember seeing Jane's Addiction on their first tour, standing in a fucking Cleveland club, unsigned and mad, thinking "these guys are fucking good – fucking assholes!" It was a good mad. Not mad like with 311, where it just sucks that you have to listen to it. But a good, humbling mad.'

By now it was clear that a pattern was emerging. Trent has the classic creative knack of becoming distracted by other – possibly irrelevant or unimportant – projects as a way to avoid dealing with the serious business of making another album. Speaking to *RayGun* magazine, he admitted that this was the case: 'When you get off the road...I'm not particularly inspired about anything. And that's when the idea of the Marilyn Manson record came up and the Quake video-game soundtrack and minor things we've been doing. Distractions for me, where I could get outside the pressure of Nine Inch Nails. With Nine Inch Nails I really feel like everything I do has to really be important. And the chance to work with Manson in the producer capacity was a challenge I hadn't really had before and it was really rewarding. I came up with shit and we got along great and they were my best friends and that was fun. What I thought would take two months ended up taking seven months, which further delayed things. And then the soundtrack to Quake, which was fun in a different capacity. Maybe my time could be spent better writing Nine Inch Nails songs from a sensible career point of view. It would be better if a Nine Inch Nails record came out every year instead of every three or four years, but I really didn't have it in me to climb back into the hole and start working, 'cause I wasn't motivated. Now I am. I'm in the trenches working on it and I feel good about it.'

Despite repeated claims that the album was under way, that Rick Rubin was producing, that he was off to a retreat in Big Sur in Northern California to write acoustic songs, that it would be a hip-hop record, that it would be a rock 'n' roll album involving the whole live band – all things that were considered – it was not until late 1997 that Trent and Alan Moulder finally set to work on the album that would be released two years later as *The Fragile*. The album was recorded in the grip of the depression that followed his grandmother's death and he was to claim after the event that it had been instrumental in helping him to get through it.

Reznor was, by most accounts, a mess after the period spent relentlessly touring with Manson, Jim Rose and Bowie. There is a famous photo of him backstage with Bowie where he looks puffed up, overweight, debauched. He looks like a man only a few more drugs away from the graveyard.

One of the jibes frequently aimed at Reznor - that he was unapproachable - had an element of truth about it. Reznor himself admitted as much, claiming that if he had exchanged phone numbers with a member of another band that he liked, he would never call them, always waiting until they called him. His method of working - essentially as a one-man band - had served him well in the past, but it now seemed that circumstances were forcing him to become more collaborative in his approach. There was also, as he told *Kerrang!*, a seismic shift in his outlook on life: 'I kind of went through an overhaul in my life when I started working on this record. It was realising that I was on a path of self-destruction that was leading nowhere but to ruination. Sitting down and working on this record turned everything into a place of repair. And maturity has crept in. I don't think it's overwhelmed the tone of NIN, but it's definitely added a different texture and outlook. I feel differently mentally. The chemicals in my brain have changed. Also I never would have considered stability or having kids. Now I'm like, "Some day I'd like to do that". I've really stopped my life to do Nine Inch Nails and I let that get to a really unhealthy level. I'd convinced myself that I only had X amount of time before no one was going to care what I had to say, so I'd got the rest of my life to be normal. But you let that go for long enough and pretty soon you need to be human, too. That's what I've been thinking I have to do. I haven't done it yet, but I at least know I have to.'

Reznor had acquired some new mentors. Bowie, Bono from U2 and Rick Rubin, all warned him to take care that he wasn't painting himself into a corner.

'I could make a million songs like "Happiness In Slavery" screaming, snarly - that's what people would expect and that's what fishnet-wearing men, skirt-wearing *Propaganda* readers would expect, but to do something that really opens me up for attack...' he told *RayGun*.

He was also in regular contact with Dr Dre (who had worked with him on the *Natural Born Killers* soundtrack) and made vague plans to collaborate on a project after he completed the album in 1998. Rather grandiosely, they decided that they would get together to 'change music forever'.

But music was changing. The climate had become more conservative, more controlled by the labels and their marketing departments. The charts were dominated by manufactured pop acts – boy bands and girl bands – churning out lightweight R&B with nice song and dance routines. It was like the dreadful period in the early pre-Beatles '60s when interchangable teen cheesecake – Bobby Vee, Bobby Darin, Fabian – ruled the charts. And given that the formula worked so well with pop, the same blueprint was being applied to rock. It was a conservative backlash as bands like Counting Crows, Bush and Live sold millions of albums of formulaic rock. There was a feeling in some labels that the day of the maverick genius was over: in the fiercely competitive music industry of the late 1990s, profit was everything. Because of the demands of shareholders, profits had to be made quickly, therefore there was less scope to invest in a band, hoping that they would develop. If the first album didn't sell, the label would cut its losses and dump them. What's more, established artists whose records were felt to have 'underperformed' – that is, if they sold less copies in the same space of time than a previous release, even though the album may have gone to number one in the *Billboard* charts – could find themselves left high and dry with marketing and PR support withdrawn. It was a harsh time for somebody like Reznor to be taking two years to record an album.

'I think it's in bad shape,' Reznor told *Circus* magazine. 'That's a very global statement, but it seems to me rock has become very homogenised, so incredibly safe and politically correct for the most part, and whatever danger might have existed at its inception has been packaged, labelled, marketed and sold as product.'

But as record companies attempted to wrest control from artists, this same power was slipping through their fingers. With the growth of the internet, rumours about the album found their way across the world faster than ever before. Snippets of information were dutifully reported by news-hungry music sites like the late lamented Addicted

To Noise and SonicNet. There were stories that Reznor had got a wino who live in the alley behind the studio to remix a track (untrue), that the Tapeworm release would be 'this year' (ie 1997 - untrue), that Steve Albini was producing (not quite true), that the album was stalled (possible) and that it would never be released (untrue, though as 1997 went into 1998, you could see why people were saying this). Possible titles started being discussed on usenet groups and fan sites: oddly along with 'Impossible Pain' and 'Septic', a few people suggested 'The Fragile', though 'Dissonance' was the one that was agreed on and news reports right into late 1998 referred to the new album by this name. Reznor, it turns out, may actually have been fuelling these rumours himself. He was an enthusiastic user and at one point in the early '90s was a regular poster on Prodigy Net, leaving details about *Broken* and *Fixed* for fans long before they were officially announced.

In a revealing interview with *Mix Masters*, producer Alan Moulder described the process of working on *The Fragile* as being akin to painstaking scientific research: 'The process changed, as you can imagine. Trent had some demos and a list of atmospheric territories he wanted to attack in different ways - electronic, or more organic and funky. So, we just started experimenting. When we'd gone through the demos, we started doing new stuff, which would involve, sometimes, just making sounds. We set Trent up in a room with a whole pile of junk, really, and four mics, and he'd just hit things and we'd record it. Sometimes we'd play a loop of something and he'd play along on different boxes, or big plastic water bottles, or shakers - he'd pick up whatever appealed to him. We spent a long time cutting that together, and we made quite a few songs out of it. Sometimes it was based on him playing to the loop, and sometimes, it was just based on the samples. Then we'd build on it - put some basses on and guitars - and then we'd move on. We never got stuck on anything for too long; we just kept moving. What was good about that was, when you'd come back, after not listening to it for a month, it was a pleasant surprise, much better than we thought. We were having a lot of fun creating stuff, and we kept doing more and more. The down side was we ended up with something like 117 tracks. I knew definitely then that we were into it for the long haul. The strong ones survived. We just kept going round, improving, and then we'd have big review sessions where we would go through everything and say, "No, that one's out." Sometimes we'd get bored and have lab days, making percussion banks or putting drum kits in different rooms and running them though PAs. A new piece of gear would arrive, and we'd spend half a day exploring it – you know how it is, when you get a new toy you always get fantastic things out of it in the beginning.'

A far cry from the days when a band would go into the studio, bash out their 'two hit singles and eight pieces of shit' (copyright Phil Spector) with all the needles in the red and the reverb up full in less than an hour, maybe rerecording some vocal parts if they were being picky.

If Interscope were nervous before the release of *The Downward Spiral* then they were positively and visibly twitchy in the run up to *The Fragile*.

A report in *Hit Parader* magazine in mid 1998 read thus: 'Like a western gun-fighter of old, Reznor seems to garner great pleasure out of making those around him squirm as they wait and wonder – coercing those caught in his blinding aura to wither under the strain of his imposing nature. Sometimes it seems like it's all just a game to Reznor – a high stakes battle of human chess with winner-take-all results. But Reznor doesn't play the game by conventional rules; never has, never will. In fact, it often seems as if he creates his own set of rules as he goes along, hoping to create as much confusion as possible in the process. Certainly as the days, weeks and months pass without a new album from Nine Inch Nails, one must begin to wonder exactly who is winning Reznor's latest game of rock 'n' roll Russian roulette.

'"It's gotten to the point where there are people at Reznor's record label that really don't have a clue about what's going on," an inside source revealed. "They don't really know when his next album is coming out. It could happen tomorrow, it could happen next year – or it might never happen."

'Could Reznor truly pack up his musical bags at some point in the not-so-distant future and walk away from his platinum-coated, award-winning musical life? Could he decide to put to rest Nine Inch Nails – one of the most commercially successful and critically lauded bands of the decade – and focus all of his abundant creative energies on producing other acts and running his own Nothing Records label? While such a notion might strike fear and loathing into the hearts of any true-blue Reznorite, those same fans know that such a scenario is far from impossible when a figure as unpredictable as Trent Reznor is concerned. They know full well that he has threatened to derail his own career before, winning a battle with his original label, TVT Records, by threatening to fall on his own sword rather than risk what he perceived as artistic prostitution. Could such a situation occur again in 1998? We may all soon find out.

'While details remain as rare as proverbial hen's teeth, there seems to be little doubt that a war of attrition has begun between Reznor and forces at his current record label. Reznor was ready to release a new album – one supposedly called *Dissonance* – as far back as last summer. But when a few label forces supposedly stepped in asking him ever-so-politely to see if he could find it in his heart to possibly "tweak this" and "refine that", Reznor promptly drew a line in the sand. Apparently he viewed such corporate intrusion as nothing short of sacrilege, manoeuvres designed solely to ruin his unique creative vision. So far neither party has been willing to cross the figurative line of Reznor's design, realizing that the consequences of such a move could turn out to be quite unsatisfying for all involved. While Reznor seems almost willing to sacrifice everything he's gained with NIN over the last half-decade in order to ensure his continued control, the folks at his label certainly are not.

'"Cooler heads must prevail," our source revealed. "Otherwise nobody wins. I think that the level of intensity between Trent and the label has been blown a little out of proportion, mostly since they're willing to do just about anything he says. But he is used to having total autonomy when it comes to his music, and anything less than that is apparently unacceptable... Trent may be playing with fire, but he seems to enjoy that," our source concluded. "He doesn't really care. He knows that somehow, someway he'll always be able to make his music and get it out to the public – he couldn't care less how far underground he may have to go to fit into anyone's preconceived notions. We all need to respect him for that.'"

Details continued to eke out from people involved. Helmet guitarist Page Hamilton said that the new material reminded him of '60s British group The Yardbirds' and confirmed that the album was a behemoth double album with at least 20 songs. Bowie guitarist Adrian Belew told press that he had been in the studio with Reznor in February '98 and had laid down guitar work for roughly 14 songs or song fragments. Steve Albini revealed that he had been involved, recording Ministry drummer Bill Rieflin to be sampled and looped on the record. A Finnish music magazine reported that Reznor told them he would 'utilise a variety of vocalists, musicians and exotic instruments'.

Charlie Clouser, speaking to *Kerrang!* after the album's release said: 'I thought we could see an end in sight when we had enough material to fill one disc. But Trent's quality control being what it is resulted in additional months fleshing it out to two discs. It didn't start to seem like a long time until the very last few months.'

'Instead of recording to tapes, I played parts of the songs into my computer and after that I could make loops and stuff', Reznor told *College Music Journal.* 'If you want to write a song, just put a loop from a drum track, and then add bass and guitars into it. After that you can do whatever you like with the song: use samples, put on the vocals and so on. This way it's easy to make remixes of a song when you have the basis of it saved in your computer.'

Charlie Clouser told reporters that he was more involved in this record, but gave away few details. *Hit Parader* continued to fuel speculation that there was a rift between Interscope and Reznor: 'Rumors continue to abound that the always-controversial Trent Reznor continues to do battle with forces at his record label over the contents of the next Nine Inch Nails disc. According to well-placed sources, Reznor has basically given the label a "love it or leave it" dictum, stating that he maintains total artistic control over the contents of every NIN album.'

This, apparently, before anyone at Interscope had actually heard the album.

'I think I've done some of my best shit ever, ever, ever,' Reznor had told *Alternative Press* earlier in the year. 'And it will be irritating to people 'cause it's not traditional Nine Inch Nails. Think of the most ridiculous music you ever could imagine...with nursery rhymes over top of it. It's probably the opposite of *The Downward Spiral*. A bunch of pop songs.'

This, apparently, before he had actually completed a track.

Expectations fuelled and stoked by the *Time* cover and the fact that *The Downward Spiral* was now starting to appear on the lists of Best Album Of The '90s/decade/last 1,000 years that were starting to be compiled in the run up to the end of the millennium.

He told *RayGun*: 'Well, everything I say will be used against me at some point...but we've been working pretty steadily the past year on it. I went into it kind of blindly, but with the intention of re-invention, which is a semi-pretentious thing to say. But I kind of came to the end of what I thought the first phase of Nine Inch Nails is or was, and it just seems like it's time to close that chapter and move on.'

The first official teaser for the new album aired in October 1998, when a 30-second commercial was shown during the 15th annual MTV Video Music Awards. It consisted of a black-and-white, pulsing NIN logo and snippets of several songs from *The Fragile*. 'It was obviously a teaser for the new album,' said Reznor's press officer Sioux Zimmerman said. 'And it was done at the last minute.' The ad, designed by former *RayGun* magazine designer Robert Hayles, opened with a piano track and the slowly flickering NIN logo, which looked as if it were part of an ancient silent-film strip. It then went into 'Into The Void'. The commercial ended with a shot of the word 'ninetynine' in orange, with the trademark NIN backwards Ns.

Confirmation, then, that the album would be released in 1999. Follow-ups appeared in print magazines as the campaign started to build.

Speaking to *Alternative Press*, Reznor confirmed that there had been a point where he considered packing music in altogether: 'I had to rediscover my passion for wanting to make music. A lot of the other shit started to take the shine off it – the celebrity aspect, the constant competitive backbiting. I've seen that with close friends. For a while it just didn't seem as appealing to get back in that arena. Not from an "I'm afraid to do it" point of view but more from an "it's not as fun as it used to be" [perspective]. But I think I've got my head turned back around.'

He told SonicNet that the sound was: 'Tom Waits on a bayou filtered through a funk blender and slowed down.'

To generate further momentum to the new album, Nothing released *Closure*, a double VHS set, the first featuring live footage and behind the scenes video from *The Downward Spiral*-era tours while the second was a back-to-back mix of all the videos for singles and tracks including 'Happiness In Slavery', for many fans their first opportunity to see it in its original uncensored gory glory.

Yet for all that it was in the home stretch, the album was delayed. The original release date given was February. That was put back until May then June. As it happened, the first single from the album 'The Day The World Went Away' was not to see the light until July of 1999.

In May, one music site ran a story that read: 'Contrary to the cajillion reports on Nine Inch Nails' new album, *The Fragile*, a few things seem certain: 1) The album is not done. 2) The album has not yet been handed into Interscope. And, 3) that Jerome Dillon guy from Howlin' Maggie we told you about is in as the drummer.'

Reznor had already previewed some tracks from the album to writers like *Rolling Stone* heavyweight David Fricke ('There was time-wasting involved in this whole thing; I won't lie to you,' Reznor told him), but it was clear that despite this he still had a lot of work to do on the release. According to producer Alan Moulder, there was a lot of wastage on the album. Trent threw away at least ten songs written for *The Fragile* because time was a factor and he couldn't wait for inspiration to strike. Some were almost completed, some were instrumentals and some were rough sketches for songs that still needed to be fleshed out. It is possible, then, that *The Fragile* could actually have been a triple album.

'It's also to do with the fact that we aren't a traditional band. You know, the bass part goes here, the guitar goes there...verse, chorus verse...drums here. For me it's a much more complicated process and it doesn't lend itself well to just getting it down. Sometimes we do work quickly, but sometimes it's the first time we've ever done something and there isn't a rulebook other than the one you write yourself. You can see why record companies would rather just work with people that they could put in a studio and turn it out but for me that isn't the way it happens,' he told me.

He told *Alternative Press* magazine that the only way to overcome his fear of writing was to actually do it: 'I can't tell you how many times I sit down at the notebook or that keyboard or that piano and walk away defeated. That's just part of the territory, but it is not fun because more often than success is failure. I got myself in a Catch-22, a self-fulfilling prophecy: Afraid to write? Well, just put it off. Then I'm more afraid to write, so I toy around and fuck off. But you add in a little life crisis and it isn't a healthy environment. But the way out of it, and through it, was just addressing it. Not being a coward. Seeing what was there. And what was there was little twinkle saying, "Remember? This worked last time, every time. You are worth something. You have a purpose; you have a gift. So use it." I sound like a fruitcake sitting here saying all this shit. But that is really what's going on - not to mention the fact that every time I pop my head out there someone's like, "When? When? When?" It's better than nobody caring, I guess, but this takes a fuckin' long time the way I do it. And I am not trying to make excuses.'

There were even some jitters that the world may actually have lost interest in Nine Inch Nails despite the head of steam that was being built up in the press and other media. With the phenomenal rise of nu metal in the period between the release of *The Downward Spiral* and *The Fragile* there was every possibility that this was just going to be yet another release by one of yesterday's men, with little or no relevance to the big jeans wearing brats in Korn t-shirts who had created a new school of rock stars.

There's a story - possibly apocryphal - that when Radiohead delivered the tapes of *Kid A* to their record company, the Managing Director, immediately after hearing it, cancelled everyone's Christmas bonus. Interscope, upon receiving *The Fragile* in its entirety, must have felt the same way. It's a dense and unforgiving album, one that won't allow you to dip in and out for a track here and there. It's all or nothing.

A few months before the album was released (or completed) Reznor teased fans by posting almost half a minute of music on the band's official website. Between *The Downward Spiral* and *The Fragile*, the internet had boomed. In late 1998 and early 1999, with the NASDAQ tech stocks index spiralling ever upwards, record companies - aware of the potential billions to be made from music online but alarmed at the ad hoc free for all taking place with file-sharing protocols like Napster - began to pay attention to what was out there on the world wide web.

Nine Inch Nails, as befits a band who demand a certain level of obsession from fans, had a huge web presence. As well as the official site, there were countless fan sites all over the world, many of them as good as or better than anything that the record label posted. There was even a Trent Reznor parody site, some of its postings so horribly believable that at least one clueless music publication reported one of its jokes as fact. The web was a better way to keep up with what was happening in Trent's world than magazines or even professional websites. But when several tracks from *The Fragile* found their way onto Napster and onto fan sites, the Interscope legal department went into overdrive.

Cease and desist letters were sent to webmasters operating fan sites who were offering free downloadable .mp3 versions of tracks that had been previewed on radio. Unlike Metallica - whose charmless legal departments ended up threatening 15-year-old school kids with the full might of their corporate legal teams - Nine Inch Nails did not actually sue any of their fans. But there was some irony in the fact that Reznor - always an early adopter of new technology - seemed to be siding with the cartel of labels conspiring to hold back the tide of history.

Initial reviews, particularly from those sections of the press that had been long time supporters of Reznor, were enthusiastic. *Kerrang!* said: 'It has been referred to as "The Most Important Album Of The Decade", its creator "The Most Influential Man In Music"… Ultimately, *The Fragile* is worth the wait and equal to the hype. The sound is readily identifiable as Nine Inch Nails, the songs a logical progression from *The Downward Spiral*, but the roots of this record are in late '70s art-rock. Reznor openly acknowledges the influence of David Bowie and Pink Floyd on his own music, and on *The Fragile* these influences are stronger and more evident than ever.

'The key references are Bowie's 1977 album *Low* and - an ambient work recorded when Bowie was based in Berlin and self-confessedly addicted to heroin - and the Floyd's 1979 concept album *The Wall*. The latter is one of the most miserable records of all time and was aired before and after every show on Marilyn Manson's *Mechanical Animals* tour. Its influence on *The Fragile* is immediately evident on "Pilgrimage", which echoes the tumultuous climax of *The Wall* as a computer-generated marching band and baying crowd create an incendiary atmosphere redolent of a fascist rally. It is no mere coincidence that Bob Ezrin, co-producer of *The Wall*, was drafted in by Reznor at the 11th hour to assemble a high-impact running order for *The Fragile*: the two albums are comparable in scope and intensity.

'Acclaimed by Reznor himself as the best work of his life, *The Fragile* is ambitious, inventive and emotive. After this, you may never want to hear Slipknot or Korn or Limp Bizkit again.'

Reznor himself did not deny his love for *The Wall*, telling *Metal Hammer*: 'I won't deny that *The Wall* had a great impact on my music and my life. Unfortunately, I do not know Waters personally but I believe I understand what bugged him when he wrote it. I grew up with this music and it's still within me. For me, this album is certainly one of the greatest works of all times. It is a perfectly composed, played and recorded album that brings extensive emotions. There is depression, anger, sadness, grief and rage, feelings that are very close to me at times.'

But there were some notes of caution. Even his most enthusiastic cheerleaders added a caveat that this was a huge, complex album and was maybe too much. Ann Powers in *Rolling Stone* wrote: 'Reznor knows that a star's torment makes for tired drama. That's one reason why he twists his music so much, to make sure unraveling it becomes the same obsessive game for the listener that making it is for him. *The Fragile* offers no insights into how people survive the assault of their own thoughts, but such wisdom has no place within Reznor's compositions. He lives to be haunted. We're lucky he keeps hammering away inside that unquiet mind.'

While Dan Silver, writing in *Metal Hammer*, seemed to have been completely blown away by the experience of listening to the album – he notes perceptively that it's a case of less is more. It is a good double album that would have been an outstanding single album: 'The first disc is phenomenal, a mesmerising tour de force in which Reznor remorselessly crushes your expectations with a stack-heeled boot and a demonic grin. It's so impenetrably dense and unfathomably textured that in the welcome moments of sonic respite your head is spinning in an attempt to merely take in what has gone before. Constantly evolving epics such as first single "We're In This Together" and "No, You Don't" are the aural equivalent of trepaning, driving tungsten drill bits through the centre of your skull, creating the breach for the likes of the haunting title track and ethereal "La Mer" to infiltrate, leading you unsteadily to a higher level of enlightenment. This is angst as high art, misanthropy made musical marvel, and the message is deafenly clear: Marilyn Manson, Fear Factory, Orgy and the like, pack up your toys 'cause daddy's home. Reznor succeeds in creating an immersive smorgasbord that not only demands but forces total submission; it is more than the sum of it's considerable parts and possibly surpasses its inspirations.

'And then he appears to lose it. The second half of the album stomps around aimlessly on *Pretty Hate Machine* synth squelches and squeaky beats, lacking much of the sang froid and grand atmospherics that have gone before; and sounds so much like a regression for it. If the first CD was akin to being transported into the nightmarish technological future of *The Matrix* then, comparatively, the concluding half is *The Phantom Menace*'s dayglo Fisher Price hamfest. Most immediately promising number "Starfuckers, Inc" is merely Trent out-Manson-ing his former protégé in his sleep, while only "Ripe (With Decay)" comes close to reaching the heights of the earlier material.

'Ultimately, you can't help but be impressed – *The Fragile* is without a doubt one of the releases of the decade. But at half the length it could have been the one.'

With the benefit of hindsight, it was probably unfair to demand that anyone made a snap judgement of *The Fragile*. Unlike previous Nine Inch Nails albums, it was not one that would instantly gratify the listener. There is just so much operating on so many layers that it actually takes a long while to pick through it all, to explore it and to appreciate what he was trying to do.

It was an album out of time. Although it sounded contemporary and leading edge, it harked back in many ways to the pre-punk world of ponderous great albums. Even the title seemed to be borrowed from English cod-classicists Yes (they released an acclaimed 1971 album called *Fragile*), while the presence of Ezrin linked him to Pink Floyd and Belew to King Crimson, bands which were the very apotheosis of serious large-concept high-progressive rock.

On one hand Reznor seemed to be fighting the prevailing zeitgeist of dumbed down kiddie rock, but on the other he was actually part of a much wider rediscovery of progressive rock. Tool, A Perfect Circle, Massive Attack, Stereolab, Aphex Twin, Squarepusher, Plaid, Radiohead, Rachels, Tortoise, Mogwai, Björk and The Verve were all unashamed proponents of a new school of prog that lacked the pomposity of the 1970s dinosaurs but revelled in experimentation and discovery, the shock of the new.

Possibly after years of relentless simpleton music – let's face it, Fred Durst ain't no fancy-pants interlectual, no sir – both bands and fans want something more in their music. A backlash against the prevailing wave of the past few years is inevitable: the 'pimp rock'/'frat house punk' axis, from Limp Bizkit to Alien Ant Farm contains the seeds of its own destruction. Having defined its own limitations so starkly, it has nowhere else to go.

'Most rock music to me is so incredibly boring right now that it's ridiculous,' Reznor told New Zealand magazine *Rip It Up*. 'I think that any time humour becomes a major factor of rock music then something's really wrong. I was watching TV today and I saw Beck, Foo Fighters, and a host of other bands all with funny videos, it's not my cup of tea. Bands like Blink 182 and all that kinda shit, I don't find it offensive, I'm just glad that I'm not in that band, you know? Like, how could I feel good about singing "Pretty Fly (For A White Guy)" every night? I want meaning out of music and depth and integrity and sincerity, I aspire to put that in my own music and I demand it from bands I listen to.'

Having been embraced by metal fans, Reznor was now seriously at odds with the mainstream of the genre. Metal has always shyed away from 'art', seeing too many embarrassing moments as bands tried to – intellectually – punch too far above their weight. There's a long tradition of 'smart' metal – wry and knowing bands like Blue Öyster Cult, high concept bands like Queensrÿche, even dumb music made by smart guys like The Rollins Band – but 'art' metal is a fairly recent innovation. Yet suddenly there are loads of groups out there bubbling under who are namechecking King Crimson, incorporating elements of 'art' and theatre into their live shows and making 'difficult' (and all the other euphemisms like 'challenging') music. Although this new 'art rock' was to reach its high-water mark in mid 2001 with the release of Tool's long awaited *Lateralus*, *The Fragile* could be said to be the first serious evidence of this shift in the base and values. Listening to a rash of new Nine Inch Nails and Tool influenced bands like Five Pointe 0, Crave and the late Earthtone 9 you can hear bands just bursting to break away from the traditional rock formula. And Nine Inch Nails on *Still*, released as a bonus CD in the *And All That Might Have Been* package may sound daring after years of industrial thrashing but to anyone unfortunate enough to be of an age to actually remember bands like Gnidrolog, Henry Cow or Caravan - look them up on the internet - it actually sounds familiar. It has always been thus. All popular music forms in the past 100 years start off as primitive, disreputable noises played by musicians who are only a notch up from the pimps and criminals they play for and end up being performed in concert halls and discussed in university seminars. From the first ragtime bands before the World War I to the 'abstract' jazz of John Coltrane in the '50s and '60s, from Little Richard standing on his piano in a pink suit pretending to fuck it to Björk performing with composer John Tavener on PBS, it starts on 'the streets' and dies in the academy.

Although it was still recognizably a rock album, the sheer density of *The Fragile* invited the listener to immerse themselves in it, to wallow in it, to decode and deconstruct it, to peel away the layers in search of meaning, to become obsessive about it. There was a danger that, like Pink Floyd's *The Wall* and other monumental works of alienation and depression, *The Fragile* was in danger of becoming the record of choice of the terminal nerd, the rock 'n' roll equivalent of a *Star Trek* obsessive 'Trekkie'.

Yet any fears that Trent had alienated his audience were allayed when the album entered the *Billboard* album charts at number one the week after its release, a feat that not even *The Downward Spiral* managed. All seemed right with the world: dummies like Creed may rule the world in the minds of bean counters at the major labels, but when it came to the crunch an album of intense, dark and uncommercial music racked with guilt, angst and pain could still scream and howl its way to the top ahead of the latest smooth R&B, plastic rap or nu punk cheapie. As Bart observed in *The Simpsons* episode 'Homerpalooza', guest starring The Smashing Pumpkins: 'Ah, making teenagers depressed is like shooting fish into a barrel.'

But week two saw it drop out of the Top Ten and subsequent weeks saw it disappear completely from the charts.

12 Beyond The Fragments

'I see that I'm saving rock 'n' roll. Billy Corgan failed, now it's up to me.'

- Trent Reznor

Reznor's tour with *The Fragile* was to take him to nearly 100 major shows all over the world, including the tragic Roskilde festival in 2000 when fans were crushed by the crowd at the front of the stage. The band once again included Robin Finck who had left to join Cirque Du Soleil and later Guns N' Roses. Their album *Chinese Democracy* was no nearer completion at his departure than when he joined. And they say Reznor takes a long time to make a record...

'I'd made the decision to come back before I'd heard the record, which is something I did intentionally. I'd been in contact loosely with mostly Danny [Lohner] through the past couple of years, so I knew what stage they were at and that they'd never replaced me – they'd never needed to for a live situation,' Finck told *Kerrang!* 'It was a difficult decision to make because I was so wrapped up in what I was doing at the time and I was proud of the work I'd done. But when it came down to it, I couldn't imagine NIN going out without me or with somebody else. I'm in a good place right now.'

But, according to Reznor himself, it was to be the last tour of this kind. He was rightly pleased that – at last – he had assembled a band that, while he was unquestionably the leader, he was able to completely trust. 'The new drummer Jerome Dillon is excellent...the musicianship level in the band is higher than it has ever been,' he said. Yet as an artist he now had a considerable stock of songs to choose from and the ones that he wanted to play were not particularly the ones that the crowd wanted to hear. The set still included songs from *Pretty Hate Machine*, for example.

'I was very proud of it and feeling that a lot of effort had paid off, the co-ordination of the production, the whole presentation,' he told me. 'And I also realised that in a good and bad way that the tour was kind of a retrospective of everything I've done. I thought then "Well I don't think I'm gonna do this again." I remember that with the band we learned pretty much every song I've ever written and whittled it down to what the folks want to hear as opposed to what we'd like to play and I based that decision on the fact that I've gone to enough shows as a fan where I generally want to hear a well-rounded collection of music that I love as opposed to the entire new album. I was torn whether to do what I wanted to do or a more crowd-pleasing show, which is what it turned out to be.'

A few years before this, David Bowie had decided that he would no longer play songs from his 'classic' albums. He played one final 'greatest hits' tour before declaring 'year zero' and playing only material drawn from more recent albums. Inevitably, many fans were disappointed, but he was determined not to fall into the trap that ensnared so many contemporaries of becoming a sort of living museum, of becoming increasingly detached from the creative heart that had actually produced all this material in the first place and becoming an irrelevant nostalgia band.

'I know that if I get this band that I have and we splatter ourselves in corn starch and play "Head Like A Hole", people are gonna like it. I pretty much know that that will happen because I've been doing it for 10 years. So the idea of – not only in the studio – trying to re-invent and try new things and push myself. I wouldn't mind trying some new things,' Reznor told me.

While the sales of *The Fragile* showed that there was still a hunger for fresh new music from Nine Inch Nails, there were enough Reznor fans who were now no longer interested in music but would happily have paid ad infinitum to see him trotting out a set of 'Head Like A

Hole' and 'March Of The Pigs' until he was getting wheeled onstage in a bath chair. It was a fate that he was keen to avoid.

The initial shows in Europe, with support from Atari Teenage Riot, exceeded any and all expectations. The band looked astounding – wearing matching black shirts and makeup – and Reznor was able to practically break the set in the middle to play 'La Mer' with a back projected film of the sea before going back into jackhammer mode.

Written at his Big Sur retreat, 'La Mer', a pastoral piano piece, had echoes of the Debussy suite of the same name.

'That was what started the whole recording process,' Reznor told *The Sunday Times*. '"La Mer" was the centre piece. The first big chunk of the album was all instrumental.'

It was an eerie sensation to be standing crammed into a vast space with a crowd of fanatical Reznor devotees all standing in absolute silence as he played this quiet piano interlude. Eerier too were the lyrics, which sounded like a plaintive suicide note: 'And when the day arrives/I'll become the sky/And I'll become the sea/ And the sea will come to kiss me/For I am going home/Nothing can stop me now'.

He said: 'I was sitting in Big Sur, losing my mind. Debussy's contribution was that you need to be regimented, with whatever you decide to do. When I was sitting there, Debussy and I had a mind meld for a second. I felt the need to plagiarise the title, "La Mer". He revolutionised the Mozart bullshit world of everything that was rigid and stabilised.'

Rock 'n' roll's flirtations with classical music were notoriously embarrassing, from Emerson, Lake And Palmer performing rock versions of Mussorgsky's 'Pictures At An Exhibition', Yes making increasingly pompous pseudo-romantic period music with quasi-mystical science fantasy lyrics to 'serious' classical musicians like John Williams unleashing the painfully awful Sky albums in the 1980s. Yet a quiet movement was taking place underground. Bands like Rodan, like Trent all classically trained musicians and composers, split to form Rachels, whose 1996 album *Music For Egon Schiel* pre-figures 'La Mer' in that it was heavily influenced by Debussy, Schumann and Erik Satie – and The Shipping News, a more post-rock version of the same.

There was a reconciliation of sorts with Marilyn Manson when he appeared in a video for 'Starfuckers, Inc'. Doubly surprising because there was some speculation that the song was actually directed at him, not least because of the line: 'Now I belong I'm one of the chosen ones/Now I belong I'm one of the beautiful ones' referring to Manson's own 'The Beautiful People'.

Reznor added a coda from Carly Simon: 'You're so vain/You probably think this song is about you.'

The song was a scathing attack on the cult of personality, the hollow world of celebrity: 'My God sits in the back of the limousine/My God comes in a wrapper of cellophane/My God pouts on the cover of the magazine/My God's a shallow little bitch trying to make the scene/I have arrived and this time you should believe the hype/I listened to everyone now I know that everyone was right/I'll be there for you as long as it works for me/I play a game it's called insincerity/Starfuckers/Starfuckers/Starfuckers Incorporated.'

Speaking to *Kerrang!* only months before there seemed to be little indication that they had buried the hatchet: 'I knew him for a while. We sat and shared ourselves. The Manson other people know is not the guy I know. I haven't run into him for some time, but all the shit that's gone on between us comes down to one thing – fame distorts people. When I signed him, I knew there was gonna be a time when he was going to want to get out from under the umbrella. He'd get tired of questions about what Trent was like. Then his popularity rises and distortion occurs. I'm not blaming everything on him – there's a shared responsibility here. I doubt if many people think I'd be a great person to have as a friend. I didn't say anything about it at the time, but that fucking book and those quips about Nothing Records are very irritating. There was a lot of revisionist history going on with the storytelling to make his position seem a little better. Some of these things are the reason there's now no communication between us.'

Manson had gone out on the road with Hole on the 'Beautiful Monsters' tour promoting his *Mechanical Animals* and Courtney Love's *Celebrity Skin*. The signs were ominous: days before, he told *NME* that she was 'a real opportunist' and that he 'wouldn't consider her a friend' while – amazingly – Courtney was worried that Manson's *laissez faire* attitude to drugs would be harmful to her daughter Frances Bean! She also took umbrage at her depiction in his book *The Long Hard Road Out Of Hell* as an out of control harridan. The two bristled at each other publicly: 'I asked myself what is the last band in the world I would ever, ever want to tour with, and it was Hole, beyond a doubt. But then I thought, I love a challenge, I like to surround myself with aggravation, it helps me perform better. And I thought, well, here's a chance to show Courtney the difference between being a celebrity and being a real rock star. We're just going to blow her off the stage – my show will be the biggest and greatest rock show of the '90s.' Manson told *The San Francisco Examiner*, 'She never talked to me until I sold a million records. Sometimes we talk and it seems OK, other times, she's just a bitch. I really don't like her too much.'

Courtney hit back by walking off the tour after two weeks, citing 'production difficulties', later saying: 'My response was "It's all camp. It's a big joke." But then I watched a little of it and thought, "Wow – this is wrong." Why willfully be a part of creating that kind of dark energy? Unfortunately for me, I've been involved with energy that's really, really dark that I wasn't trying to create, and all of a sudden, years later, I'm allowing myself to be a part of that. It was very regressive and ridiculous, and it was wrong.'

The ground was tilled for a reconciliation and at Nine Inch Nails' New York show, Manson joined Reznor onstage for 'Starfuckers, Inc' and Manson's own 'The Beautiful People'.

'It feels good to be back united again, because I think that the bad guys have taken over,' Reznor told *MTV News*.

'We shouldn't be competing. There's much more terrible music out there that we should unite against,' Manson added.

In the video, Reznor takes a date (Manson in drag) to a carnival, where they toss balls at plates adorned with the faces of Fred Durst, Billy Corgan, Michael Stipe and even Manson himself.

'We remember a phase where every time you opened up *Rolling Stone*, there's a picture of Michael Stipe popping out of somebody's underpants, and then it was Billy Corgan everywhere,' Reznor said.

'We didn't want to make a video that was like, "We're bitchy because Limp Bizkit's doing better than we are...in their minds,"' Manson explained.

'Look, I'm not going to say Limp Bizkit sucks,' Reznor added. 'You know it. I know it. I'm not going to say it.'

Courtney Love, who is portrayed by a lookalike in the video as an aging, overweight, overly made-up former prom queen who resides in the carnival's dunk tank atop a vat simply marked 'waste'.

'Manson said it best: There's mean, and then this is just brutal,' said Reznor.

Inevitably, after being pelted by custard pies, she is dunked in gunk.

It was rather like walking into a room and punching everyone there: a few people that deserved a punch would be hit along with the innocent bystanders. Why Reznor would single Michael Stipe out rather than his buddy Bono – a much more ubiquitous and self-righteous figure – is mysterious. Courtney was an easy hate figure: revelations that Billy Corgan had helped her write most of her album *Celebrity Skin* and the discovery of demos where Kurt Cobain played songs from *Live Through This* seemed to add credence to the belief that she was a talent-vampire, regardless of the fact that both were good albums whoever actually wrote the songs. She was also in a sense her own worst enemy, from assaulting fans in the crowd to her odious fawning at the oscars where she was felt to have 'gone Hollywood'. Her film career had taken off with her role in *The People Vs Larry Flynt* and films like *200 Cigarettes* proved that she was a competent actress. But to many of the alt.rock crowd this smacked of heresy. Fred Durst, on the other hand, despite Manson's protestations, was a much harder target. Limp Bizkit were riding high on the momentum of their album *Significant Other*; 'Starfuckers, Inc' coincided with the release of *Chocolate Starfish And The Hotdog Flavored Water*, their breakthrough album. They have been singled out as the cause of everything from teenage suicides and killings – in the wake of the Columbine shootings in 1999, there were reporters desperate to establish a link between the band and the deranged high school gun rampage killers – to the decline of standards in rock 'n' roll. They are everybody's scapegoat. If Limp Bizkit did not exist, it would be necessary to invent them.

Durst was no reluctant celebrity, unlike Reznor. He would turn up to the opening of an envelope, dispense controversial quotes that made for great news stories and regularly got into celebrity spats. As one-time producer Ross Robinson told *NME*: 'Fred's willing to put his face in front of every camera and that's pretty rare for bands because they get tired of it. He's always out there. He's willing to do whatever it takes and so is she. I don't know, maybe it's a race to sell more records. Y'know, that's their game. It can't last too much longer, but if it does, good for them.'

Trent and Manson seemed removed from Limp Bizkit: pale, pasty and clad in black, they looked like quasi-aristocratic vampires from the novels of Reznor's New Orleans neighbour Ann Rice. Durst, in comparison, came on like a man of the people, a regular beer drinking guy who watched Monday night football, wore his back to front baseball cap to hide his growing bald patch and carried a slight paunch from too much barbecue.

The rift between Manson and Durst opened with a posting on the official Marilyn Manson website where he described Durst as 'one of the illiterate apes who used to beat you up at school for being a fag'. With Reznor, as we have already seen, the problem was more deep rooted.

In 1999 Trent told *Rolling Stone*: 'I like the challenges of flirting with the mainstream. I think we can do it honestly. Let Fred Durst surf a piece of plywood up my ass.'

Durst responded by saying: 'Trent Reznor is obviously unhappy with how he's alienated the world, how long he took to make a record, and how he thought he was immortal. We're just here doing what we do and we have nothing to say about anybody. I wish [him] luck and I feel sorry that [he's] so jealous and mad at [himself] that [he has] to talk shit.'

Both Nine Inch Nails and Limp Bizkit were signed to Interscope but there may have been a sense in which Trent was no longer the favoured son, replaced in their affections by Durst, who was taken onto the board of the label in 2000. Although Reznor had his own imprint, apart from Manson, they had not exactly enjoyed a string of commercial success. Durst on the other hand had brought them bands like Cold and Puddle Of Mudd.

When Bizkit parodied Reznor on 'Hotdog' they had to seek his permission to quote the lyrics. Trent gave it, saying that it would be petty to stop the release of their album.

And while Reznor paid lip service to the fact that hip-hop had replaced rock as the most creative music in America, it was Durst who was actually making the explicit connections between rock and rap.

The feud was one sided, since Durst was a long-time fan of Nine Inch Nails, particularly of the highly commercial *Pretty Hate Machine* and in early 2002 told a German magazine 'I'm pretty sure that the upcoming Limp Bizkit album will be the most heavy and best that we've ever done. I just contacted Trent Reznor's management to ask if he wanted to produce a few tracks of the next album. That probably shows how serious we are about the intensity and being heavy.'

'I made no bones in the press about my displeasure with Limp Bizkit, and I've kind of rethought that,' Reznor told Launch.com. 'I mean, one time I was getting barbed in an interview by somebody, prompted to say bad things [about Durst], and I said, "Look, I said what I have to say. I don't need to be the bitter guy pointing the finger at the successful band with zero integrity... I really don't want to do it."'

Although it was certified double platinum by the Recording Industry Association of America (RIAA), *The Fragile* almost bounced back out of the charts as quickly as it had entered. This was partly due to the fact that upon its release Nine Inch Nails were touring Europe – apart from the Night of Nothing club shows and a secret launch gig in New York, it had been five years since they had toured the US.

'The tour we did in Europe, Australia and Japan was a bit more well-rounded, a greatest-hits-style package. I feel that the American audiences are more scrutinizing. We've restructured every element of the show to the point where I wouldn't take out projections this time because we had already done that here. Even though somebody who is 15 now would have been 10 the last time we played, I don't want to repeat myself.' But the changes in the musical climate meant that an artist like Reznor whose main goal is to make music is squeezed by an artist whose main goal is to be famous. The all pervasive celeb culture – where people become famous for being famous rather than for actually achieving anything – was taking its toll. Why wait five years for somebody like Trent Reznor to deliver his masterpiece when you could sign up one of the contestants from *Survivor*, put them in a studio with some professional songwriters and session men and churn out an album that – however bad – would chart and recoup its initial investment within a year?

'A lot of artists – including myself – are getting squeezed and it's not about art anymore, but about being on *Total Request Live* and being shiny and golden, wearing the right clothes and kissing the right ass. I got D'Angelo's record the other day, because I like some of what he does. I read the liner notes, and he's kinda just ranting, but he's got some good points in there. You're complimented much more on your business affairs than on your talent.'

Trent was not above making money: he made no bones about the fact that he did remixes, including Puff Daddy, for dollars rather than for arts sake. But it seems that the tyranny of market forces means that from now on there will be less and less scope for anyone to create something worthwhile unless they are in the superstar league like REM. There was some evidence, then, that things were starting to go awry in Trent's relationship with Interscope.

'I'm on a major label now that I don't think believes in me very much. I hope they do, but I don't think they do. I made a record that I think is...I cried when I heard it. As an artist and a human being, it's the most I can make in my life, but I don't want to kiss ass to get it played. 'Cos I think it's art. You should frame it on your wall. Maybe I'm pretentious,' he said in an online chat with fans.

'I don't think there's any sort of commitment from record labels now in an artistic sense to cultivate a band that might be around 10 records later – a Cure, a Depeche Mode, a Jane's Addiction,' he said. 'If they came out right now, you wouldn't hear about them. Because they're not a commodity,' he told the *Cleveland Plain Dealer*. 'If you're not a Backstreet Boy or you're not a disposable hip-hop act or you're not the alternative to the 14-year-old demographic, the Limp Bizkits, it's difficult to exist right now.'

The fightback started with the launch of 'The Fragility V 2.0' tour in 2000, his massive North American tour.

'Interscope used to be a label that believed in artists. Now it's all about profit, period... I can either sit back and bitch about it and let the record drop off the charts, or I can promote it myself. We funded this tour ourselves. Not Interscope. Us. The reality is, I'm broke at the end of the tour. But I will never present a show that isn't fantastic. I've adopted a philosophy of the way to present Nine Inch Nails live that incorporates a theatrical element. I want it to be drama. I want my rock stars to be larger than life, you know? The Kurt Cobains of the world, I'm sick of that shit. I don't want a gas station attendant being my hero. I grew up with Gene Simmons. I grew up with Ziggy Stardust.'

Despite initially poor ticket sales, Reznor was determined to push forward, maintaining quality control over the live shows rather than cut losses.

The visual highlights of the show included mid-set videos done by Bill Viola, an acclaimed figure who produces video installations in museums and art galleries.

'I'd just like to elevate the concept of a rock performance, rather than have it be the same thing all the time in a venue designed for sporting events,' says Reznor. 'I'm just trying to notch up the intellect a couple of levels. That's what appeals to me.'

He also wanted to document their tour on film and took a crew on the road to shoot some footage on digital video for release at a later date.

'We hired a bunch of DV cameras and filmed the last 15 shows of the tour from seven positions and recorded the audio in a DIY fashion. It's not like an HBO special with Bon Jovi with swooping crane shots. We're compiling it on Apple Macs,' he told *Kerrang!*

The shows were well received by fans, kicking off – symbolically – in Cleveland. The critics were initially rather sniffy, sensing blood given the comparatively poor sales of *The Fragile*. Countless pieces with the headline 'Nine Inch Stale' appeared, rather unimaginatively berating Reznor for not being Korn and for having had his initial success in the 1990s.

Wall Of Sound's Laura DeMarco noted: 'The audience seemed far less interested in songs from Reznor's new album, which made up half the show. The ominous, opening "Somewhat Damaged" elicited some cheers, but the linear, laid-back instrumentals from *The Fragile* that Reznor chose to feature in the middle part of the set left the crowd cold, even when he stepped behind the keyboards on the delicately pretty "La Mer". The group's playing on these songs was perfectly competent, though the accompanying Discovery Channel-esque footage of falling raindrops and beaches added to the background-music, soundtrack-like feel.'

The *Cleveland Free Times* said: 'After a solid start, Reznor and his band would content themselves with delivering a competent, solid performance that never reached the overblown proportions needed to really make an arena show work. Throughout their set they performed at a degree just below boiling. Some of the band's strongest numbers, such as the usually searing "Wish" and their biggest hit, "Closer", were fairly toothless, garnering surprisingly docile crowd reactions. The show certainly had its moments, particularly in a bruising take on "Gave Up" and "Head Like A Hole". But for the most part, NIN turned in a precise, machine-like performance that played like Nintendo in the year of the Dreamcast.'

Chicago's *Sun Times* said: 'It was as if a five-piece band was trying to deliver music scored for a 40-piece orchestra. The outline was there, but it just wasn't the same in terms of power, grandeur, or complexity... It was a losing battle. On their worst night, Chicago's industrial pioneers Ministry were ten times better – and even their act was old by 1992.'

'Unlike Korn, a band that manages to convey a spirit of celebration and community within its tales of alienation, Reznor comes across as being self-immersed and emotionally paralyzed...obsolescence – the current rallying point for '90s superstars such as Reznor and the Smashing Pumpkins' Billy Corgan. Perhaps Reznor, who feels commercially sucker-punched by boy bands and Britney, can find inspiration in something other than his misery. An attempt to find the way out – whether he succeeds or fails – would make a great starting point,' said the *Indianapolis Star*.

Support band, A Perfect Circle, had some difficulty, meeting not so much hostility as indifference, despite the fact that their presence on the tour had garnered a lot of interest. Maynard James Keenan, their singer, was an established artist with Tool. A Perfect Circle were almost like a side project that he and room mate Billy Howerdel cooked up to fill in time while Tool were on hiatus between *Aenima* and their 2001 masterpiece *Lateralus*. But it was a side project that threatened to outshine Tool and actually caused some consternation in the ranks of America's premier progressive band, wondering if their singer would actually return after enjoying major success touring with Nine Inch Nails.

A Perfect Circle's *Mer De Noms* sold 188,034 copies in its first week of release in 2000. Maynard was also involved in the long-mooted Tapeworm project with Trent and would also debut the one and only Tapeworm song – 'Vacant' – at a show (and resulted in the track turning up on Napster minutes later!).

But the tour was comparatively successful despite odd dates that did not sell out. Yet some of the criticism must have got to Trent: he prided himself with being at the cutting edge, yet here were people claiming that he was stuck in the past. They say that nothing dates quite as quickly as the future and to some extent Reznor's imagery – quasi cyberpunk 'dark' techno-fetishist futurism – was dated, like a 1950s concept of a rocket ship or a ray gun.

In Chicago, Reznor was invited to play a show for a local radio station.

'They said, "Do whatever you want." I thought it'd be interesting if we went in with a deconstructed vibe – I played grand piano and Robin played acoustic guitar,' he told the *Denver Post*. 'It wasn't an "unplugged" situation, but the songs sounded surprisingly good out of the context you normally hear them in. It got me thinking...'

The songs from this show – which were to appear on *Still*, a mini-album included in the live package *And All That Could Have Been* in 2002 – were quite unlike anything that Reznor had attempted before.

In late 2000, Nine Inch Nails released *Things Falling Apart*, a remix album featuring reworkings of tracks from *The Fragile* as well as some unreleased material left over from the album sessions, including a cover of Gary Numan's 'Metal'. Adrian Sherwood and ex-Skinny Puppy man/Manson co-producer Dave Ogilvie were among the remixers.

He told radio station KROQ: 'During the process of recording *The Fragile*, there would be times when some of the other key people around here – like Keith Hillebrandt my programmer, Danny Lohner the bass player and Charlie Clouser the keyboard player – would take songs and ask if they could reconstruct them, or deconstruct them or try different approaches. Some of these have different instrumentation than the versions that appear on *The Fragile* and some are just deconstructed to be barely like the original. There were a bunch of these lying around that I thought were pretty cool. We debated about offering them for free on the internet or using them as B-sides of singles that ended up not coming out. It just seemed a good idea to put out an EP of them, as kind of a coda or side note to *The Fragile*. It's not for the masses as much as it is for people who like *The Fragile* and want to hear some alternate approaches. The thing that appeals to me about that format is that it's not meant to be the next major work. It's a place where I can experiment and present some things that I didn't overanalyze, which I tend to do on a lot of Nine Inch Nails records. I also brought in a few different friends of mine. Adrian Sherwood did a remix of "Starfuckers, Inc". Dave Ogilvie did a mix. But it's not like, "Let's take the new Madonna song and have everybody that's hot at the moment remix it for every current dance style, so it can be played in the Latin clubs and at a rave..." It's the anti-approach to that. This is more like headphone music. Or stuff to put on on rainy Sunday afternoons.'

Inevitably, people started asking about what the follow-up to *The Fragile* would be like. There were all sorts of these tantalizing hints and an agreement even from Trent that he couldn't do anything like his previous Nine Inch Nails work again, despite the fact that he had actually perfected his sound and was at last working with a great band.

After the US shows, Trent returned to Europe, appearing at the ill fated Roskilde Festivals, where nine fans were killed during Pearl Jam's set. It was a scar that was to haunt them subsequently. Reznor was set for a London date at a two day metal festival called the Lost Weekend the following day but cancelled, reportedly because drummer Jerome Dillon had gastric flu, much to the chagrin of fans: half of the 9000 strong crowd walked out after the cancellation was announced.

The tour wound up in Italy. More shows were considered - Reznor had told one interviewer that he would 'tour until the end of time' to promote *The Fragile* if he had to - but in the end Reznor cut his losses, unwilling to burn himself out as he had done with *The Downward Spiral* and accepting that *The Fragile* was destined to be a cult item. It was an album that everyone felt would grow in stature as time passed and new generations discovered it, but that was not good news to the bottom-line boys in the record business.

He told the *Chicago Tribune*: 'I'd love it if 20 years from now one of my records is referenced like Talking Heads' *Remain In Light* or Bowie's *Low*. But the troubling aspect to me is that in the 1970s music was still looked at more as art than as just product. The only thing I can do about it as a musician is make music I think matters to me, and inspires me and motivates me. I hope if nothing else somebody puts on my record and goes, "What the hell is that?" That would be great, because I got a reaction.'

'Being quite frank, when I released this record we didn't have great commercial hope for it, necessarily. A long time had passed [since *The Downward Spiral*] and the climate had changed. Now I'm delivering a record that's very unfashionable. It's long, it requires a lot from the listener in the day of the short attention span, and there's no real obvious single on it,' he told the New Orleans *Times-Picayune*. 'It's been a weird roller coaster. It took me, once again, sitting myself down and saying, "This is the record I wanted to make. It's the best record I could make, and I'm proud of it. Success or failure is not based on the amount of records sold." That sounds like a defensive stance, like I'm trying to make myself feel better. But I love that record. I'm doing what I can do to try to get people to give it a chance, take a listen to it, and maybe open their minds a little bit.'

13 And All That Might Still Be

'Unfortunately *The Fragile* became the poster-boy for flop albums.'

- Trent Reznor

Live albums stink. Half-arsed cruddy sounding sub-standard bum-note laden toss, cynical contractual obligations that only the most cloth eared or anal-retentive collector would ever actually want to own. Live albums (and by extension live videos/DVDs) have neither the raw excitement of a great gig or the hard hewn perfectionism of a great studio song. There are exceptions – AC/DC's *If You Want Blood, You've Got it*, Hawkwind's *Space Ritual* and The MC5's *Kick Out The Jams* are as good as or better than any of their studio records – but mostly they are cheap and shoddy cash-ins designed to milk the last few bucks from the diminishing fan base of creatively washed up bands on the road back to nowhere.

And All That Might Have Been is one of the rare exceptions: a live audio and DVD video retrospective of the first decade of Nine Inch Nails caught on the Fragile tour, it perfectly conveys the same madness, the beautiful destructiveness that is Nine Inch Nails onstage.

The DVD package, filmed on tour by Rob Sherridan using digital video and mixed in surround sound even brings a new dimension to the usual lame concert films.

Nine Inch Nails in the studio and Nine Inch Nails onstage are two completely different entities, and it was as a control-freak studio boffin, playing all the instruments himself, that Trent Reznor moulded the sound. But history will judge the Nine Inch Nails line-up here – Robin Finck and Reznor on guitars and keyboards, Danny Lohner on bass and keyboards, Charlie Clouser on keyboards and theremin, and Jerome Dillon on drums – as one of the classic live acts of the past decade. 'Head Like A Hole' and 'Closer' still retain the visceral punch-in-the-gut power that they have when played live.

It's not the usual live album second-best version of the studio recordings: it's a worthy addition to them, an interpretation that enhances them.

Live albums are usually a watershed in a band's career. For Trent Reznor *And All That Might Have Been*, released in early 2002, is a full stop to over a decade of apocalyptic noise. It also marks the beginning of the next phase of Nine Inch Nails, which will be radically different to anything that has gone before.

'We were nearing the end of the tour supporting *The Fragile* and I'm standing onstage one day and – not that I do this that often – I was congratulating myself on getting the tour together,' says Reznor. 'I was very proud of it and feeling that a lot of effort had paid off, the coordination of the production, the whole presentation. And I also realised that in a good and bad way that the tour was kind of a retrospective of everything I've done. I thought then "Well I don't think I'm gonna do this again." I remember that with the band we learned pretty much every song I've ever written and whittled it down to what the folks want to hear as opposed to what we'd like to play and I based that decision on the fact that I've gone to enough shows as a fan where I generally want to hear a well rounded collection of music that I love as opposed to the entire new album. I was torn whether to do what I wanted to do or a more crowd-pleasing show, which is what it turned out to be in fact. I wanted to document that we did this and to act as a kind of look at what we had done up until that point as a way to move away from it into the future.'

From the release of *Pretty Hate Machine* in the early '90s through its follow-up *The Downward Spiral* to *The Fragile*, Reznor has always been unsatisfied, always pushing the work a little bit further. Even when he has finished a song, he keeps going back to it, reworking and remixing. It's as though there is no actual definitive version of a Nine

Inch Nails song, as though the version he releases on record is only the latest one, and that others – equally good – preceded it and will follow it. That he is now looking at a drastic overhaul of the very concept of Nine Inch Nails itself – which has been everything from Trent playing all the instruments in the studio to the fully fledged 'proper' band who went on the road with *The Fragile* – is hardly a surprise.

Trent, speaking in early 2002, sounds comparatively upbeat; the man who has been the ultimate miserable goth icon for the past decade often lived up to his image, going through phases of sullen pique and monosyllabic mutterings in interviews. The idea that he would play a live set as a crowd pleaser – and admit that that's what he had done – would have been anathema to the younger Reznor. But as he repeatedly makes clear, this album is the end of an era, the end of Nine Inch Nails as we know Nine Inch Nails and maybe it's this process of laying to rest a lot about what Nine Inch Nails stood for that has filled him with optimism.

'I need to risk failure to move into whatever is next. The whole format of the band needs to evolve,' he says.

Does that imply personnel changes?

'Personnel will probably change to fit whatever the new format is. It needs to be a bit more fresh and daring from my perspective.'

When you say failure do you mean commercial or artistic failure?

'Say I decided to go out and play with an acoustic piano on the next tour. That may be risking failure because I know that if I get this band that I have and we splatter ourselves in corn starch and play "Head Like A Hole", people are gonna like it. I pretty much know that that will happen because I've been doing it for ten years. So the idea of – not only in the studio – trying to re-invent and try new things and push myself. But also in terms of the live presentation, I wouldn't mind trying some new things.' Going on tour with an acoustic piano is actually one of the possibilities that Trent is looking at. He's also adamant that he is never going to tour in the way that he has done in the past.

'From the point of view of practicalities, the guy who sets up the tour would like you to play seven shows a week. Whereas I might like to play two or three shows a week so that I can rest in between and my voice isn't ruined and every time I walk out onstage I'm ready to kick ass rather than thinking "Well I really wouldn't have minded getting more than one and a half hours of sleep" because we had to leave right after the show to get to the next show.'

On the bonus CD *Still* – recorded at a Chicago radio show – that accompanies the live album, Trent 'deconstructs' songs from *The Fragile*, performing them at a piano in a live setting.

'In the middle of "The Fragility" tour I had new resources that I didn't have before. The new drummer Jerome Dillon is excellent...the musicianship level in the band is higher than it has ever been. We messed around at sound checks and took songs that we enjoyed playing but that for one reason or another didn't fit with the live set and somebody asked us to do a radio show that was "deconstructed" – I don't want to say "unplugged" – where I played piano, there was no drum kit, where it wasn't a big rock production. And I wanted to be sure that this live album had value when it wasn't part of the DVD set, so we remixed the stuff and felt that these tracks showed a different side to the band. A sort of rainy day melodies that showed a more melancholy side to counterpoint the bombast of the live show. It's the hangover for the next day...it's not all forks in the eyeballs!'

Reznor is adamant that *Still* is a little curiosity rather than a signpost to the future direction that Nine Inch Nails will take and that while an acoustic club tour is on the cards, it's not necessarily the only path that Reznor will take in future.

'My favourite venues are clubs, where you can see the audience and the audience can see you without 30 feet [10m] of security barriers in between,' he says. 'At the same time the other things I'd love to do would be to actually score a movie.'

Reznor's involvement in the soundtracks for both Oliver Stone's *Natural Born Killers* and David Lynch's *Lost Highway*, both for the Nine Inch Nails contributions and the other artists that he brought in

– most notably Marilyn Manson who actually appeared at the end of *Lost Highway* – was instrumental in the way that movie soundtracks began to change in the 1990s, at best standing as entities in themselves (and at worst as spurious cash-ins bearing only a tenuous relationship to the songs that you actually heard on the screen).

'Actually my big dream is that David Cronenberg calls me up and tells me that he's got a project that he wants me to work on from start to finish,' admits Trent. 'I'd love him to say I've got an uneasy film and I need some uneasy music to go with it. I'm not saying that this would replace what I want to do with Nine Inch Nails, but I'd like to go in and find out what I don't like about it!'

If you see Trent Reznor only as some missing link between Al Jourgensen and Marilyn Manson, the results may be quite shocking. For fans reared on the frothing at the mouth cyberpunk of *Pretty Hate Machine* and the deep negativity of *The Downward Spiral*, it may even smack of betrayal and heresy (and you should never forget that Reznor's first stage appearance was as Judas in the school production of *Jesus Christ Superstar*). There's an obvious comparison to be made between the nine songs on *Still* and the stark, atonal minimalism of Radiohead's *Kid A* and Björk's recent *Vespertine*. It's the sort of record that must have had all the high-ranking label bods cancelling Christmas the moment they heard it.

The Fragile was Trent Reznor's most ambitious work: at nearly two hours, it required the sort of commitment that you give when you sit down to read *Crime And Punishment*. But in a dumbed-down post-dotcom age when the corporate marketing chimps have trouble reading their own nametags never mind Dostoevsky, Nine Inch Nails had made an album that his record company Interscope simply could not understand or deal with. Despite entering the *Billboard* album charts at number one, selling double platinum, the album is still perceived as a monumental commercial failure.

'I knew it was a pretty difficult record in a disposable climate. It was asking a bit much to put a two hour album out and expect people to deal with it. But I guess I'm more disappointed in the fact that the media seem to equate commercial success with things being good. I have to admit that I get defensive when that starts coming up because it's an album that I loved and I still love. In the long run it probably hurt it more because it went into the charts at number one. If you'd asked me when I put out *The Downward Spiral*, I'd never have thought then that it would even sell a tenth of what it did and I think in the long run the success of that album was damaging to my career in a way in that now the stakes have gone up. As a musician you're put into this competitive race to see who sells more record in the first week than the other guy. And that's not a good thing if you're in music for the reasons that I'm in it. My anger at the distributor stems from their inability to understand what they're trying to sell. When you push my record through the same hole that Eminem goes through, it doesn't fit, and when it started to not fit, it was left to die on the floor.'

Trent is also understandably pissed off that Radiohead's *Kid A*, an album as musically 'difficult' in every way as *The Fragile*, is perceived as being a success.

'I love Radiohead and this isn't anything against them. Those albums *Kid A* and *Amnesiac* were two of my favourite records of last year,' he says. 'With the distributors I have, if they had tried to understand or put a little more thought into presenting it to the right people. On that label alone, the Radiohead machinery, the people behind them, succeeded. Our machinery failed. Radiohead's team of people that sold you that record also sold you the perception that it worked, it was a success. The actual numbers would challenge that [*The Fragile* actually sold more than *Kid A*, shifting 800,000 double albums in the US to Radiohead's 300,000] but it didn't matter. They won, you didn't question it. Interscope dropped the ball. And it's not like they're doing me a favour with this album because they are still taking the lion's share.'

Tellingly, Interscope did not understand why Reznor wanted to include *Still* - which contains new songs - as a bonus disc in the package and wanted to promote it as the 'new' Nine Inch Nails album.

'They were saying "Well what is this? A new album? Why are we giving it away?"'

Although it was well received, the live album, DVD and *Still* rather crept onto the market apologetically, unlike the splash made by *The Fragile*. Reviews were positive: 'All the songs are quiet, lyrical and deeply unsettling – persuasive proof, if any is even needed at this point, of the musicality that underlies Reznor's most ear-shattering work, and of his ability to disturb even at his moments of greatest beauty,' said *Rolling Stone*.

But the world had changed and like it or not whatever he did in future would attract less attention.

Speaking to *Kerrang!* he said: 'I wish I had released more music and I can only really blame myself for that. Every time I've been approached by the media to represent a group of people or a movement I've told them not to look to me for that. But, yeah, I wish things had been slightly different. But I have enough faith in the music-listening public that they'll soon have had enough of look-a-like blonde Barbie doll singer fluff music, or enough comic book scary bands, or enough fucking rap-metal, or enough bland power rock bands. I mean with that last one, my fucking God, what has happened there? Eddie Vedder should start suing these people for sounding like him, for fuck's sake. But myself as an artist, if I don't have anything to say, then what is the point of saying anything? And I would imagine that the guy from Bush probably never asked himself that question. "Wow, I can sound a lot like Nirvana! Kick ass! We'll get a deal". Unless he's that stupid that this never occurred to him. But what's the point of imitation apart from the fact that it begets more imitation? And you do have to wonder what is going on in these people's heads. The eternal answer to why I haven't had more music out is that I didn't ever sit down and say, "Let me make a band that's about this, where I'll write about this..." It just came out. When I first started making music I had no idea what I was going to write about. I knew I liked The Clash but I didn't know shit about politics, so either I could fake it or I could try and make it honest. So in the end I resorted to journal entries that had almost been written as lyrics, stuff that I thought I could never let people hear. But when I did it had a power to it because it was so honest and I was saying things from the heart. Even though I'm not particularly proud of what I'd said, it did have a certain truth to it. But it got to the point where I was giving so much of myself away that I could almost predict where I was going to head, so I'd written an album about it before I'd even done it. And that was basically despair, drug addiction, isolation, desolation and suicide. And I began to wonder if this fatalistic approach was my destiny? And all the while the band is getting bigger, so you think, "Well, I must be doing something right." And I wonder if that has been a little bit corrupting.'

The past few years has seen a lot of clear outs from labels of bands that they no longer considered to be commercial. Ultimately if a band like Sonic Youth is no longer associated with a major label, it makes little difference: many artists have actually found that they were able to thrive – financially as well as artistically – outside the protective indentured-labour of major labels. If Reznor parts company with Interscope by the time the next album hits, it will come as little surprise, though whether this move is initiated by Trent or by the label remains to be seen. It is clear that the honeymoon is over.

But *The Fragile* is an album that continues to sell, albeit at a low level, and, as those who have already bought it will testify, it is an album that seems to be continually remade with every listen. Its future is in the long term: like all classic albums that died when they were first released – The Velvet Underground's debut, Love's *Forever Changes*, Iggy And The Stooges' *Fun House* and *Raw Power* – *The Fragile* has already passed into rock 'n' roll history and the actions of a few short-termist marketing men and bean counters will not affect this.

But the rock 'n' roll market is volatile and just because we are going through a phase where the labels are not so much following the dictates of the market as trying to create those dictates for their own convenience does not mean that things will always be thus. Trent Reznor has always been at odds with the prevailing mainstream, even if sometimes that just seemed like tantrums from a spoiled noisy goth kid. What is interesting is that every so often the mainstream approaches him. Although he's no fan, there are a whole school of bands who grew up on *Pretty Hate Machine* and *The Downward Spiral* who have access to gear that Reznor could only have dreamed of in 1988. Static X, Orgy and Disturbed have all to some extent borrowed bits and bobs from various points in the career of Nine Inch Nails. And while the straight copyists like Stabbing Westward and Filter made little headway, these are all popular bands. And if, as has been mooted, there is an alliance between Limp Bizkit and Trent Reznor, could such a combo really be stopped from global domination?

And Reznor himself has always been open to what's going on. There is a rich subterranean seam of new electronic music from the wilder and funkier shores of UK garage to the extreme noise terror of Digital Hardcore DJs and bands like Atari Teenage Riot (who supported Reznor in Europe), patric C, Shizuo and EC8OR. The dummy bands like Creed and Westlife are just the scum on the surface.

In my fantasy world, Trent will come back with an album that has guest appearances from PJ Harvey and Tom Waits, additional production by Alec Empire and maybe some guitar and vibes from Spiritualized's Jason Pierce. Well, you can dream...

It took two years in the studio before *The Fragile* saw the light of day. Other projects - like the long mooted Tapeworm collaboration involving Trent, Charlie Clouser from Nine Inch Nails, Maynard James Keenan from Tool/A Perfect Circle, Danny Lohner, Phil Anselmo of Pantera, various members of Prong and Helmet - may be already with us by the time you read this book or be about to arrive soon. But are we going to be drawing our pensions when the next Nine Inch Nails studio album hits?

At the time of writing, the Tapeworm website was updated with a picture showing a studio log with completed titles (though blurred within Photoshop so as to be actually unreadable) with Reznor's name at the top. The driving forces behind Tapeworm were initially Charlie Clouser and Danny Lohner, who were supposed to have more musical freedom in this project.

'Tapeworm's music is electronic with big guitars, beats and melodic yet aggressive vocals,' said Danny Lohner.

Clouser started working all out on Tapeworm in 2000: 'Every time I would be doing a remix, Danny would hear it through the wall and come in and give me shit and say, "What the hell are you doing that for? You should be working on the Tapeworm shit that's in your computer waiting for you to mix it!" So I've had enough of the damn guilt trips and I'm only working on Tapeworm for the next few months.'

It all seemed to be on hold again until March 2002, when the official Nine Inch Nails website showed a snap of Maynard James Keenan, Danny Lohner, Atticus Ross (12 Rounds) and Trent Reznor during Tapeworm recording sessions at the Nothing Studio in New Orleans. Nine Inch Nails drummer, Jerome Dillon, confirmed in June 2002 that Trent, Danny and Dillon were working on some demo tracks with Reznor playing bass and programming.

'"With Tapeworm I'm just a member of a band. Obviously I'll have studio expertise and so on, but I'm not the one calling the shots."

"Which is a new situation for you?"

"Which is a new situation for me."'

With musical technology making yet more leaps forward – Trent experimented with holographic sound on the DVD of *And All That Could Have Been* – the next official Nine Inch Nails album could hit any time this decade, though as of 25 June 2002, the Nine Inch Nails official website was updated with a picture showing Trent in the studio with Alan Moulder. Whether he was just stopping by the mixing desk or actually working on an album, we have no real clues. There was also a suggestion that some of the 70-odd minutes of music left over from *The Fragile* would finally see the light of day, though Reznor was adamant that, while he did not rule this out, he was intending to start afresh.

'Actually I'm writing a lot at the moment. I've got a notebook full of stuff and quite a bit of semi-finished music waiting to be worked on. I'm still in the process of editorial, deciding what makes sense for Nine Inch Nails proper, but in my head right now I feel like I've unloaded a lot of baggage that's made me a lot more appreciative of my life and my reason for making music. My enthusiasm level is high right now,' he laughs. 'I'm just ready to get beat back down again!'

As to what the next level of Nine Inch Nails will actually sound like, we can only speculate based on the evidence of *The Fragile*'s more out-there moments and the stripped down approach on *Still*. Asked what he's listening to he mentions Radiohead, Julian Cope's *Autogeddon* and *20 Mothers*, Spiritualized, Mercury Rev and Beethoven's Piano Sonatas. Clues or red herrings? When can we expect this?

'In a perfect world...well, I'm starting on it now. 2008 or something? No, I'd love for it to be completed by the summer. That's my goal.'

The clock is ticking.

Tommy Udo
London
July 2002

14 With Teeth

'I was getting sane while the world was going crazy.'
- *Trent Reznor*

If you're Nine Inch Nails, you can't go out with *The Fragile,* an effort that was - to be kind - rough going even for diehard fans and - to be blunt - hard evidence of a particular type of drug-addicted self-obsession and paranoia that was plaguing Trent Reznor.

If you're on *Time*'s 1997 list of the 25 most influential people in America, you don't bid farewell two years later with an album that hits the charts at number 1 only to slide down ignominiously, like a drunk propped against a wall, in the weeks that follow.

If you're Trent Reznor, you always have something more to say.

For all his efforts to cultivate the image of a reclusive loner, Reznor gives shockingly good interview. He clearly likes to let the world know what's on his mind, even if his thoughts are messy and even if he contradicts himself entirely later on. Sometimes, however, it can take a painfully long time for him to express himself.

The Fragile was years in the making; years of false starts and second-guessing. There were the standard 'creative differences' with the record company, a horde of collaborators, retooling, reworking, re-recording. It must have been an agonizing slog, yet in looking back on the creative process that led to *The Fragile* it's possible to come away with the impression that the biggest obstacle to the album's fruition was Reznor himself and the demons he was fighting: the pressures of fame, emotional insecurity and most importantly substance abuse.

As he would later admit to the *Daily Telegraph,* when he listened to *The Fragile* some five years on, 'It sounds like a paranoid, terrified person.' And after two years of touring in support of the album, with all the excess and exhaustion that entailed, 'I was ready for death, there's no other way to put it.'

It took more than five years from the release of *The Downward Spiral* in early 1994 to the release of *The Fragile* in mid-1999. In that time, Reznor wrote or conceived of 117 tracks, by producer Alan Moulder's count. Undoubtedly more than that if every bit of noodling and knob-twiddling were added into the total. The resulting double album, clocking in at some two hours of playing time, thrilled but ultimately confounded the fans who had spent half a decade panting for its release.

In the end, it was just all too difficult: for listeners who couldn't figure out the record and for Reznor, who had to contend with the arduous production process, the tour that followed and its often-lukewarm reception. In fact, the Fragility tour in early 2000 lost millions in Reznor's own money. (How much he lost and why he lost it would come to light years later.)

The question now was: Did Trent Reznor want to go through all that again?

The answer: Not in a hurry.

Time between *The Downward Spiral* and *The Fragile:* five-plus years. Time between *The Fragile* and the next album: even longer.

Yet Reznor could not expect the music industry to remain in neutral gear while Nine Inch Nails took stock. He had to hope NIN fans would wait for him. And he had to hope he could give them something worth waiting for - something with teeth.

Following *The Fragile* - of which Dan Century wrote in Legends Online, 'Trent is furious, confused, disgusted, disappointed, depressed, desperate - you name it. He's everything but happy.' - Reznor had determined to quit using drugs and alcohol. Ironically, it was a decision that left him more 'fragile' than ever before.

The alternative, of course, would have been considerably worse, exemplified as it was by a near-fatal heroin overdose in 2001 during the Fragility tour. 'I was unable to keep my act together,' he later recounted to Ben Wener of the *Orange County Register*. 'I couldn't make art anymore in that condition.' Checking into rehab in New Orleans was a predictably humbling experience. 'It's tough to feel really cool when you're throwing up in a psych ward.'

Following rehab: an upward spiral of sorts. 'When I got sober, my first priority was trying not to want to kill myself,' Reznor told *Rolling Stone*. 'After that I was aware that drugs and alcohol had not only taken away my soul but also took away my love for music. It'd become a job...and the competitive nature of business consumed me.'

Which is not to say that Reznor had lost his taste for competition. Last time out, the music industry tide was lifting the proverbial boats of Fred Durst/Limp Bizkit, Korn and Foo Fighters among others. The last being the new pet project of Dave Grohl, late of Nirvana and out from behind his drum kit. True to form, Reznor had nothing nice to say about any of them, and the fact that these bands might have derived some of their fan bases from the NIN fans who couldn't wrap their heads around *The Fragile*.... Well, it was best not to think about that.

Now, in the early years of the 21st century, as Reznor prepared to work on the next NIN release, he began to take stock of the state of the industry.

As usual, rumors began to fly as soon as word leaked that Trent Reznor was recording. In April 2004, *Rolling Stone* reported that Reznor was in Los Angeles working with Rick Rubin. 'I'm re-energized, my life's in order and I'm ready to combat shitty music,' Reznor told the magazine.

Per *Billboard*, the top-selling modern rock singles and albums for 2004 belonged to Linkin Park, Incubus, Three Days Grace, Jet, Blink-182 and Hoobastank. Which was producing the so-called shitty music? Or maybe Reznor was griping about Usher, Alicia Keys and Outkast, who ruled the pop charts that year. Surely he wasn't referring to Johnny Cash, who topped the year's country singles chart with his cover of NIN's 'Hurt.' (Of which, more later.)

Reznor promised that the new album would be a 'complicated concept record reduced to simple songs...minimal and a bit brutal.' According to *Rolling Stone,* it was to be titled *Bleed Through.* Eventually Reznor decided that the studio boffin term had too many alternate interpretations and he retitled the disc *With Teeth.*

The year 2004 would find Reznor leaving his home in New Orleans and relocating to Los Angeles, ostensibly to be closer to the music industry. 'The fake tits and celebrity bullshit is all there, but it's not *all* there is there,' he would later argue to *Revolver.*

In November of that year, perhaps as an offering to the fans who'd waited so patiently for a new release they could embrace, the remastered, 'deluxe,' tenth anniversary edition of *The Downward Spiral* was released on Nothing Records. Disc 1 of the two-disc set was Reznor's own SACD Surround Sound remaster of the album. Disc 2 had 13 B-sides, remixes and rarities, including previously unreleased demos of 'Ruiner' and 'Heresy.'

Part of *With Teeth* was recorded at Reznor's Nothing Studios in New Orleans. Reznor, Rick Rubin, Alan Moulder and Atticus Ross also recorded and produced tracks at The Village Recorder, Sound City Studios and Grandmaster Recording Studios in Los Angeles.

'The Hand That Feeds' was released as a single more than a month before the album would hit stores. On April 2, 2005, it debuted at number 8 on the *Billboard* Modern Rock Tracks chart and the magazine postulated that it was 'poised to become the biggest single of NIN's career.'

Clearly Reznor had plenty of fans among the music press and within the industry who were pulling for him to return to form with the new album. Not least of those would have been the folks at Interscope - Trent Reznor's nemesis Fred Durst included. When 'The Hand That Feeds' went to number 5 on the *Billboard* Modern Rock Tracks chart one week later, Interscope became the first label ever to hold four of the top five positions on the chart in a single week. Audioslave's 'Be Yourself' was number 1, 'E-Pro' by Beck held the number 2 slot and 'Little Sister' by Queens of the Stone Age (who would soon embark on a tour with NIN) was number 4.

There was a caveat here for those who chose to acknowledge it. The marked departure from the 'grandiose' (*Arizona Daily Star*), 'sprawling' (*Florida Times Union*), 'difficult, overambitious opus' (*Orange County Register*) known as *The Fragile* - which even Reznor had conceded was challenging for listeners - indicated that the new album would be notably more accessible. '*With Teeth* follows more closely on the patterns established with the first two albums,' the *Arizona Daily Star* noted.

'Sure,' wrote Brian Teitelman in *Billboard*, 'some purists will claim that it is too commercial. But this will be supplanted by new fans that may have been in diapers during the band's early- to mid-90s heyday.'

'Commercial' and "Nine Inch Nails' in the same thought? For a moment the earth tilted ever-so-slightly on its axis.

In a review of the album, *USA Today*'s Edna Gundersen wrote, 'This time Reznor aims for radio with a straight-ahead rock cruncher, "The Hand That Feeds," and scattered tunes with compact, accessible structures.'

That's not to say that anyone was accusing Nine Inch Nails of selling out. (Who would dare?) But there was a palpable sense of relief over the fact that Reznor seemed to be easing up just a bit after the sonic assault of *The Fragile*.

When *With Teeth* was released on May 3, 2005, reviewers received it with cautious optimism. 'There are far more hits than misses, and die-hard fans will be elated,' wrote Katy Kroll in a *Billboard* review, adding that the new album was a departure from the 'somewhat indulgent' *The Fragile*.

Fans were elated. The album sold more than 270,000 copies in its first week and came out on top of the *Billboard* 200. 'The last thing I expected was to debut at number one,' Reznor told the *St. Louis Post-Dispatch*.

And everyone - *everyone* - remarked on NIN's enlisting the services of Foo Fighters' Dave Grohl for live drumming on the album. 'Grohl brings ballistic punch to the party,' wrote Gundersen in *USA*

Today. The music sounds 'deceptively less electronic than anything NIN has released in recent years,' said Teitelman in *Billboard.*

But perhaps Stephen Thomas Erlewine said it best, writing in *All Music Guide*, 'Quite frankly, this is the record that NIN should have released if Reznor had wanted to capitalize on the success of *The Downward Spiral*. It's loud and angry, doesn't skimp on hooks and is heavy on both sexy, robotic dance beats and crashing rock rhythms (some supplied by everybody's favorite drummer, Dave Grohl, but not that you'd know it from reading the CD; the chintzy packaging not only has no credits, it has no booklet.)' In fact, Dave Grohl played drums and/or percussion on seven of the album's 13 tracks.

Of course, Reznor had previously slagged off Foo Fighters for their 'funny' videos, but that was typical Trent Reznor modus operandi.

Name a band or an artist that was enjoying success at a time when NIN was about to release an album, and you'll find an interview in which Reznor belittled their efforts: from Marilyn Manson to Beck to Radiohead, Korn and Limp Bizkit. Following the release of *With Teeth,* it was Glaswegian rockers Franz Ferdinand - of all things - that drew Reznor's ire.

'All the cool people say they're good, but it sounds like I'm getting bullshitted by somebody,' he told *Rolling Stone*. 'Their record kind of sucks,' he said to the *St. Louis Post-Dispatch*. 'It doesn't speak to me on any level emotionally or purposefully. They're a band you're meant to think is cool because they're marketable.'

Rivalry and competition fuel Reznor's fire, and if no genuine animosity exists between NIN and whoever is climbing the charts in a given month, Reznor will try to create some.

Then, just as quickly and inexplicably he'll invite them into the studio or onstage or both. 'I wrote some of these tracks [for *With Teeth*] with a Grohl-esque performance in mind,' Reznor told *Rolling Stone*. 'I asked him if he was into it and that was that.'

Even more surprising, perhaps, was the live band Reznor had assembled to tour in early 2005 before the album's release. It included a bass player known to his mum as Jeordie White and to the rest of the universe as Twiggy Ramirez, late of Marilyn Manson. (Interestingly, around the time that Reznor was writing and recording *With Teeth*, Twiggy Ramirez was auditioning to replace Jason Newsted as Metallica's bassist. He didn't get the job. Nor did former NIN bassman Danny Lohner, although both auditions are documented in the 2004 film *Metallica: Some Kind of Monster*. One wonders what Reznor had to say about that.)

Discussing the band with Austria's Go TV in July 2005, Reznor noted that Jeordie White had been a friend for a long time and 'I like being around him.' He added, 'I've been much less of a dictator in terms of what people play this time around because I trust that what they're doing is good and I respect their musicianship.'

The tour preamble kicked off in late March 2005 - a week before the single's release and more than a month before the album would drop - with dates at small venues, mainly in California. 'We are punishing you with new songs,' Reznor would warn the audience before launching into a handful of tracks from *With Teeth*.

Yet Reznor had learned, albeit reluctantly, that it was advisable to give the people what they want. NIN's two sold out shows at New York's Hammerstein Ballroom in May 2005 included a strong representation from NIN works going back to *Pretty Hate Machine* and *The Downward Spiral*, among them 'Terrible Lie,' 'Sin,' 'Gave Up' and 'The Big Come Down.' (Keep in mind that although the NIN back catalogue was not large it did span more than 15 years, and such songs were veritable chestnuts.)

The *With Teeth* tour, which would ultimately run nonstop for more than a year, kicked off at the 2,000-seat Saroyan Theatre in Fresno, California, on March 23, 2005. Even the Fresnonians couldn't understand why. NIN had never played there before. But the locals - not to mention the loyalists who hadn't seen the band perform live for years - were not complaining. When tickets went on sale, they were gone in 10 minutes; according to the *Fresno Bee*, it was the fastest sellout in the theatre's history.

Reznor's first choice for an opening act was Queens of the Stone

Age. 'I truly, really like that band,' Reznor (remarkably!) told the *Fresno Bee.* 'I talked to Josh [Homme, lead singer] and he was all for it.' The two bands made the rounds of arenas in 2005 along with other supporting acts.

During the 'amphitheatre' leg of the tour (leg 4 if you're counting) in 2006, NIN was joined by the reunited Bauhaus - singer Peter Murphy, guitarist Daniel Ash, bassist David J and drummer Kevin Haskins - who even broke out some new tunes and began writing together again. They still refused to cop to the 'goth' label - 'That was just how we dressed,' David J told the *Virginian-Pilot* newspaper. 'We thought we were punk gone elegant.' - but their presence on the tour was a tribute to what they hath wrought all those years ago.

There were setbacks of course. No tour is without them. Early on was the loss of drummer Jerome Dillon, who had to bow out early when he began to suffer chest pains. They turned out to be atrial fibrillation brought on by the combination of the adrenaline in a prescription medication Dillon was taking and the natural adrenaline rush of playing drums onstage in front of thousands of screaming fans. In fact, Dillon was forced to leave the stage during a September 2005 performance in San Diego just 45 minutes into the show and he suffered similar symptoms days later in Sacramento. He was replaced a few weeks later by Alex Carapetis, who was replaced a few months after that by Josh Freese.

Despite the fact that Dillon had worked with Reznor and NIN since 1999, and could presumably have been considered part of the 'team,' his departure could easily be mistaken for an unceremonious sacking. Following the October 1, 2005, show at the Hollywood Bowl, Dillon received an e-mail that 'led to me leaving the band,' he later told the *Columbus* (Ohio) *Dispatch* (his boyhood hometown paper). 'On a human level, it was a very big disappointment. When you work for somebody for that long, you would think that your time would account for more.'

One could hardly blame Dillon for feeling hurt. Not only was his working relationship with Reznor comparatively long and fruitful, but Dillon had also soldiered through the agonizing Fragility tour as an eyewitness to Reznor's drug-fueled self-destruction. Watching a colleague whom you respect and admire slowly, purposefully poison himself takes its toll. Reznor wasn't the only one to come off the Fragility tour feeling miserable. Dillon - and undoubtedly the other band members - felt it too.

Other members of the live band for the With Teeth tour, in addition to bassman Jeordie White, included guitarist Aaron North, late of The Icarus Line and Alessandro Cortini, an Italian-born keyboard player who came to Nine Inch Nails after reading about auditions on a flyer posted at the Hollywood music school where he worked. 'I was a little nervous,' Cortini later told the *Grand Rapids* (Michigan) *Press.* 'I remember having to learn the stuff for the audition off the live DVD [*And All That Could Have Been*], and I was like, man, I don't know if I'll be able to stand up and play with all this stuff flying around.'

Speaking of 'stuff flying around'... Cortini's comment could not have been more prescient. Just a few nights later at a show in Grand Rapids Trent was hit in the face by a projectile thrown by an overly enthusiastic fan. Hurling a few choice epithets at the audience, Reznor upended his keyboard and stormed offstage. Show over. That the interruption occurred during the opening bars of 'Hurt,' acknowledged by every reviewer as an unquestionable show highlight, was a pity.

In Madison, Wisconsin, another incident. This time, in the heat of performance, guitarist Aaron North allegedly clocked a security guard with his mic stand, knocking the man unconscious. A lawsuit against both NIN and North himself soon followed, with the victim demanding compensatory damages for negligence and assault.

When the tour moved from small theatre venues to arenas, the stage show expanded to include more visuals. 'I get involved with the set design, lighting and the use of film because I always hated seeing bands in arenas,' Reznor told the *St. Louis Post-Dispatch.* 'I [try] to make it unique, help frame the music and make it more like theatre so it starts at one place and winds up at another.'

And while there were plenty of NIN 'classics' in the set list, most of them had been retooled to give the audience something new to ponder and, in no small part, to keep the band from growing bored banging out the same versions of the same songs night after night.

Sense of nostalgia and nightly heartfelt renditions of 'Hurt' notwithstanding, Reznor still had plenty of spleen to vent at the live shows, and his target of choice was U.S. President George W. Bush. Playing 'The Hand That Feeds' before a giant scrim showing footage of 'Dubya' waltzing with his wife was one of the most incendiary moments of NIN's live performance.

Yet that particular 'special effect' caused some consternation among the brain trust at MTV when it came time for the 2005 MTV Movie Awards. NIN was scheduled to perform on the broadcast and planned to adapt the visuals from the stage show as a backdrop. The network expressed misgivings about attacking the Commander in Chief on air so pointedly and suggested that NIN forgo the visuals. Reznor suggested that MTV might be more comfortable if Nine Inch Nails decided to forgo the performance altogether (though he probably did not suggest it in quite those words). MTV thought that was an excellent suggestion and NIN was dropped from the lineup. They were replaced by Foo Fighters.

15 Men in Black

'I think it's probably the best anti-drug song I've ever heard,
but I don't think it's for me.'

- Johnny Cash

With the release of *With Teeth* and the relentless tour schedule that
followed - the U.S., Europe, Japan, Australia, back to the U.S., Canada,
Brazil, U.S., Canada, U.S., Europe...Crikey! - 2005–2006 shaped up
to be one of the busiest periods in NIN history.

Reznor also found time to wage war in court against his former
business manager and partner John Malm. In the classic artist-versus-
management complaint, Reznor alleged that Malm and his company,
J. Artist Management, had fraudulently withheld millions of dollars
over the course of their 15-plus-year working relationship with Trent
Reznor and Nine Inch Nails. The official charges, filed in 2004,
included fraud, breach of fiduciary duty and breach of contract.

Among the gems unearthed during the three-week jury trial in
New York was the fact that Malm had essentially tapped Reznor's
personal accounts to fund the Fragility tour and to keep the
struggling Nothing Records afloat, even though both were expenses
that Reznor and Malm were to have shared. In addition, Malm had
given Reznor trademark registrations to sign that made Malm part
owner of the iconic NIN 'backwards N' logo, and thus entitled him to
a percentage of the proceeds from its use. In sum, Malm had not
done right by his star client, Reznor, and had kept entirely too much
of the NIN revenues for himself. Ironically, the whole issue would not
have come to light - let alone gone to trial - if Malm had not initiated
a lawsuit for unpaid fees against Reznor the year before.

For Reznor, spending May 17, 2005, testifying in court, when he should have been out celebrating his fortieth birthday, was a small sacrifice to make. The jury found for Reznor, awarding him nearly $3 million in compensation for overpaid commission fees and other damages. It was now time for Trent to move beyond his past.

Trent Reznor circa 2005 was a changed man. He'd mellowed in the way that only a hardcore rocker facing 40 could; he began looking outward.

'The tone of Nine Inch Nails...has been focused on darker subject matter and that's been a way for me to exorcise it out of my system and examine it and explore it and figure out what's going on in my own head,' Reznor told the *Boston Herald* in 2005. 'There's still plenty of things to think about and examine that I can do with a functioning brain. I don't feel like I have to write depressing music to be Nine Inch Nails.'

The demons inside his head were still wielding their pitchforks, but Reznor had also realized there were plenty of things to be outraged about in the world around him. Not that he was in danger of turning into 'Sir Bono' and hobnobbing at think tanks - at least not yet - but the clean and sober model of Trent Reznor was preparing to take on some of the problems of the world.

As it turned out, one of the greatest problems, and one of the greatest causes of outrage in the United States in late 2005, struck very close to home indeed for Trent Reznor. That was Hurricane Katrina and its aftermath.

Reznor had become an honorary citizen of New Orleans during the 14-plus years that he lived and worked there. For an artist seeking inspiration - not to mention chemical stimulation - New Orleans has always been fertile ground. Reznor was a regular at Tipitina's, one of New Orleans' best live music venues, and a frequent visitor to just about every other club and bar in town, partaking of all the Big Easy had to offer.

Then on September 2, 2005, everything changed.

Hurricane Katrina slammed through New Orleans; Biloxi,

Mississippi; and the entire region in between, leaving behind devastation that had not visited the southern United States in such proportion since the American Civil War.

Tears and heartache over the loss of life and the destruction of one of America's most individual cities quickly turned to outrage, as the federal government blundered through a mishandled 'relief' effort to assist the thousands (many of whom were already living below the poverty line) who were left homeless by the storm and resultant flooding. In a flash, Katrina became yet another rallying cry for the millions of Americans who were disillusioned - nay, disgusted - by the Bush Administration. And leading the rally: one Michael Trent Reznor.

'When it's a place that you're intimately familiar with...to see it just destroyed and to see the people treated in a disrespectful, inhumane way by our government, it went from disbelief and shock and grieving to just outrage,' he told Mike Osegueda of the *Fresno Bee*. 'I honestly don't know how many more glaring, crystal-clear examples of incompetence and criminal negligence and greed and inhumanity and racism we can see from this administration before we do something about it.'

So Reznor did something about it.

To benefit hurricane relief, he signed guitars for auction on eBay and allowed 'Leaving Hope' (off *Still*) to be used, free of charge, in public service announcements. He performed on the ReAct Now: Music & Relief benefit concert broadcast on MTV, VH-1 and CMT (Country Music Television). He even gave props to Kanye West, whom he met for the first time soon after the hurricane, for West's harsh criticism of the Bush Administration's apparent disregard for black people. And he used his name-brand clout - perhaps not for the first time, but certainly for the most significant time - to get things done in his one-time hometown.

Before Katrina, NIN had signed on to play the Voodoo Music Experience, then a seven-year-old New Orleans music festival traditionally held on Halloween weekend. (Foo Fighters reportedly were on the original bill as well.) But in October 2005, just over eight weeks after the hurricane, New Orleans was in no condition to host a music festival. The organizers considered canceling it entirely, but Mr. Reznor, among others, was having none of that.

In the end it was agreed to move the main event to Memphis. But first there would be a Voodoo Music Experience prelude - a free show for 20,000 police, firefighters, military, National Guard and rescue personnel in New Orleans. It was a concert that show organizer Stephen Rehage emphasized would not have happened without Reznor's involvement and Reznor's insistence that a show be performed in New Orleans. As Reznor would tell the *Houston Chronicle*, he did it 'to send the message out that the city isn't dead.' (That particular interview in late October was especially well placed, as many New Orleans residents had been evacuated to Houston after the storm.)

The Memphis show at AutoZone Park, a minor league baseball stadium, featured 25 bands on three stages, a mix of local favorites and headliners. Proceeds from the ticket sales for the Memphis show were donated to the New Orleans Restoration Fund (NORF), also at Reznor's suggestion.

NIN headlined both shows, along with stalwarts Queens of the Stone Age and a reconstituted New York Dolls featuring Sylvain Sylvain and David Johansen. (Foo Fighters dropped out.) And while the Memphis performance was outstanding, it was the New Orleans show that steamed with raw passion. Reznor had spent the day before the show touring storm-ravaged neighborhoods and had sat down with New Orleans mayor Ray Nagin, both of which fueled his sense of purpose.

Describing what came next, Keith Spera wrote in the New Orleans *Times-Picayune:* 'All coiled energy, [Reznor] focused and released his emotions via an intense 90-minute set [that] opened strong with "Head Like A Hole" and "Terrible Lie".... Reznor's final gesture was his most potent. Alone at an electric keyboard, he unspooled "Hurt," his memoir of addiction's isolation.' And while Spera acknowledged that the 2003 Johnny Cash version of 'Hurt' had already supplanted NIN's original in the minds of most listeners, he added, "At Voodoo, Reznor reclaimed "Hurt" as his own. It became a communal moment of mourning for the city. The full band crashed in for the final coda against a blaze of white light.'

Closing the show with 'Hurt,' something Reznor had been doing quite a bit on the *With Teeth* tour, did indeed seem to be a way for Reznor to reclaim the song that, more than once, he'd said 'isn't mine anymore.' And the evolution of 'Hurt,' from what might be considered Reznor's most intimate, most personal composition to a career highlight for someone else, is an interesting milestone on Trent Reznor's own career path.

Originally released on *The Downward Spiral,* with Chris Vrenna playing live drums on the recording, 'Hurt' was a soul-bearing song of addiction, alienation and despair. (At the time, Reznor was the de facto poster child for all three.)

'I hurt myself today/to see if I still feel/I focus on the pain/the only thing that's real,' Reznor sang achingly. It was the type of song that seemed always to evoke a new bout of torment within Reznor. He'd write something so raw and true, leave himself exposed and vulnerable, then he'd feel crushed by the inevitable criticism and analysis - the picking over the bones - after a song or album had been released. That sensitivity, and an understandable unwillingness once again to lay his soul bare for others to poke sticks at, was one of the things that had delayed Reznor's return to the studio before *With Teeth.*

All artists experience moments of self-doubt, and Reznor, so famously trapped inside his own head, seems more susceptible than most to such things. 'Those voices [in my head], left to their own devices, have no problem convincing me how worthless I am,' he once told the *Orange County Register.* The voices will never be silenced entirely, which is good in a perverse way since Reznor would not be Reznor without them. Yet once in a while, something, or someone, intercedes to smother them for a bit.

As Reznor embarked on the early stages of *With Teeth*, that someone was Rick Rubin.

Rubin had become a mentor of sorts for Reznor on his road to sobriety. Most importantly, he was able to instruct Reznor in the fine art of making an album without killing yourself in the process - something Reznor had not quite mastered on his own. And Rubin was a large part of the reason that Reznor took himself out of his comfortable Nothing Records studio - a former funeral parlor in New Orleans - and off to Los Angeles to work. 'By nature...I will isolate,' Reznor told MTV during a pre-*With Teeth* interview, 'so I try to make myself do some things to avoid that.'

The man who founded Def Jam Records with Russell Simmons in the 1980s had produced records for everyone from the Beastie Boys to The Bangles, Red Hot Chili Peppers, System of a Down, Jay-Z and Nusrat Fateh Ali Khan. Besides a demonstrably eclectic taste in popular music, Rubin was known for possessing Zen-like patience and the ability to shepherd artists - particularly 'troubled' artists - gently and constructively on the path to creative rehabilitation.

'I think the act of creation is a spiritual act. [Great songs] are just kind of in the universe. The best artists are the ones with the best antennae that draw it in,' Rubin told the *Los Angeles Times* shortly before winning the Grammy for Producer of the Year in 2006. (Three of the five albums nominated for 2006 Album of the Year - The Dixie Chicks' *Taking The Long Way*, which won, Justin Timberlake's *FutureSex/LoveSounds* and Red Hot Chili Peppers' *Stadium Arcadium* - had been Rubin productions.)

Another Rubin trademark: allowing artists as much time as they wanted or needed to write material for an album. No concerns about booking studio time, appeasing anxious record company execs or selecting singles. For Mr. Five-Years-Between-Albums Reznor, that must have been appealing.

More valuable, though, would be Rubin's ability to suggest ways in which disparate pieces of a vast creative jigsaw puzzle might fit together to form an unexpected whole. That's how he convinced

Anthony Kiedis to open up his journal and to reveal the poem that would become the lyric of Red Hot Chili Peppers' 'Under The Bridge' - an unprecedented melodic departure for the erstwhile funk-rappers, and the song that ultimately launched the band on a global scale.

Rubin already had two disparate pieces of a new creative puzzle in his hands. One was Johnny Cash, then in his seventies, ailing, and working, albeit with modest expectations, to revive his musical career. The other was Trent Reznor, newly sober and shell-shocked by self-doubt, wondering if he would ever write music again - or if the chemicals, more than his own creativity, were responsible for his past success. His Buddhist spiritual leanings might have led Rubin to suggest that the idea of fitting those two particular pieces together simply came from the universe. Fortunately, he had the antennae to draw the idea in.

Reznor's antennae, on the other hand, weren't quite as receptive to those messages from the universe. 'Rick Rubin had been a friend for a long time, and he called me asking how I felt about Johnny covering "Hurt,"' Reznor told Geoff Rickly of *Alternative Press*. 'I was flattered, but frankly, the idea sounded a bit gimmicky to me.'

On his American Records label, Rubin had been working with Cash on a series of albums. They had already put out *American I* through *III*. Now they were working on *American IV: The Man Comes Around*. On the first three albums, Cash had covered a number of MTV-generation songs, Tom Petty's 'I Won't Back Down,' U2's 'One' and Soundgarden's 'Rusty Cage,' among them. This time, in addition to 'Hurt,' the album would include covers of The Beatles' 'In My Life,' Sting's 'I Hung My Head' and Depeche Mode's 'Personal Jesus.'

Rubin brought 'Hurt' to Cash and asked what he thought. Cash immediately related to the song's message: 'A song about a man's pain and what we're capable of doing to ourselves and the possibility that we don't have to do that anymore,' Cash would explain to *USA Today*. Yet, as he later recounted to *Time* magazine: 'I said [to Rubin] "I think it's probably the best anti-drug song I've ever heard, but I don't think it's for me. It's not my style...not the way I do it."'

Reznor, too, had reservations about the Cash cover, beyond the thought that it might be 'gimmicky.' For one thing, past covers of NIN songs - Trixter's version of 'Terrible Lie' and Devo's take on 'Head Like A Hole' are two that he's mentioned - left Reznor a tad underwhelmed. But there was more than that to worry him.

'I thought "Here's this thing that I wrote in my bedroom in a moment of frailty, and now Johnny Cash is singing it,"' Reznor told journalist/author Anthony DeCurtis. 'It kind of freaked me out. When I write a song, I'm only considering myself as the one narrating it. It's my voice. [This] was like building a home, and someone else moving into it.'

Yet Rubin's instinct to match Reznor's song with Cash's performance had a certain symmetry. Both Cash and Reznor had suffered through, and conquered, drug addiction. Both had embarked on a similar long road back to find their artistic cores. And both favored a certain sartorial palette - although while Reznor might be *a* man in black, Cash is *The* Man in Black, now and forever.

Rubin sent Reznor a CD of Cash's recording. (In addition to Cash's personalized vocal performance - more restrained and declarative than Reznor's - one lyric change was made: In Cash's version the 'crown of shit' became a 'crown of thorns.') 'You did a very tasteful job with it,' Reznor told the producer after giving it a listen. Polite, for the 'new' Trent Reznor had vowed to treat those around him with more consideration, and in any event, he had genuine respect for both Rubin and Cash. Nevertheless, it was hardly a ringing endorsement.

Then one more piece of the cosmic puzzle fell into place when Mark Romanek convinced Rubin to let him direct Cash in a video for 'Hurt.' So eager was Romanek to direct the clip, he even offered to do it for free. It's hard to know if Rubin was resistant to the idea, mainly because it's hard to understand why he would be, especially since Romanek's video proved to be the elusive, final piece of the puzzle - that bit of blue sky that completes the picture.

Reznor was in the studio in New Orleans, working with Zack de la Rocha, formerly of Rage Against the Machine, when the package arrived bearing Romanek's video. 'I pop the video in and...wow,' Reznor recalled, 'tears welling, goose bumps. I told [Zack] to take a look. At the end of it there was just dead silence. There was, like, this moist clearing of our throats and then, "Uh, ok, let's get some coffee."'

The throat-tightening, tear-welling reaction to the video was universal. Even years later, it has the power to mesmerise. So much so that a panel of 31 musicians, video directors and music industry professionals - R.E.M.'s Michael Stipe, Björk, Jamie Cullum and Amy Winehouse among them - voted it number 1 on a list of the Top 20 videos of all time. 'The video is just devastating,' said Stipe in a 2005 interview with the *Observer* in the U.K.

Mark Romanek was no stranger to Nine Inch Nails. He'd directed the deeply disturbing video for 'Closer' that quickly entered MTV's hot rotation despite lyrics and visuals that were the scourge of censors. He'd also directed the futuristic video for the Michael and Janet Jackson duet 'Scream,' the video for Lenny Kravitz's thomping 'Are You Gonna Go My Way?' and videos for Madonna, Beck, Fiona Apple and Jay-Z. Oddly enough, Romanek did not direct the NIN video for 'Hurt,' which was shot by Simon Maxwell before a show at the Omaha Civic Auditorium. (Maxwell went on to direct videos for a 'Christian rock' band called DC Talk, who reportedly fell in love with his work after watching the 'Hurt' video. Maybe it was the decomposing fox carcass....)

Perhaps Romanek had wanted to get his hands on 'Hurt' ever since *The Downward Spiral* days. His video treatment of Cash's version was haunting and reverential. A few cynics called it 'hagiography,' but they missed the point by fixating on the Christ images that Romanek intercut at the end. In fact, the video, shot in Tennessee at Cash's home and at the derelict House of Cash Museum and peppered with images of the younger, harder-living Cash, gave extraordinary dimension to the song by placing it in the context of a much older man, with much more to regret. Trent Reznor's battle with drugs and addiction undoubtedly caused him to make those around him hurt, yet his real-life struggles and his rendition of the song - pained and raw as it always has been - paled in comparison to Cash's. No wonder the song and video were immediately embraced as 'definitive' Johnny Cash.

'In the video, Cash is shown holing up at home...his once jet-black mane gone white and wispy, the bullets of his eyes reduced to useless shards of sea glass,' wrote James Sullivan in the *San Francisco Chronicle*. At the end, Sullivan added, 'Cash gently closes the lid over the piano keyboard. In close-up, his thick fingers gently follow the contour. It's a coffin.'

The original video concept was quite different, however. Romanek had envisioned Cash in Los Angeles in a more theatrical environment. He'd even planned a cameo appearance by Trent Reznor. Unfortunately, Cash's declining health prevented him from traveling to L.A. and at the same time forced the shooting schedule to be speeded up. Romanek grabbed a flight to Nashville, then quickly scouted his locations and made his decisions. Many shots were conceived on the fly, from Cash's gold record for *Johnny Cash at San Quentin* discovered with its frame smashed on the floor of the House of Cash to an appearance by Johnny's wife June Carter Cash. ('June came down from upstairs to watch him perform,' Romanek told *Mojo*. 'I saw her expression of sadness, pride and love. I was so moved, I suggested she appear in the video and she agreed.')

Overall, Romanek described the finished video as a 'sucker punch' for the typical viewer, whose expectations of music videos are understandably low. As he explained to *Rolling Stone,* 'Mortality is a very unusual topic for this medium. I think that's what grabs people.' He later told MTV, 'Videos are supposed to be eye candy - hip and cool and all about youth and energy. This one is about someone toward the twilight of his career, this powerful legendary figure dealing with issues and emotions you're not used to encountering in videos. [Cash's] music has always been extremely candid. That's what I wanted to draw from. I didn't want to make a phony video.'

Romanek admitted that neither he, nor Rubin, nor Cash expected any sort of widespread recognition, let alone commercial success, from the video. The director genuinely wanted the gig because he was a Cash fan from way back and didn't want to miss a chance to work with the man. That he wound up receiving 'letter after letter' from people - including David Bowie and Bono - who were profoundly moved by the video was immensely gratifying, 'But I ascribe most of the power to the Johnny Cash-ness of it all,' he said.

More than ever before in his long, convoluted career, Johnny Cash was resonating with audiences across the spectrum. Naturally, CMT was playing the video for 'Hurt,' but MTV and VH-1 were playing it too. The song received airplay on country radio stations, which was predictable, but also on rock and pop stations that might not have had Cash on their playlists since 'A Boy Named Sue' went to number 2 on the pop charts in 1969. Suddenly, everybody 'got' Johnny Cash, and by extension they 'got' Trent Reznor, whose name was being bandied about among country music - and even Christian music - enthusiasts.

Then the award nominations began to roll in. Romanek's video was nominated for six MTV Video Music Awards (it won one for cinematography) and it won a Grammy for Best Short Form Video. At the Country Music Association Awards in 2003, the video was named Music Video of the Year, but more notably - and unexpectedly - Cash won for Album of the Year (*American IV: The Man Comes Around*) and Single of the Year ('Hurt').

'This artist deserves and demands respect from a new generation that wasn't that aware of him,' Reznor told Anthony DeCurtis. 'The MTV exposure - even though they were cowards not to give him the awards he deserved - might open a lot of people up who weren't that aware of Johnny Cash, or of his importance. I felt honored to have been involved in that in any way.'

Sadly, by the time of the CMA Awards in November 2003 something more significant than any awards ceremony had occurred: Johnny Cash had died. And what no one had wanted - but many had feared - happened at the same time: 'Hurt' became Johnny Cash's epitaph. No one could separate the images of the 71-year-old Cash singing his regret directly to the camera from Trent Reznor's poignant, personal words and music. For all intents and purposes, Johnny Cash now owned 'Hurt.'

Yet remarkably - and in a true testament to the man Trent Reznor had become - the songwriter accepted what had transpired, and he saw what he had gained. Cash's treatment of Reznor's song - indeed his interest in recording it at all - provided confirmation to Reznor that his career in music was far from over. It was a critical, tangible indication that his work had more weight, importance and worth than he'd realized.

'It took my breath away,' Reznor told the *Orange County Register*. 'This legend from another walk of life I never thought I would intersect with on any level chooses this song I wrote in a private moment of pain, makes it his own, a breathtaking video is made for it and it becomes something else. It just reminded me how powerful music is. It filled me with this sense of worth, this feeling I could do this again.'

'It was like a pat on the back in a way,' Reznor added to MTV. 'Like, "You can do this. Go out there and write an album."'

Feeling stronger and better about himself than perhaps he ever had, Reznor set to work writing new music with renewed purpose. That was the music that would eventually become *With Teeth*.

And on September 13, 2003, the day after Johnny Cash died, nin.com, the official Nine Inch Nails web site, paid tribute to him in a way that only NIN and Reznor himself could do: It faded to black.

16 Countdown to Zero

'I'm not saying I can change the world, but now I feel like it's my duty as a human to try and do something,'

- Trent Reznor, 2007

Now it is 2008 - mid-2007 actually, close enough at any rate - the time that, back in 2002, Trent Reznor predicted he'd release the follow-up to *The Fragile.* He underestimated himself.

Trent Reznor and Nine Inch Nails have been more productive than Reznor ever anticipated. There have been albums, EPs, tours and natural disasters; none of which we might have predicted when we left our hero after *The Fragile.* There was even Reznor's first solo gig, a 2006 performance in northern California to benefit The Bridge School during which he was accompanied by a string quartet.

There was the re-release of *Pretty Hate Machine* on Rykodisc in 2005 - plus a vinyl edition that dropped in 2006. There was the release of *Nine Inch Nails: Beside You In Time* - a testament to the 2006 North American Live: *With Teeth* winter tour, and the first music programme to be released in DVD, HD and Blu Ray formats simultaneously. It also featured rehearsal footage, videos for 'The Hand That Feeds' and 'Only' along with various other gems.

At the same time we're still waiting for the delivery of *Chinese Democracy* from Axl Rose, and it's entirely possible that we'll see the geopolitical version before the sonic one.

Marilyn Manson married and (by the time your read this) divorced stripper Dita Von Teese and took up with underage actress Evan Rachel Wood. (She's 19 years his junior.) He released *Eat Me, Drink Me* in May 2007 and was scheduled to take to the road with Slayer in July.

Even Smashing Pumpkins, who melted away around 2000, are back on tour - minus James Iha and D'Arcy Wretsky, plus a new album called *Zeitgeist* released in summer 2007.

And at this brief and shining moment, the world and Trent Reznor have caught up with each other. For how long the two will be in synch, and whether this is a benefit or detriment to either the world or the outsider cred of NIN, who can say. Is it disconcerting to think that the thrumming, seething voice-inside-your-head that has been NIN's stock in trade is now so comfortable - even comforting - that it's embraced like a long-lost friend whenever it makes an appearance?

"Clean and sober" - a phrase included in virtually all the coverage of NIN these days - Trent Reznor isn't scary anymore. What you might consider frightening though: Look fast at a photo of the new-and-improved Reznor, with his close-cropped hair and pecs to rival Henry Rollins', and you might mistake him for the actor Luke Wilson of *My Super Ex-Girlfriend* fame.

Trent Reznor is growing old gracefully. He might even be in danger of approaching elder statesman status, tackling, as he does, nothing less than the future of the world on the NIN 2007 release, *Year Zero*.

'For the first time in my life, I wanted to break away from opening up my journal and transferring that into song lyrics,' he said in an interview following the release of *Year Zero*. 'I thought about what was at the forefront of my concern and the state I'm in right now and the age I'm at...just the state of being an American citizen and a lot of concern I have about the direction our country's headed in and the erosion of freedoms...and the way we treat the rest of the world. It felt like something I needed to comment on.'

But let us begin at the beginning: at the countdown to *Year Zero*.

No longer spending hours getting shit-faced and even more hours sobering up left Reznor with lots of free time on the road during the *With Teeth* tour. 'It's fun to play a show,' he told *Revolver*, 'but the rest of the day is just waiting around.'

So, while he was 'waiting around,' Reznor whipped out his laptop and began to experiment. The limitations of the software he had available combined with the brief snatches of time backstage, in hotel rooms and on the tour bus weren't viewed as obstacles so much as parameters in which Reznor and producer/collaborator Atticus Ross could work. Far from stifling his creativity, Reznor found the constraints inspiring. 'If I had a spare 20 minutes, I could come up with a cool beat or passage or a chunk of sound so I had the time to stumble into the thing that felt good to me musically,' Reznor told *RockSound*.

Year Zero began to take shape when Reznor set up digs for three months in the woods near Malibu, California, at a house that was isolated enough to satisfy his need to be alone, but still within striking distance of the Los Angeles nerve center. That's where he began writing lyrics, inspired to a great extent by his lifelong love of science fiction. 'I thought I'd see what would happen if I wrote a story about the future and what it could be like if we continue down this path of madness that we, the United States, seem to be on,' he said to *RockSound*. 'Then I thought of writing the songs as if they were from the points of view of people living in this world, and that's how the record came about. It happened quickly and it happened as an experiment.'

Just as he had set about to reclaim 'Hurt' by performing it live to stunning effect, Reznor was working to reclaim his artistic freedom. *With Teeth* had proved to Reznor himself and to the record company that he had returned to form, or more aptly in Reznor's case, to fighting trim. 'Usually when I finish a record, I have to go into battle with the people whose job is to figure out how to sell the record,' he wrote on his nin.com blog. 'The only time that didn't happen was *With Teeth*. This time, however, I'm expecting an epic struggle. This is not a particularly friendly record and it certainly doesn't sound like anything else out there right now. Artists these days are not encouraged to experiment or take risks, and my punishment is on its way.'

What Reznor had in store as 'punishment,' however, went far beyond his unfriendly album. In fact, it was to be one of the most brilliant overall concepts in music industry history. If the record company was not supportive of his efforts from the start - and, other than Reznor's speculation, there's no indication that they weren't - they certainly got behind him in a hurry, even if the new album did not promise to be *With Teeth* Mark II.

Unlike *With Teeth,* which admittedly possessed a hit-oriented sensibility, *Year Zero* would be a concept album. And Reznor did not have to look far to find his concept; it was everywhere around him. 'I wanted to be honest about what I've been thinking about in recent years, and that hasn't been me,' he told *Terrorizer.* 'It's been the state of the world and just exactly where the hell we're heading morally as Americans. The major emotion behind *Year Zero* is disgust...concern growing into dawning horror.'

While it's clear that Trent Reznor has George W. Bush to thank for providing him with mountains of angst and outrage, *Year Zero* attempts to take the issues of 2007 and cast them on a wider canvas. Officially, the album is set in 2022 - 15 years in the future. 'I took time to imagine what the world would be like politically, ecologically, spiritually,' Reznor explained. 'I wanted to do it in a way that didn't feel preachy and that didn't feel rooted in 2007.'

Nevertheless, *Year Zero* with its 16 thematically-linked songs - from the instrumental 'Hyperpower,' with live drums by Josh Freese, and 'The Beginning Of The End' to the closing 'Zero Sum' - speaks volumes about the state of the world at this very minute. 'There are a couple of things giving doomsaying an extra urgency at the moment,' Reznor admitted. 'One is how close we are to running out of resources, and the clear, visible way we can all see the environment collapsing. Another is the way that radical evangelical movements in the States are coming to the forefront.'

'Don't give a shit about the temperature in Guatemala/don't really see what all the fuss is about/ain't gonna worry bout no future generations and a/I'm sure somebody's gonna figure it out,' Reznor sings on 'Capital G,' a stab at a certain someone who 'signs his name with a capital G.' It's an NIN song that could reasonably be described as catchy, with Josh Freese on drums and a full brass section chiming in.

'Survivalism,' with backing vocals by Saul Williams, a spoken-word artist/poet and Rick Rubin protégé who opened for NIN in Europe in 2005 and joined Reznor onstage at the Voodoo Music Experience in New Orleans, was tapped as the first single. It went to number 1 on the Billboard Modern Rock chart, making NIN only the second act to score four consecutive number 1s on the chart.

Yet, the song that is arguably the most impactful is 'The Good Soldier,' an ode to the young men and women fighting for God and country in far-off lands. It's sad, it's chilling and it embodies what Reznor was trying to achieve with the album by stepping outside his own personal and emotional concerns to write songs from the point of view of other 'characters.' Who is the 'good soldier' who is 'trying to see...trying to believe'? It could well be one of the all-American kids Trent Reznor grew up with in Mercer all those years ago. 'I'm not from New York,' he explained. 'I'm not from L.A. I'm from Pennsylvania so I know these people.'

While reviewers did not embrace *Year Zero* as fervently as they did *With Teeth,* they didn't roll their eyes (or hold their ears) as they did with *The Fragile.* Many pointed to the fact that Reznor had opened up his sonic doors just enough to let hip-hop, funk and new wave beats sneak in. 'Din arm-wrestles melody at every turn,' wrote Edna Gundersen in *USA Today,* 'and while he excels at whipping up storms of industrial-strength static and synthesized freak-outs, Reznor can't camouflage the pure pop craft, gonzo hooks and emotional drama in surprisingly tuneful songs.'

In other words, if you're going to make an album admonishing people about the state of the world and what they should do about it, you have to make it something they'll actually listen to. Or as Malcolm X. Abram wrote in the *Akron Beacon Journal,* 'Reznor [pushes] the abrasive industrial textures to the front while not forgetting that his fans also like to tap their toes.'

One of the things that make Reznor likeable (no that's not a misprint) is his commitment to his fans and his willingness to invite them into the process of making and releasing a new album. It's an old-school way of thinking that has been lost to a great extent as the music industry continues to be homogenized. There was a time, however, when the impending release of a new album was an event in the lives of a band's fans. Trent Reznor has not forgotten this.

'You let [your fans] get straight to the source by answering their questions on your web site and letting them download and remix songs. Why do you give them such access?' asked Mike Osegueda of the *Fresno Bee.*

'Why not?' Reznor replied. 'I try to put myself in the role of the fan and think about what would be cool...what would be exciting. [At gigs] I try to sneak out in the crowd and check out the opening band, or watch people showing up and remember, for most people, this is a big deal. I remember what it was like for me. I saved up money to go to a concert...I planned my ride and saved enough money for a T-shirt. It was an event. It helps me to remember that.'

So long before the release of *Year Zero,* the event began - with a complex and clever multimedia alternate reality game cum scavenger hunt that true NIN fans sussed through a peculiar configuration of letters on a *With Teeth* tour T-shirt and mysterious USB flash drives left in the toilets at NIN gigs. The scheme was put into action by viral marketing firm 42 Entertainment, but it was Reznor's concept and it was all produced with his blessing, and reportedly with his money.

The letters on the tour T-shirt spelled out 'I am trying to believe' - the refrain of 'The Good Soldier' (but of course no one knew that then). Adding .com to the phrase takes you to a creepy web site about Parepin, a fictitious chemical that was to be added to the water supply of Orlando, Florida, in Reznor's futuristic dystopia.

The random USB drives, discovered in loos at gigs in Lisbon, Barcelona and Manchester, England, contained MP3 files of 'My Violent Heart,' 'Me, I'm Not' and 'In This Twilight,' respectively. Selflessly, the fans who found the drives wasted no time in sharing them on the Internet with friends far and near. And the event was in full swing.

Not only had Trent Reznor captured the imagination of rabid fans, who immediately began hitting web sites such as echoingthesound.org where they could pool information about clues they found on their electronic scavenger hunt and decipher what it all meant. He had drawn the attention of marketing wizards, who were in awe of both the cleverness of the campaign and the speed at which it spread.

'Reznor's deviating from the norm and it's blowing people's minds,' said James Montgomery, an MTV News staff writer quoted in *USA Today*. 'Not many bands have the intelligence to do this.'

'He's saying an album is not this fixed piece of media, and it's not just music, it's way bigger,' added *Wired* contributing editor Eric Steuer. 'It's art and interactive entertainment. He's pretty geeky and very technical, and he recognizes that you're not dealing with passive consumers anymore.'

Or as *Rolling Stone* writer Elizabeth Goodman noted, 'It's *The Da Vinci Code* for rock geeks.'

Reznor was putting it all together as only he could, with equal parts rock, sci-fi, classic literature, technology and doom. It certainly didn't hurt that Reznor had always been a bit of a geek - a label he might willingly cop to now - but one could look back on his boyhood fascination with Kiss to find the seeds of the *Year Zero* assault. After all, Reznor's music heroes were also known as the original multimedia music marketing machine. He might have picked up a thing or two by watching what they did. (Does that mean we can expect to see NIN comic books? Thought not.)

Other *Year Zero* alternate reality web sites were soon discovered, including bethehammer.org, the diary of a mercenary soldier/assassin called the Angry Sniper that opened with the uplifting line: 'I kill people'; churchofplano.com, the site for a fictitious evangelical sect; and anotherversionofthetruth.com, where clicking and dragging the computer mouse across the screen revealed a post-apocalyptic farm scene and links to a message board that led the faithful farther into Reznor's dark future-world.

Shortly before the album's release, Reznor posted multitrack files for 'Survivalism' on the NIN web site, inviting fans to remix or to 'reconstruct/deconstruct' the song to their hearts' content. About a week after the album's release 'My Violent Heart,' Capital G' and 'Me, I'm Not' were available online for the same treatment, 'as a reward for stealing *Year Zero,*' so nin.com said, adding that the plan was to have the entire album available in multitrack format within months of its release. 'The Beginning of the End,' 'Vessel' and 'God Given' were added in June.

Explaining his decision to make the music available on the Internet, Reznor told *The Guardian,* 'I've always been open to the idea of letting people behind the scenes with my music. As to what I'm looking to gain from doing this, I'm not really sure...it just seemed like something I'd want as a fan. Of the many remixes and reconstructions that get made, some end up being truly great.'

To the astonishment of many in the record industry, leaking the tracks, opening them up for remixing and even streaming the entire album on the Internet didn't hurt sales a bit. The album peaked at number 2 on the Billboard 200 in May 2007. 'Survivalism' hit number 1 on Billboard's Hot Modern Rock Tracks and number 14 on Hot Mainstream Rock Tracks. On those charts, 'Capital G' went to number 7 and number 26 respectively. And weirdly, after 63 weeks on the charts, NIN's 'Every Day Is Exactly The Same' from the 2006 *Every Day Is Exactly The Same* EP, caught residual buzz and went to number 1 on the Billboard Hot Dance Singles chart. Go figure.

Meanwhile, the games continued. A toll-free telephone number printed on the album cover invited listeners to call the U.S. Bureau of Morality to report subversive acts or thoughts - only to discover that by calling they were 'reporting' themselves. And while said bureau is not an official arm of the U.S. government (yet!), the warning was printed in a fashion strikingly similar to the official FBI Anti-Piracy warning beside it.

Additional clues trickled out in various ways, including heat-sensitive paint on the CD itself, which changed from black to white and revealed a puzzling binary code of zeros and ones on the disc. And let us not forget the literary references - everything from Kurt Vonnegut, Jr., to JRR Tolkien, Walt Whitman, Stephen King, John Milton and the Bible - that seeped into the web sites, e-mails and telephone messages.

On the package of the Blu Ray edition of the *Beside You In Time* DVD, were printed the seemingly incongruous words 'secure,' 'broadcast' and 'informatics.' Slap a .com on the end of that and you're launched into yet another alternate reality where an IT guy named Francisco will e-mail you with cryptic German messages. And the 'news' section of the site reports that a 'notorious underground figure' named Darren Kroupa had been apprehended. (Eagle-eyed fans noted that Kroupa was also thanked on the *Year Zero* liner notes, and further investigation found that he was in fact a fan from New Jersey who was suffering from cancer and who had hooked up with NIN through a charitable foundation. Sadly, Darren Kroupa didn't survive to fully enjoy his viral marketing moment in the spotlight. He died less than a month before *Year Zero* was released.)

Music industry reactions to the contrary, in Reznor's mind the alternate reality game is really a visual and interactive component of the whole, far-reaching *Year Zero* concept. 'This is a concept record and it's part of a bigger picture of a number of things I'm working on,' Reznor told *Kerrang!* 'Essentially, I wrote the soundtrack to a movie that doesn't exist.'

Following the release of *Year Zero*, the tour schedule was remarkably limited, taking in venues and festivals throughout Europe and into Australia and the Far East during the summer, but with no U.S. dates announced as of June.

When they weren't speculating on the end of the world and the Year Zero apocalypse, once the album came out, fans immediately began speculating on how the tracks would play live. The answer: They wouldn't - at least not at first. Of the 16 tracks on *Year Zero*, only one - Survivalism - made it onto the set list for the Brixton

Academy show in March. A free stealth concert for (incredibly fortunate) fans in Los Angeles two days after *Year Zero* dropped also included 'The Beginning Of The End,' but everything else came from earlier albums. By the time NIN got to Melbourne and Tokyo in May 2007, there were six tracks from *Year Zero* circulating through the set list.

Why Reznor had chosen to make his U.S. fans wait to see the Year Zero tour is anyone's guess, but by now everyone understands that he has his reasons for everything his does. And more importantly, his instincts consistently prove to be on target.

Gone - hopefully forever - are the days when Reznor would hole up in the studio for years, paralyzed by indecision and self-doubt. Our man has a new work ethic and a new attitude. He's not messing around anymore. It's a busy life for Trent Reznor and Nine Inch Nails.

Not long ago, there was a swift cease-and-desist order to the conservative, Rupert Murdoch-piloted Fox News network for using 'La Mer,' 'The Great Below' and 'The Mark Has Been Made' in a documentary without permission. In a classic 'it pays to be nice to your fans' moment, Reznor only found out about the piracy when it was mentioned on ninhotline.net a Nine Inch Nails fan site.

One thing is certain, though, he's working on his own stuff...all the time. And he seems proud of the fact that after promising there would not be a typical, frustrating five-year gap between *With Teeth* and the next album, he was true to his word.

So, what's next? Well, the comment to *Kerrang!* spawned rumors of a Year Zero movie - perhaps the realization (at last!) of Reznor's desire to work on scoring films. He's made some noise about bringing in new collaborators (Sade? Lauryn Hill? Seriously, Trent?).

What's next? Who knows? In any event, Reznor has made it clear that the *Year Zero* story is not over.

'I've begun working on the conclusion, part two,' he told *Rolling Stone*. 'The fate of the world is in my hands.'

You have been warned...